organization behavior in
American public administration

public affairs and administration
(editor: James S. Bowman)
vol. 15

.

Garland reference library
of social science
vol. 320

the public affairs and administration
series: James S. Bowman, editor

1. career planning, development,
   and management
   an annotated bibliography
      Jonathan P. West

2. professional dissent
   an annotated bibliography
   and resource guide
      James S. Bowman
      Frederick A. Elliston
      Paula Lockhart

3. American public administration
   a bibliographical guide
   to the literature
      Gerald E. Caiden
      Richard A. Loverd
      Thomas J. Pavlek
      Lynn F. Sipe
      Molly M. Wong

4. public administration in rural areas
   and small jurisdictions
   a guide to the literature
      Beth Walter Honadle

5. comparative public administration
   an annotated bibliography
      Mark W. Huddleston

6. the bureaucratic state
   an annotated bibliography
      Robert D. Miewald

7. labor management relations in
   the public sector
   an annotated bibliography
      N. Joseph Cayer
      Sherry S. Dickerson

8. public choice theory in
   public administration
   an annotated bibliography
      Nicholas F. Lovrich
      Max Neiman

9. public policy analysis
   an annotated bibliography
      John S. Robey

10. public personnel administration
    an annotated bibliography
       Sarah Y. Bowman
       Jay M. Shafritz

11. news media and public policy
    an annotated bibliography
       Joseph P. McKerns

12. equal employment opportunity
    and affirmative action
    a sourcebook
       Floyd D. Weatherspoon

13. voluntary associations
    an annotated bibliography
       Donato J. Pugliese

14. administration and development in the
    Arab world
    an annotated bibliography
       Jamil E. Jreisat
       Zaki R. Ghosheh

15. organization behavior
    in American public administration
    an annotated bibliography
       Aurora T. Payad

organization behavior
in American
public administration
an annotated bibliography

Aurora T. Payad

Garland Publishing • New York & London
1986

Library of Congress Cataloging-in-Publication Data

Payad, Aurora T.
   Organization behavior in American public administration.

   (The Public affairs and administration series ; 15)
(Garland reference library of social science ; vol. 320)
   Includes indexes.
   1. Public administration—Psychological aspects—
Bibliography.   2. Civil service—Psychological aspects
—Bibliography.   3. Public officers—Psychology—
Bibliography.   4. Organizational behavior—Bibliography.
5. Bureaucracy—Bibliography.   I. Title.   II. Series.
III. Series: Garland reference library of social
science ; v. 320.
Z7164.A2P39   1986   [JF1601]   016.35′00001′9   85-45111
ISBN 0-8240-8685-6 (alk. paper)

Cover design by Alison Lew

Printed on acid-free 250-year-life paper
Manufactured in the United States of America

contents

Series Foreword   vii

Foreword   ix

Preface   xi

User's Guide   xiii

1. In Search of Organization Behavior   3

    A. State of the Art   3

    B. First Job Dilemma: Recruitment and Placement   11

    C. Retention Dilemma: Promotion and
       Staff Development   22

2. Ecology of Public Organizations   37

    A. Political Economy and Citizen Participation   37

    B. Budgetary Strategies and Constraints   53

    C. Technology and Office Modernization   68

    D. Administrative Ethics   75

    E. Management Philosophy: Issues and Prospects
       for the Future   91

    F. Organization Design: Pyramids, Adhocracy, and
       Quality Circles   100

3. Individual Behavior   109

    A. Motivation and Productivity   109

    B. Creativity and Innovation   134

4. Intergroup and Intra-group Behavior   145

   A. Group Dynamics and Communication   145

   B. Matrix Organizations and Relationships   155

   C. Unionism and Group Norms   157

   D. Group Conflicts and Office Politics   166

5. Managerial Behavior   171

   A. Challenge of Leadership   171

   B. Decision Making Models and Perspectives   188

   C. Management of Change   199

   D. Management of Power   213

   E. Management of Conflict   222

   F. Management of Managers   231

Directory of Professional Associations   245

Author Index   247

Subject Index   255

series foreword

The twentieth century has seen public administration come of age as a field of study and practice. This decade, in fact, marks the one hundredth anniversary of the profession. As a result of the dramatic growth in government, and the accompanying information explosion, many individuals—managers, academicians and their students, researchers—in organizations feel that they do not have ready access to important information. In an increasingly complex world, more and more people need published material to help solve problems.

The scope of the field and the lack of a comprehensive information system has frustrated users, disseminators, and generators of knowledge in public administration. While there have been some initiatives in recent years, the documentation and control of the literature have been generally neglected. Indeed, major gaps in the development of the literature, the bibliographic structure of the discipline, have evolved.

Garland Publishing, Inc., has inaugurated the present series as an authoritative guide to information sources in public administration. It seeks to consolidate the gains made in the growth and maturation of the profession.

The Series consists of three tiers:
1. core volumes keyed to the major subfields in public administration such as personnel management, public budgeting, and intergovernmental relations;
2. bibliographies focusing on substantive areas of administration such as community health; and
3. titles on topical issues in the profession.

Each book will be compiled by one or more specialists in the area. The authors—practitioners and scholars—are selected in open competition from across the country. They design their work to include an introductory essay, a wide variety of bibliographic materials, and, where appropriate, an information resource section. Thus each contribution in the collection provides a systematic basis for managers and researchers to make informed judgments in the course of their work.

Since no single volume can adequately encompass such a broad, interdisciplinary subject, the Series is intended as a continuous project that will incorporate new bodies of literature as needed. Its titles represent the initial building blocks in an operating information system for public affairs and administration. As an open-ended endeavor, it is hoped that not only will the Series serve to summarize knowledge in the field but also will contribute to its advancement.

This collection of book-length bibliographies is the product of considerable collaboration on the part of many people. Special appreciation is extended to the editors and staff of Garland Publishing, Inc., to the individual contributors in the Public Affairs and Administration Series, and to the anonymous reviewers of each of the volumes. Inquiries should be made to the Series Editor.

James S. Bowman
Tallahassee

foreword

Dr. Aurora T. Payad's bibliography is timely for a number of reasons: (1) increasingly more people, including public servants, erroneously believe that government can be run like a business enterprise, (2) more privatization efforts are being considered and effected without a thought to the consequences, (3) a growing number of public-private efforts are being implemented and/or considered for implementation, and (4) public administrators are being forced to manage with "less."

To be sure, anyone concerned about these areas, whether academic or practitioner (public and private sector alike), will be well served by this annotated compilation. Not only will many readers gain some understanding of the distinction between the public and private sectors, and how they may or may not be meshed together, but also they also will gain an enhanced appreciation for the environmental contexts of the public service.

Academics should find this book particularly useful, since there are no books, to my knowledge, which deal with organizational behavior within the context of public administration. Indeed, the typical course syllabus in public administration designed to address organizational behavior consists of books having a private sector focus and/or context, complemented by a scattered collection of articles which may or may not inform the utility of such books for the public service. This book is a mid-way step in filling that void. By virtue of the magnitude and organized thrust of the literature compiled, it directly and comprehensively shows the relevance of the organizational behavior literature to the public sector.

Employing an organizational development (OD) perspective to guide her selection of bibliographic materials, Payad characteristically focuses on those human interpersonal dynamics believed relevant. This trust of her compilation stimulated a tighter focus for a number of areas of ongoing conern:

- How does one stimulate citizens to revitalize the public service?
- In what way are motivational techniques in the public sector different from those of the private sector?
- How much more different and/or complex are the measures of productivity between the two arenas?
- How different are the contexts of creativity?
- How much does the interjection of the electorate affect union negotiating efforts (in contrast to union negotiations in business)?
- How much more (or less) dynamically responsive is the public sector to the electorate to the private sector's responsiveness to its clientele? In what way is this responsiveness reflected in: leadership strategy, power, management, style, and conflict resolution differences?

I trust that the users of Dr. Payad's bibliography will be similarly stimulated.

> David Lopez-Lee
> Professor of Public Administration
> University of Southern California

preface

I owe the idea for this project to Dr. Roberta Baade, a former colleague and a good friend. Having been assigned to teach a class on organization behavior in public administration for the first time, she enlisted my help in finding appropriate textbooks. The assistance she was expecting ended in a futile search.

The publications on organization behavior in the public sector were few and far between, mainly addressing very specific behavioral issues or directed towards organization development strategies and experiences. Prescribed textbooks for behavior classes are written within the context of corporate experiences and designed to resolve private sector behavioral problems. Pertinent journal articles are usually used to supplement these textbooks to provide governmental flavor and perspective.

The preparation of this volume started in the summer of 1982 and was facilitated by research funds and assigned time granted by the California State University at San Bernardino. The School of Business and Public Administration likewise provided graduate assistants who helped in culling entries from journal publications. Particular mention goes to Normita Recto, who took precious time off in the summer of 1983 from her doctoral studies at the University of Southern California. Karen Kessinger, Karen Winn-Aquino and Alan London, among others, contributed their time and efforts in accumulating the entries. Special mention goes to Connie Lao, who not only joined me on weekend trips to Los Angeles but also started the task of word processing this manuscript, including the author and subject indices.

The expression of my gratitude also goes to Dr. David Hartl and Dr. David Lopez-Lee of the School of Public Administration, University of Southern California; to Dr. Steven Levy,

School of Business and Public Administration, California State University at San Bernardino; and to Dr. Roberta Baade of General Dynamics, Convair Division at San Diego, California. They have all graciously consented to serve as referees for this volume when this proposal was submitted to the Series Editor, James Bowman.

Terri Hope, the Department of Public Administration secretary, presided over the tedious job of printing the first draft of this manuscript on the School's IBM-PC computer. She had to do a lot of thinking and experimenting to conform to the prescribed format since even Micropro telephone consultancy could not assist her. Her patience and perseverance gave birth to the draft copy of this volume. Alan Weiner, a former student, installed my Diablo 620 printer and became my printer consultant. The final responsibility, however, for overseeing the completion of this project and in printing the camera-ready copy of this book rests squarely on my shoulders.

user's guide

Organization behavior cuts across spheres of the political system and government levels, meanders through civilian and military career services, and encompasses the lowest to the top rungs of the hierarchical ladder in bureaucracy. Thus, leadership behaviors involve those of mayors, governors, members of Congress, the President of the United States, Supreme Court Justices, Brigadier Generals, and agency managers. The field of organization behavior encompasses the actions, reactions, motivations, ethics, conflicts, challenges, leadership styles, individuals and groups. Organization behavior, as defined here, also goes beyond the confines of public agencies and is directed at how to attract and retain qualified people into the public service. This book, then, views both the internal and external environment in which the government workforce operates. Organizational behaviors aimed at improving performance productivity and effective service delivery, are examined here from individual, group, and managerial perspectives.

An organization development (OD) approach guided the choice of entries for this book. Nigro and Nigro in *Modern Public Administration* (1984) describe OD as a planned, long-term social science-based approach to the analysis of organization problems and to effecting guided change by utilizing trained consultants or in-house specialists. They suggest that an OD program focuses on "(1) relationships between the organization and its environment; (2) intergroup relations within the organization; (3) interface between the employee and the formal system; or (4) interpersonal relations."

OD change interventions are directed at "motivational patterns, power relationships among individuals and groups, communication processes, ways of perceiving situations, organizational values and norms, problem-solving procedures, interpersonal relations, and the handling of conflict" (Nigro and

Nigro, 1984: 161–162). In short, the OD approach differs from other strategies in that "it tends to be more concerned with human variables and values" (Nigro and Nigro, 1984: 162).

The purpose of this volume is to fill a gap in public administration literature relative to a major area of specialization—organization behavior in government—by using this approach. The absence of any comprehensive work on organization behavior in the public sector, consolidating the various findings and experiences of American government administrators and subordinates, is a glaring omission in the discipline.

This book intends to address this problem in three parts. The first is this user's guide. The second is the bibliography itself which is divided into five major areas, each area being subdivided into two or more sections. References are entered alphabetically with numerical sequence across the five areas. Cross-references indicate when an entry falls under more than one area. Finally, the last part consists of a resource guide and author and subject indices. The guide lists national professional societies and their addresses. The author index identifies all the annotated works of the authors by reference number. The subject index includes all reference numbers corresponding to each subject entry. It provides cross-references to facilitate accessibility to various entries.

organization

In the compilation of relevant organization development literature on individual, group and managerial behaviors, this book focuses on what types of behavior contribute to efficient and effective service delivery. The choice of entries illustrates the motivations and creativity of individuals, group dynamics, and managerial styles that mesh together towards productive performance in organizations.

An efficient, cohesive, and productive government bureaucracy can exist only when the recruitment process seeks the best qualified and altruistically motivated candidates to enter the public service. Conversely, qualified candidates must be willing to join and remain civil servants. Such willingness should be strengthened by a healthy organizational climate and a management culture that enhances and provides opportunities for creativity and growth and is conducive to work satisfaction.

Chapter 1 of the bibliography, "In Search of Organization Behavior," introduces the sparse literature on organization behavior in government in Section A: State of the Art. The section indicates the paucity of coverage and specificity in the publications in recent years. It is followed by Section B which involves the first job dilemma. The entries deal with the various strategies that candidates and government administrators employ in seeking to fill vacancies in bureaucracies. The recruitment function marks a change from purely technical activities to providing guidelines on how and where to recruit candidates for public jobs and how to imbue a desire for public service in the government. This attitude has to be fostered among students as early as their high school education through collegiate and graduate work (see, e.g., items 17, 20, 23, 26, 32, 41). Section C, retention dilemma, emphasizes the need for training and staff development to encourage government career personnel to stay in public service (consider, for instance, items 54, 55, 56, 62, 70, 74, 77).

Chapter 2 looks at a major variable which distinguishes and influences behavior in government organizations: ecology of public organizations. This area presents, in six sections, the internal and external climate in which public sector agencies operate. Section A starts with the political economy (items 98, 100, 103, 108) and citizen participation (most notably, items 91, 92, 130) as significant determinants of how bureaucrats behave. It brings to light a two-fold focus on the interrelationships among vested interests, citizens, bureaucrats, and legislators. The first involves the dynamics of interactions between bureaucrats and elective officials; the second stresses the mutual accommodations in relationships between appointive and elective officials and the various publics they serve. Of noteworthy mention is the existence of a "shadow government" which overlays the policy decisions of government appointive and elective officials.

Section B, budgetary strategies and constraints, underscores the need for resources and responses to scarcity of same. It cites experiences of public administrators who are forced to manage cutbacks with more efficiency, rationality, and flexibility (items 135, 136, 155). The impact of technological advance on manpower planning and the use, misuse, or non-use of new technology is treated in Section C on technology and office modernization. Items 171, 183, and 184, for instance, raise issues and provide insights into the utilization of modern technologies in management.

Section D, administrative ethics, shows how the ethical orientations of people in government vary from one level to the next. It discusses their susceptibility to, and moral strength against corruption, waste, and abuse in the public agencies. It emphasizes that no branch or level of the political system or of the bureaucracy is untouched by unethical behavior. It contains some recommendations toward responsible and responsive behavior by administrators (items 190, 194, 198). Items in Section E argue that a participative, managerial philosophy encourages a humanization and professionalization of the public service. They contend that organizations would benefit from more creative employee-management participation by increasing morale, performance, professionalism, and prestige (items 235, 236, 250, 252).

Some desirable and future trends in structure and processes of government agencies are projected in Section F on organization design. It cites the importance of changes in examining behavioral adaptation through shifts in personnel function, integration of functions, and non-hierarchical organizations (items 259, 260, 264).

Chapter 3 is concerned with individual behavior. The two sections correlate motivation and innovation to productivity of workers. Section A on motivation and productivity stresses the desirability of implementing productivity programs; barriers to institutionalization of these programs are also discussed (items 281, 284, 286, 287, 292). The literature also demonstrates that job satisfactions and role expectations come from different directions and motivational incentives (296, 298, 302, 320, 323). Section B covers the impact of innovations on productivity, such as technology-transfer, flex-itime, medical audit, process accountability, and incentives (items 349, 351, 354, 358, 368). A particularly important article by Donald Stone (item 366) discusses the requirements for innovative organizations and innovative managers.

The four sections in Chapter 4 delve into inter-group and intra-group behavior. Section A views communication in forging positive dynamic interactions within organizational boundaries, across departmental lines, and between civil servants and the general public (items 370, 375, 377, 379, 385). Matrix organizations and relationships are the topic of Section B. Some entries deal with matrixing as a means for overcoming organizational formalization and civil service rigidities (item 391), improving employer-employee relationships (item 393), and increasing capacity for decision making (item 394). However, problems in using matrix organizations are explored in items 392 and 395. Unions and group norms in Section C contend with the interplay of union-management behaviors within the public environment (items 402, 405, 410, 413). Section D on group conflicts and office politics describes tensions between career and political executives (items 423, 425, 426).

Chapter 5 on managerial behavior is divided into six sections. The sections address specific perspectives that public managers encounter in effectively running their respective agencies. Section A reports on the challenge of leadership on institutional and personal levels, as well as on the development of women managers (items 431, 432, 434, 436, 443, 462). Section B on decision making models and perspectives contrasts "muddling through" decision making with analytical problem solving (items 478, 479) and analyzes uncertainties, problems and outside influences encountered by decision makers (items 481, 484, 486, 491, 504, 505). The management of change in Section C examines the application of organization development (OD) efforts in government. It details several strategies and problems in OD experiences in several government agencies, discusses the role of consultants, and cautions against direct transfer of OD technology from the private to the public sector (items 507, 516, 517, 523, 529, 532, 536).

The management of power, covered in Section D, balances the intricate task of managing power vis-a-vis political demands and rationality in service delivery and resource allocations (items 538, 546, 555, 560, 562). Management of conflict in Section E explores the stresses in organizations arising from comparable worth controversies, innovations, sociological and psychological factors, and collective bargaining (items 565, 566, 569, 571, 572, 573, 577). And finally, Section F culminates the bibliography by focusing on the management of managers. It urges the training, development and establishment of motivational programs to recruit, retain, and develop effective male and female managers at local, state, and federal bureaucracies, in both civilian and military services. It also directs attention to the need of professionalization of the public service to strengthen the execution, selection and retention process in government (items 591, 595, 597, 601, 603, 604, 607).

methodology

The entries that form these sections cover journal articles, books, book chapters, reviews, and dissertations. The period of study includes publications from 1940–1984, with the bulk of the entries published within the last decade (1974–1984). The starting date coincides with the first year of publication of the *Public Administration Review*. Primary materials constituted the largest number of entries. Secondary materials, mostly dissertation abstracts, also form part of this bibliography.

Library collections of three libraries were consulted: University of Southern California, University of California at Los Angeles, and California State University at San Bernardino. The following journals were reviewed:

Administration & Society
Administrative Science Quarterly
American Behavioral Scientist

American Journal of Political Science
American Political Science Review
American Review of Public Administration
The Bureaucrat
Gao Review
Group and Organization Studies
Harvard Business Review
International Dissertation Abstracts
International Journal of Public Administration
Journal of Social Issues
Management Review
Management Science
Monthly Labor Review
National Journal
Personnel Journal
Public Administration Review
Public Budgeting & Finance
Public Leadership
Public Management
Public Personnel Management
PS
Southern Review of Public Administration

Computerized literature searches for data bases before 1976 could not be used because they were not available at that time. The compilation of those entries was, therefore, accomplished by manually searching early journal issues and other publications.

*   *   *

It can be readily seen that this bibliography attempts a comprehensive, albeit selective, collection of available literature on organization behavior in American public administration. It is with high expectations that the joy in completing this work will be shared by colleagues in the discipline, as well as by students and practitioners of the art of public management. If the void in public administration literature is even partially filled by this work, the hard work of everyone who contributed to the making of this book will have been adequately compensated.

organization behavior
in American
public administration

1. IN SEARCH OF ORGANIZATION BEHAVIOR

A. State-of-the-Art

1. Anderson, Jack. AMERICAN GOVERNMENT...LIKE
   IT IS. Morristown, N.J.: General Learning Press, 1972. 117 p.

   Supplements the textbook for American government classes by hanging the flesh on the
   skeleton of theory. Throws some light on the
   hidden side of government by providing a cur-
   sory sketch of the most obvious waste habits
   of federal agencies. Views the study from
   the perspectives of Congress, the lobbyists,
   the Presidency, the judiciary, and foreign
   policy.

2. Bollens, John C., and Henry Schmandt. POL-
   ITICAL CORRUPTION: POWER, MONEY AND SEX.
   Pacific Palisades, CA: Palisades Publish-
   ers, 1979. 282 p.

   Deals with all major types of political
   corruption in the American governmental system. Uses case material in examining the
   different forms of abuse of public office,
   the kind of people that get involved, the circumstances in which such behavior arises,
   its impact on the political system, and the
   efforts to eliminate it.

3. "Congressional Quarterly." CONGRESSIONAL
   ETHICS, Washington, D.C.: Congressional
   Quarterly, Inc., 1980. 150 p.

   Provides detailed analysis of constitu-

tional, judicial, and legislative developments, as well as background, on previous
attempts by Congress at self-policing and
reform. Reviews recent developments, outlin-
ing congressional scandals in 1976 and efforts in 1977 at reform. Examines pay and
perquisites, campaign financing, seating
and disciplining, and ethics and criminal
prosecutions.

4. Davis, R.V. "OD in the Public Sector:
   Intervening in Ambiguous Performance Environments." GROUP AND ORGANIZATION STUDIES,
   4, 3 (September 1979), 352-365.

   Notes important differences existing between corporate and public sector organizations. Identifies some of the major external and internal variables in the literature that affect public sector organizations.
   Develops an integrated conceptual framework
   used as an orienting device for an OD intervention in a division of a state welfare
   system. Describes the tactics of change
   in an ambiguous performance setting. Focuses on some of the internal influence variables that may typically be expected to
   affect change attempts in public sector
   organizations.

5. Eddy, William B. PUBLIC ORGANIZATION BEHAVIOR
   AND DEVELOPMENT. Cambridge, Mass.: Win-
   throp Publishers, Inc., 1981. 210 p.

   Undertakes study of organization behavior
   in government settings from the manager's
   perspective. Attempts to provide insights into managerial behavior. Discusses management skills, leadership strategies, and change
   techniques for administering more effectively.
   Explores the basic philosophy that not only
   are people the most important component of
   public organizations, but that people are
   public organizations. Presents some of the
   differences between public and private organizations pertaining to utilization of people

and formulation of management techniques.
Mentions some characteristics affecting employee behavior: emphasis on rules and procedures, few objective performance criteria, and
lower status. Deals with the dimension of
human interaction processes--communication,
cooperation, control, conflicts, commitment,
cohesiveness, trust, and intimacy.

Explores the skills, styles, attitudes
that may increase the manager's ability to
perform effectively. Suggests some strategies for planned change through organization
development, job redesign, management by objectives, and imposed change. Concludes that
modern managers need to view organizations as
socio-technical systems; scan the environment
continually for new techniques, new opportunities, points of view and bits of knowledge;
learn from self-examination and feedback from
others; and stay one step ahead of subordinates in the growth process.

6. Fried, Robert C. PERFORMANCE IN AMERICAN
      BUREAUCRACY. Boston: Little, 1976. 470 p.

Accents the performance of American public
administration, i.e., the ability of American
systems of public administration to cope with
and satisfy the demands and expectations of
the American people in their local,
state, and national communities. Analyzes
American systems of administration in terms
of their comparative ability to provide service and   protection of high quality.
Places accent also on organizational behavior,
on bureaucratic politics, on structure, and
on decision making processes, with the view
of the ability of administrative systems
to translate citizen demands and preferences into desirable patterns of stability
and change. Deals with comparative performance of administrative systems in terms of
responsiveness and liberalism: work   ethic,
democratic ethic, and legal ethic.

7. Goetze, David B. "The Impact of Inputs, Em-
       ployee Characteristics, Organizational Ar-
       rangements, and Activities on the Environ-
       mental Effectiveness of State Air Pol-
       lution Control Agencies." Ph.D. Disserta-
       tion, Indiana University, 1980. 214 p.

       Reports findings of study involving five
   state air pollution control agencies in Illinois, Indiana, Minnesota, Ohio and Wisconsin. Suggests that air quality emis-
   sions data are consistent dimensions but that
   compliance data behave in a different manner.
   Finds effectiveness to be associated most
   predictably towards the intentions of industrial pollutors, and the jurisdictional
   scope of agencies. Determines that other
   variables examined surprisingly had little
   connection with the performance of the air
   pollution control agencies.

8. Golembiewski, Robert, and William B. Eddy,
       eds. ORGANIZATION DEVELOPMENT IN PUBLIC
       ORGANIZATION. New York: Marcel Dekker,
       1978. Part I, 268 p. Part II, 326 p.

       Presents book-length resources in organiza-
   tion development tailored to needs and environment of the public sector. Provides, in
   Part I, a generic perspective on OD and directs attention to issues particular to
   public sector usage. Emphasizes motivators
   and constraints specific to the public
   sector. Describes, in Part II, the numerous
   OD designs and details their consequences.
   Illustrates the application of these designs
   in public agencies.

9. Hummel, Ralph P. THE BUREAUCRATIC EXPERI-
       ENCE. New York: St. Martin's Press, 1977.
       238 p.

       Examines the assumption that we will be
   better able to live and work with, in,
   or against bureaucracy if we: (1) view it as
   an entirely new world; (2) become aware of

the practical impact of its differences from
the world with which we are familiar;
and (3) understand how that impact will vary
from each of us depending on the form of our
involvement with bureaucratic life. Declares
that the study of the new form of power
applied by bureaucracy will be essential to
opposing its more blatant claims to hege-
mony over mankind.

Asserts the self-destructive impulses of
bureaucracy because for most of its func-
tionaries, bureaucracy which is designed to
have widest and fullest use of reason has
become the grave of reason. Concludes that
three tasks have to be confronted: (1) recognizing bureaucracy so that actions can
be oriented towards it; (2) controlling
bureaucracy to insure survival of people within it and still retain human potential; and
(3) overcoming or transcending bureaucracy.

10. Katz, Elihu, and Brenda Danet, eds. BUREAU-
CRACY AND THE PUBLIC: A READER IN OFFICIAL-
CLIENT RELATIONS. New York: Basic Books,
1973. 534 p.

Investigates the variety of factors which
influence the relationship between bureaucratic organizations and their publics. Focuses specifically on the interaction between officials and clients in varied organizational settings. Includes in the term
"officials" the practitioners and professionals of all kinds who deal with clients
within the context of formal organizations.
Takes the client's point of view rather
than that of the official, in identifying
the organizational and extra-organizational
factors which influence the interaction
and its outcome. Concludes against the
kind of bureaucracy that is unresponsive
to its clients, that usurps the goal-
setting functions, that undermines autonomous and creative personalities, that in-
vades domains which belong to the individuals or to other kinds of organizations.

Advocates continued attention to the harnessing of bureaucracy.

11. Medina, William. CHANGING BUREAUCRACIES: UNDERSTANDING THE ORGANIZATION BEFORE SE- LECTING THE APPROACH. New York: Marcel Dekker, Inc., 1982. 140 p.

Studies limitations to the power of the President over executive branch arising from well-established work patterns, individual values and habits, enacted legislation, and congressional intervention. Uses force field analysis in understanding the failures of some programs designed to improve the per- formance of bureaucracy. Observes that best reasons for change are: willingness of beneficiary to use products of change, meeting existing priorities, satisfying felt needs, fitting existing management ethics and power relationships, appropriate- ness of technology to existing circumstan- ces, and usefulness to working staff.

12. Neuse, Steven M. "Professionalism and Public Responsibility in State Government." Ph.D. Dissertation, University of Texas at Austin, 1976. 239 p.

Focuses on the development of profes- sional attitudes among Texas state em- ployees and the effect of such attitudes on public responsibility values. Defines and measures public responsibility in terms of the civil servants' perceptions of respon- sibility both to population and hierarchical elements. Finds that different professional groups reported widely varying responsibi- lity norms--service-oriented professions had higher responsibility norms toward clien- tele and citizen interests than the tech- nical professions.

13. Richards, Francis M. "A Sociotechnical Experience in Government Organization:

Learning Systems in Organizations."
D.P.A. Dissertation, University of
Southern California, 1978. 261 p.

Undertakes to ascertain the conditions
under which a work group in a government
organization (letter sorting machine opera-
tors in the United States Postal Service)
can become an adaptive learning system.
Employs the sociotechnical systems approach
which holds that the understanding of an
organization requires consideration of its
technological and social elements and their
reciprocal effects. Indicates that the action
research effort resulted in improving opera-
tor productivity, accuracy and job satisfaction. Shows improvements in morale,
opportunities for growth and development,
communications, ability and technical operations. Notes less improvement in supervision
and holding of conflicting views by participants regarding improvement in training and
the working environment. Finds that the
action research committee provided a medium
for self-regulation and self-transformation
of the system, served as a forum for
problem-solving, and promoted communication
among participants.

14. Ridgley, Edward Earl. "Acceptability of
    Mandated Organizational Change." Ph.D.
    Dissertation, University of Southern
    California, 1984. 178 p.

    Investigates the acceptability of man-
dated change by members of the FBI through
the implementation of the Quality versus Quantity Program initiated by Dir. Clarence
Kelley. Examines the program which forced
the redistribution of organizational resources toward prioritized investigative
matters. Compares Hoover and Kelley relative
to their leadership styles and approaches
to change. Makes it clear that Quality
versus Quantity was not unilaterally accepted
as a significant organizational change by
street level agents who were chosen to gain

a bottom-up perspective of change.

15. Weiss, Carol H. "Bureaucratic Maladies and
    Remedies." AMERICAN BEHAVIORAL SCIEN-
    TIST, 22, 5 (May-June 1979), 477-482.

    Gives an overview of the special issues
    dedicated to the effort to see public bureau-
    cracies'in their multidimensional variety.
    Assesses their shortcomings from a range
    of perspectives. Considers the likely ef-
    fects of a number of interventions that
    have been proposed as remedies for current
    problems.

16. Zawacki, Robert A., and Warrick, D.D., eds.
    ORGANIZATION DEVELOPMENT: MANAGING CHANGE
    IN THE PUBLIC SECTOR. Chicago: Interna-
    tional Personnel Management Association,
    1976. 308 p.

    Contains readings which discuss the
    characteristics, mood, process, and techni-
    cal aspects of OD. Analyzes the frustra-
    tions, failures and successes of OD ef-
    forts in some government agencies. Pre-
    sents some practical approaches for agency
    administrators and political policy makers.
    Includes: (1) meaning of OD development,
    behavior, and change; (2) special consi-
    derations of applying OD in the public
    sector; (3) discussions of all phases of
    the OD process; and (4) insights on
    change agent skills, managing the change
    process, and preparing for future deve-
    lopments in OD.

B. First Job Dilemma: Recruitment and Placement

17. Andersen, R., and D. Thomas. "Advice to Candidates." PUBLIC MANAGEMENT, 65, 3 (March
1983), 11-12.

Presents six guidelines a candidate should
follow to maximize chances of success: career
development, initial investigation of position, resume preparation, contact with
executive recruitment firm, job interview
and final negotiation with executive recruitment firm, job interview, and final
negotiation.

18. Ash, Philip, Noreen Taylor, and Louise Hall.
"The University Civil Service System of
Illinois: Updating a Merit System."
PUBLIC PERSONNEL MANAGEMENT, 2, 6
(November-December 1973), 456-461.

Discusses a new approach to validation of
employment tests. Includes a Digitek answer
sheet to (1) facilitate scoring; (2) generate
reports and analysis of blacks versus
whites test-taking experiences; and
(3) facilitate systemwide performance evaluation. Hopes to provide a system that
is "Griggs" clean (reference to the case
Griggs versus Duke Power Co.).

19. Berkely, Charles S., and Charles F. Sproule.
"Test-anxiety and Test-unsophistication:
The Effects, the Cures." PUBLIC PERSON-
NEL MANAGEMENT, 2, 1 (January-February
1973), 55-60.

Examines the relationship between test-
anxiety and test-unsophistication in ap-
praising performance of examinees. Suggests
that more anxious individuals and persons
who are unsophisticated in test taking
do not perform up to their capabilities
on tests. Also suggests that public

personnel agencies can improve the validity of these tests through coaching and distribution of instructional materials.

20. Bollens, John C. "Hiring and Training Assistants." PUBLIC MANAGEMENT, 31, 10 (October 1950), 221-224.

Discusses the different training methods and selection processes done by city managers for assistant positions. Advises applicants on qualifications needed which include educational training, work experience and public relations abilities, and the assignments and responsibilities involved in the job. Shows an average of two trained men assuming the city manager position. Concludes that city managers are making an important contribution to the development of the city manager profession.

21. Bruno, Cam J. "The Relationship of Demographic Factors to the Perception of Recruitment Advertisement." PUBLIC PERSONNEL MANAGEMENT, 2, 6 (November-December 1973), 439-448.

Evaluates the perceptions of varying age, sex and academic classified groups to recruitment advertisements. Found that men were more responsive to "reader oriented" advertisements than women; ages 17-22 were more susceptible to recruitment advertisements; freshmen and sophomores, more sensitive. Considers factors present in the recruiting ads: advancement opportunities, salaries, bonuses, etc.

22. Campbell, Joel T. "Tests are Valid for Minority Groups Too!" PUBLIC PERSONNEL MANAGEMENT, 2, 1 (January-February 1973), 70-77.

Presents the results of a study that

aptitude tests can predict the job performance of minority groups. Uses intensive research on three ethnic groups:
Blacks, Mexican-Americans, and Caucasians.
Applies different experiment instruments
such as job knowledge tests, work sample
problems, job analysis of duties and responsibilities, and job performance rating
scale done by supervisors. Finds that on
a general scale, higher ratings were given by supervisors to their own ethnic
group.

23. Davy, Thomas J. "Competing for Adminis-
    trative Brainpower." PUBLIC ADMINISTRA-
    TION REVIEW, 19, 4 (Autumn 1959),
    227-232.

    Approaches the issue of how government
can improve its efforts to attract and
retain more of the outstanding college
students for administrative careers in the
public service. Discusses the advice of
young career administrators and professors
of political science to government recruit-
ers: (1) emphasize satisfactions of serv-
ing the public; (2) convey sense of accomplishment in public service employment;
and (3) bring university professors into
the recruitment process.

24. Goldich, Robert L. "The Need for Posi-
    tive Change." MILITARY REVIEW, 53, 4
    (April 1973), 44-53.

    Calls for an analysis of the socio-
cultural aspects of current military policy to induce Americans to pursue a career in the volunteer military. Proposes
application of new ideas on human organization, management and control that have
led to success in business, government
and other areas of American life. Predicts that these concepts, if properly
applied, could contribute to military

success as well.

25. Grode, George, and Marc Holzer. "The Per-
    ceived Utility of MPA Degrees." PUBLIC
    ADMINISTRATION REVIEW, 35, 4 (July-
    August 1975), 403-412.

    Presents the findings of a research
    project in which a sample of MPA degree
    holders were contacted. Reports on the
    usefulness of their MPA training degrees
    to find the utility and the relevancy of
    MPA programs.

26. Hauptmann, Jerry. "Initiation into Public
    Administration." PUBLIC ADMINISTRATION
    REVIEW, 27, 3 (September 1967), 256-258.

    Addresses the need to educate high
    schol students about public service.
    Feels a need for a cooperative effort of
    professional organizations and educational
    institutions to do this.

27. Howell, Margaret A., and Marjorie C.
    Ginsbury. "Evaluation of the Profes-
    sional and Executive Corps Within the
    Department of Health, Education and
    Welfare (HEW)." PUBLIC PERSONNEL MAN-
    AGEMENT, 2, 1 (January-February 1973),
    37-42.

    Proves that the use of part-time em-
    ployees in the Professional and Executive
    Corps of the Department of Health, Educa-
    tion and Welfare is successful. Suggests
    that the corps can be used to attract
    highly qualified individuals for part-time
    positions.

28. Kenned, Giles W. and A. Grayson Walker III.
    "Graduate Students Recruitment in Ame-
    rican Public Administration: A Survey
    of NASPAA Member Institutions." PUBLIC
    ADMINISTRATION REVIEW, 41, 2 (March-

April 1981),   249-252.

Reports   the   results   of   a   survey   of
recruiting practices   evidenced   in   NASPAA
member   institutions.   Finds   that   current
practices   range   from   limited   involvement
to   expensive   promotions.   Concludes   that
targets of   recruiting   efforts   and   requirements   of   recruits   vary   according   to
institutional   characteristics,   but   practices   of   waiving   admissions requirements
are   widespread.   Asserts   that   schools
feel   current   recruiting   practices   will   be
inadequate   in   the   future.

29. Kranz,   Harry.   "Are   Merit   and   Equity   Com-
      patible?"   PUBLIC   ADMINISTRATION   REVIEW,
      34,   5   (September-October   1974),   434-440.

      Explores   whether   it   is   possible   to
   have   both   a   "representative   bureaucracy,"
   in   which   women   and   minorities   are   equit-
   ably   distributed,   and   a   "merit   system" of
   selecting   government   employees.   Concludes
   that   they   are   possible.

30. Loehr,   Virginia   M.,   Esther   Arellano,
      Edward Levine,   Wayne   Porter,   and   John
      Posegate.   "Personnel   Selection   Methods
      Used   in   Arizona   Local Government."   PUB-
      LIC   PERSONNEL   MANAGEMENT,   2,   5
      (September-October   1973),   327-331.

      Looks   at   the   impact   of   employment   va-
   lidation procedures   promulgated   by   the
   Equal   Employment Opportunity   Council   on
   the   personnel   selection policies   of   Arizona   local   government. Concludes   that   few
   jurisdictions   follow   the   EEOC-set   guidelines   and   there   is   substantial   resistance
   to   employment   of validation   methods.   Notes
   that   oral examinations   are   widely   used.
   Stresses   need   for cooperative   effort   among
   governmental   units   to help   understand   importance   of   new   personnel   testing   programs.

31. Malek, Frederic V. "The Development of
    Public Executives: Neglect and Reform."
    PUBLIC ADMINISTRATION REVIEW, 34, 3
    (May-June 1974),230-233.

    Outlines the need for capable public
    managers, who are competent and well-
    trained, to insure that program implement-
    ation is successful.

32. Malone, James E. "Minorities, Women and
    Young People in Local Government."
    PUBLIC MANAGEMENT, 55, 5 (May 1973),
    16-17.

    Reaffirms belief in providing opportu-
    nities to minorities and women in local
    government. Advances two approaches in
    implementing this program: (1)"job raid-
    ing," that is, stealing from other em-
    employers who have trained the protected
    classes in the position; and (2) employ-
    ing inexperienced persons with good po-
    tentials and proper motivations. Encoura-
    ges people to be open-minded about new
    hiring practices because the program
    brings fruitful and rewarding experiences
    and benefits for both the city and the
    citizens.

33. Mandell, Milton M. "Some Hypotheses on
    Administrative Selection." PUBLIC ADMIN-
    ISTRATION REVIEW, 19, 1 (Winter 1959),
    12-18.

    States that administrators often sub-
    consciously accept the personnel selec-
    tion process as something mechanical.
    Examines selection process for administra-
    tors as it relates to other aspects of
    administration as well as to filling spe-
    cific jobs. Presents hypotheses that can
    provide firmer guides to personnel action
    and identification and placement of ad-
    ministrative talent.

34. May, Geoffrey. "Day Dreams of a Bureaucrat."
    PUBLlC ADMINISTRATION REVIEW, 5, 2
    (Spring 1945),   153-161.

    Presents an argument for good govern-
    ment and good bureaucracy staffed with
    people who know the goal of government
    and how to attain it as opposed to more
    government and people.

35. McCaffery, Jerry L.   "Perceptions of
    Satisfaction-Dissatisfaction in the In-
    ternship Experience." PUBLIC ADMINISTRA-
    TION REVIEW, 39, 3 (May-June 1979),
    241-244.

    Explores the adequacy of the internship
    as a supplement to classroom learning by
    interviewing undergraduate and graduate
    interns through two questionnaires.

36. McClung, Glenn G.   " 'Qualified' versus Most
    Qualified': A Review of the Issues of
    Competitive Merit Selection."   PUBLIC
    PERSONNEL MANAGEMENT, 2, 5 (September-
    October 1973), 366-369.

    Reviews the merit system existing in
    the public sector. Weighs the relevance
    of the selection process to the needs
    of the total system--court-mandated cor-
    rection of discriminatory ills versus
    public interest. Suggests that an over-
    haul in the merit system is needed.

37. McKinley, Tina Macaluso. "One by One:
    Training the Unemployed." PUBLIC AD-
    MINISTRATION REVIEW, 39, 6 (November-
    December 1979),532-536.

    Reviews CETA and Oak Ridge Association
    University and the Union Carbide Corpora-
    tion Nuclear Division's Training and
    Technology Program (TAT). Uses Lindblom's
    Science of Muddling Through in analyzing

the decision making and planning of the program.

38. Mills, Claudia. "All-Volunteer Force: Second Thoughts." THE BUREAUCRAT, 13, 1 (Spring 1984), 48-52.

    Examines effectiveness and justice in all-volunteer force (AVF). Argues that training in military skills and effective leadership is probably more important than high school diplomas and test scores in determining the effectiveness of an armed force. Concludes that the AVF seems to merit a cautious thumbs-up assessment. Cautions that a brighter and better educated force can be attracted by offering competitive pay and benefits of civilian sector.

39. Morris, Robert B. "Trainees for City Management." PUBLIC MANAGEMENT, 35, 8 (August 1953), 174-178.

    Acknowledges the development of an administrative trainee program in the city government. Finds that it helps both city managers and department heads in administrative paperwork and in providing practical training for young persons interested in a career in city management. Outlines the first recruitment program for two college-trained trainees for the city of Illinois in 1953. Reaffirms belief in the administrative trainee positions to attract high-grade applicants.

40. Muchmore, Lynn. "Youth in Government Service." PUBLIC ADMINISTRATION REVIEW, 32, 2 (March-April 1972), 152-155.

    Attempts in an editorial to induce young people into public service as a means of changing society. Contains generalizations with no specific arguments to back them up.

41. Murray, Michael A. "Strategies for Placing
    Public Administration Graduates." PUBLIC
    ADMINISTRATION REVIEW, 35, 6 (November-
    December 1975), 629-635.

    Identifies the problem areas of find-
    ing jobs for Public Administration gradu-
    ates. Presents strategies to make find-
    ing jobs successful.

42. O'Harrow, Dennis. "How to Recruit a City
    Manager." PUBLIC MANAGEMENT, 31, 11
    (November 1950), 242-244.

    Outlines the efforts of the Park Fo-
    rest Village Board in attracting good
    candidates for the city managership. In-
    cludes a detailed description of job
    responsibilities, organizational structure,
    salary and benefits, rigid screening of
    job-related information, intensive adverti-
    sing, personal interviews, and final se-
    lection.

43. Pati, Gopal C. "Ex-offenders Make Good
    Employees." PUBLIC PERSONNEL MANAGEMENT,
    2, 6 (November-December 1973), 424-428.

    Analyzes employment problems and re-
    sults in hiring ex-offenders. Perceives
    social responsibility as the key factor
    in assimilating ex-cons into society.
    Shows that there are pay-offs in hiring
    ex-cons, ranging from: (1) tax allocation
    in supporting the inmate's stay in pri-
    son to other areas of greater human
    concerns; (2) reduction in crime rates;
    (3) retention of productive workers to
    keep business in operation; (4) reduction
    in rate of absenteeism and turnover.
    Points out society's resistance in em-
    ploying ex-offenders for a variety of
    reasons: (1) lack of awareness; (2) lack

of believability at the middle management
level regarding job development for ex-
cons; and (3) lack of support. Believes
that cooperation among prison administrators and employers can surmount all obstacles and achieve goal of rehabilitation.

44. Perkins, John A. "Finding Jobs in the
    City Hall." PUBLIC MANAGEMENT, 24, 3
    (March 1942), 80-82.

    Discusses reasons why academically
    trained professional administrators find
    limited job opportunities: absence of ci-
    vil service systems (if any exists, em-
    phasis of examination is on experience
    and practice and not on educational qua-
    lifications), local residence require-
    ments, prejudice against college-trained
    men, and recruitment of persons with
    strictly technical attainments. Suggests
    value of administrative assistants and
    municipal student workers.

45. Reaume, Paul A. "A Professional Process
    Benefiting Councils, Candidates, and
    the Profession." PUBLIC MANAGEMENT,
    65, 3 (March 1983), 13-14.

    Discusses key activities involved in
    finding a fully qualified group of can-
    didates from which to select a city
    manager: development of qualifications
    criteria and position expectations, posi-
    tion vacancy announcements, consultant re-
    search and candidate solicitation, ac-
    knowledgment of applications, screening
    credentials, reviewing candidates for in-
    terviews, interview arrangements, candidate
    interviews and council evaluation of can-
    didates, final background inquiries and
    appointment confirmation.

46. Roberts, Norman C. "Myths About Executive

Search in Government." PUBLIC MANAGE-
MENT, 65, 3 (March 1983), 9-10.

Debunks myths about executive search in
government: favoritism, use of ICMA conferences, candidate pressure, prejudice
against women and minorities, narrow
searches, and resistance of constituents
in supporting costs of hiring executive
search firms.

47. Rosenbloom, David. "A Note on Intermi-
      nority Group Competition for Federal
      Positions." PUBLIC PERSONNEL MANAGEMENT,
      2, 1 (January-February 1973), 43-48.

Discusses the problems of the federal
employment opportunity (EEO) programs in
the future as competition increases for
federal positions among minority groups,
primarily between Blacks and Spanish-
surnamed groups.

48. Shapek, Raymond. "Breaking Barriers: Urban
      Managers and Academics Working Toge-
      ther." PUBLIC ADMINISTRATION REVIEW,
      37, 5 (September-October 1977), 581-585.

Presents a case study demonstrating
the value of practitioner cooperation and
involvement in the development of future
public administrators. Studies Kent State
University and the Northeast Ohio city
managers. Discusses the results of the
study which led to a new working relationship between practitioners and academics at Kent State University

49. Sommers, William A. "Job Hunting in Mu-
      nicipal Government." PUBLIC MANAGEMENT,
      36, 2 (February 1954), 29-32.

Offers constructive suggestions for
city managers and would-be managers in
looking for a management position. Points

out to many cities the inadequacies of
their recruitment process from the job-
seeker's perspective. Seeks to add job-
seekers into municipal administration by
retelling municipal jobhunting experience
of George B.

50. Yeager, Samuel, Jack Rabin, and Thomas
    Vocino. "How Do MPA's Find Jobs?"
    THE BUREAUCRAT, 13, 2 (Summer 1984),
    48-51.

    Surveys the various ways used by MPA
    graduates in seeking work. Finds in-
    service status, internship and trainee
    positions as most effective means of
    finding a job after graduation.

        C. Retention Dilemma: Promotion
           and Staff Development

51. Barlotta, Samuel J. "Basic Training:
    The Verge of Destruction. " MILITARY RE-
    VIEW, 60, 11 (November 1980), 47-62.

    Identifies the weaknesses in the cur-
    rent philosophy of basic training that
    does not produce mentally and physically
    complete soldiers. Warns that the cur-
    rent basic training program is on the
    verge of destruction unless certain im-
    provements are made.

52. Beaumont, Roger A. "The Field-Expedient
    Factor: Adaptation and Survival in the
    First Battle." MILITARY REVIEW,
    60, 10 (October1980), 69-75.

    Emphasizes the importance of the
    "field-expedient" factor, i.e., innovation
    and invention in response to immediate
    need.   Recommends that military occupa-

tional specialty (MOS)-oriented training
and testing system must be balanced by
selection and training techniques toward
developing special improvisational and
adaptive skills.

53. Bollens, John C. "Municipal Training: An
    Appraisal." PUBLIC MANAGEMENT, 31, 7
    (July 1950), 146-149.

    Evaluates the in-service program con-
    ducted by the Institute for Training in
    Municipal Administration established by
    the International City Management Associa-
    tion (ICMA), fifteen years after its in-
    ception. Uses training manuals and les-
    son sheets to allow enrollees to work
    at his own speed, after which a certi-
    ficate is granted upon completion of as-
    signments and examinations. Concludes
    this unique program is a success because
    of the widespread acceptance of its form
    and the increase in the number of text-
    book sales all over the country.
    [Achieves the objective of improving the
    standards of performance in local govern-
    ment employees.]

54. Brockman, Paul R. "Meeting the Young
    Employee Halfway." PUBLIC ADMINISTRA-
    TION REVIEW, 31, 5 (September-October
    1971), 571-573.

    Suggests five ways in which an orga-
    nization can effectively involve a new em-
    ployee in the organization: (1) comprehen-
    sive low-key briefing for each candidate
    before job offer; (2) joint planning of
    first work assignment by agency and new
    or prospective employee; (3) encourage-
    ment of other employees to evaluate and
    relate to young employee; (4) involvement
    of new employee in evaluation of his
    work at the very beginning; and (5)joint
    "stay-no stay" decision no later than se-
    cond year of employment.

55. Dodson, Charles and Barbara Haskew.
    "Why Public Workers Stay." PUBLIC
    PERSONNEL MANAGEMENT, 5, 2 (March-
    April 1976), 132-138.

    Examines reasons why public workers
    stay on their jobs--approximately 600 em-
    ployees in a major division of a state
    government. Provides interesting implica-
    tions for managing retention, and improv-
    ing productivity. Concludes that public
    personnel practices need to be concerned
    not only with why workers leave, but
    why they stay. Recommends that if rea-
    sons for staying do not involve factors
    contributing toward productive job per-
    formance, then public personnel managers
    must search for ways to emphasize the
    development of job-intrinsic motivator
    factors as reasons for retention. Sug-
    gests that the directions this approach
    will take may involve substantial redefi-
    nition of certain job tasks in the
    search for job enrichment as well as
    further study into the work ethics of
    many levels of state employment.

56. Flanders, Loretta R. "Qualifications and
    Competence." THE BUREAUCRAT, 12, 1
    (Spring 1983), 48-50.

    Claims that many promotions into and
    upward in the federal managerial hierar-
    chy generally are based more on the in-
    dividual's technical expertise than on
    managerial competence. Addresses the
    process of identifying the content and
    forms of the executive qualification
    areas and how these provide a framework
    for SES candidate development. Proposes
    that differences in the nature of senior
    and middle management roles and responsi-
    bilities support the need for highlight-
    ing managerial competence requirements for
    SES jobs through processes of executive
    qualifications certification and executive
    development.

57. Floyd, Picot B. "Some Aspects of Staf-
    fing for the Urban Crises." PUBLIC
    ADMINISTRATION REVIEW, 31, 1 (January-
    February 1971), 36-40.

    Urges that responsible public adminis-
    trators must find new techniques to im-
    prove municipal employment in reducing
    the urban crisis of increasing manpower
    needs. Presents some issues that must
    be considered in staffing: (1) innova-
    tion in recruitment; (2) new ways of
    managing; (3) professionalization;
    (4) training opportunities; (5) new staf-
    fing patterns; (6) militancy of employee
    organizations; (7) minority group employ-
    ment; and (8) joint appointments with
    local colleges and industries for
    difficult-to-find professionals.

58. Gulick, Luther. "Cities Need More Advisory
    Services." PUBLIC MANAGEMENT, 30, 6
    (June 1948), 158-161.

    Argues for the creation of a local
    government technical advisory service by
    the Tennessee State government. Cites
    following arguments: (1) expansion of
    services provided by cities and counties;
    (2) similarity of technical problems en-
    countered by local governments; (3) need
    for technical assistance by local govern-
    ments; (4 economical basis in providing
    such service by experts on Tennessee af-
    fairs, law and practice; and (5) non-
    political nature of the service.

59. Harrison, Evelyn. "The Working Woman:
    Barriers in Employment." PUBLIC ADMIN-
    ISTRATION REVIEW, 24, 2 (June 1964),
    78-85.

    Identifies and debunks some of the
    conventional assumptions concerning compa-
    rative employment characteristics of men
    and women workers. Concludes that the

personal insistence that women play a
larger role in government is found to
provide significant impetus in advancing
their employment status in the federal
service.

60. Ingraham, Larry H. and Frederick J.
    Manning. "Psychiatric Battle Casualties:
    The Missing Column in a War Without
    Replacements." MILITARY REVIEW, 60, 8
    (August 1980), 18-29.

    Analyzes the causes for psychiatric
    combat casualties. Makes recommendations
    for appropriate preparations to turn psy-
    chiatric casualties from liabilities to
    assets. Warns that psychiatric casualties
    could become permanent losses without
    these preparations, and could represent
    recoverable manpower on the battlefield.

61. Jones, Roger W. "Developments in Govern-
    ment Manpower: A Federal Perspective."
    PUBLIC ADMINISTRATION REVIEW, 27, 2
    (June 1967), 134-141.

    Describes some of the important and
    interesting developments in executive
    training since the passage of the 1958
    Government Employees Training Act: (1) man-
    power planning and career development;
    (2) employee mobility and analysis of
    losses and turnover; (3) pay and fringe
    benefits; (4) labor-management relations;
    (5) use of modern technology in person-
    nel administration, and (6) intergovern-
    mental personnel matters.

62. Katzell, Raymond A. "Reflections on 'Edu-
    cating Executives'." PUBLIC ADMINISTRA-
    TION REVIEW, 19, 1 (Winter 1959), 1-6.

    Analyzes apparent similarities and dif-
    ferences in array of educational programs
    to develop executives in industry and

public agencies in terms of objectives,
content, method, educational agency, and
job level of trainees. Discusses three
possible weaknesses in the educational
programs for public executives: (1) non-
integration into a total executive development program by employing agency for
each individual; (2) little attention to
emotional barriers to effective action as
opposed to the barrier of inadequate
knowledge; and (3) over-emphasis on administrative technique as against program
knowledge.

63. Lyden, Fremont J. and Ernest Goriller.
    "Why City Managers Leave the Profes-
    sion: Longitudinal Study in the Pacific
    Northwest." PUBLIC ADMINISTRATION RE-
    VIEW, 36, 2 (March-April 1976), 175-181.

    Provides information on why indivi-
dual city managers leave the profession.
Compiles results from a questionnaire
answered by city managers in the Pacific
Northwest. Finds the principal negative
aspects were salary and council relationships. Notes that those who left had
found related occupations.

64. Marsh, Julian T. "Preparing the Combat
    Aviator." MILITARY REVIEW, 62, 5 (May
    1982), 23-39.

    Explains the direction of aviation
training to prepare aviation crews for
operation and survival in future conflicts. Describes institutional and unit
training to attain and sustain job pro-
ficiency.

65. Merriam, Charles E. "Some Aspects of
    Loyalty." PUBLIC ADMINISTRATION REVIEW,
    8, 2 (Spring 1948), 81-84.

    Presents various factors which create

loyalty and hatred of outsiders: great-
ness in freedom of life and spirit,
customs, democratic loyalty, propaganda
relating to political behavior, and
larger loyalties to the global organization of mankind.

Outlines a constructive program to
promote loyalty in public servants: adequate compensation, in-service training, and
halting stream of bitter, smearing attacks
upon public servants and service.

66. Nigro, Lloyd G. , and Kenneth J. Meier.
    "Executive Mobility in the Federal
    Service: A Career Perspective." PUBLIC
    ADMINISTRATION REVIEW, 35, 3 (May-June
    1975), 291-295.

    Presents the results of a survey con-
    cerned with the mobility of federal exe-
    cutives (GS 16-18). Shows that they are
    highly mobile over a career but there
    were variations found which lead the au-
    thors to conclude that statements on mo-
    bility should be made with caution.

67. Odom, Thetus C. "Management Development
    at Kelly Air Force Base." PUBLIC AD-
    MINISTRATION REVIEW, 16, 1 (Winter
    1956) 3-36.

    Reports that to meet the needs of
    more airpower and the demand for less
    money, Kelly Air Force Base developed a
    program to train all supervisors in man-
    agement areas, both at the executive le-
    vel and at the middle management level.

68. Olsen, Allan S. "Group Training for City
    Employees." PUBLIC MANAGEMENT, 35, 8
    (August 1953), 178-179.

    Summarizes the results of a survey
    carried in 175 council-manager cities on

in-service programs. Concludes that in-
service training of employees costs com-
paratively little and show a higher return on effective government management
than any other government expenditure.

69. Paulionis, A.N. "The Value of Practical
    Promotional Examinations for the Police
    and Fire Ranks." PUBLIC PERSONNEL
    MANAGEMENT, 2, 3(May-June 1973),
    179-181.

    Suggests that practical promotional
examinations in the police and fire departments have long-term consequences. Al-
lows employees to be tested for leadership and human skills needed at the supervisory levels. Proposes three parts
in examinations: written which could also
be the qualifying exam; oral; and practical which includes three elements for
effectivity--candidate orientation as to
limitations of authority, assumption of
situations and familiarization of the
scene, creation of a decision-making situation which requires a candidate to
apply sound practices, and rater's orientation in which guidelines and acceptable
actions are to be taken.

70. Pernick, Robert. "An Integrated Approach
    to Human Resource Management." GAO
    REVIEW, 16, 2(Spring 1981), 71-78.

    Serves four purposes: (1) gives a
background on a variety of personnel
management changes that could occur;
(2) defines the need for the benefits
of HRM and suggests its relevance to
GAO; (3) gives a context for considering
several of GAO's own programs; and
(4) notes several reasons why an organization needs to establish a comprehensive
policy and a systematic approach to Human
Resource Management. Discusses one integrated system that could enhance GAO's

management of human resources in the
1980's.

71. Pfiffner, John M. "Selection and Training
    of Supervisors." PUBLIC MANAGEMENT,
    30, 2 (February 1948), 30-34.

    Emphasizes the role of supervisory
    personnel in getting the job done and
    the importance of training development
    programs for qualified personnel in muni-
    cipal government. Suggests scientific se-
    lection approaches, training methods, and
    constant evaluation of supervisors for
    promotional purposes to make the training
    program a success.

72. Pickering, Thomas J. "The Enlisted Equa-
    tion: Reality-Ritual = Retention." MILI-
    TARY REVIEW, 60, 12 (December 1980),
    2-9.

    Examines certain "rituals" and "reali-
    ties" that influence the soldier's deci-
    sion to remain in or leave the army.
    Offers some ideas on improvements that
    can be made to retain a significant
    number of quality soldiers in today's
    army.

73. Ridley, Clarence E. "Twenty Years of
    Management Training." PUBLIC MANAGE-
    MENT, 36, 9 (September 1954), 194-197.

    Evaluates the cumulative impact of in-
    service training, both on local and na-
    tional scales. Poses the challenge of
    expanding training programs that result
    in a higher standard of service for in-
    dividuals and cities pioneering in admin-
    istrative training.

74. Ring, Peter Smith, and James L. Perry.
    "Reforming the Upper Levels of Bureau-

cracy: A Longitudinal Study of Senior
Executive Service."ADMINISTRATION &
SOCIETY, 15, 1 (May 1983), 119-144.

Investigates the impact of first two
years of implementation of Senior Executive Service (SES) on improved individual and agency performance. Reviews SES
theoretical underpinnings which indicate
negative effect of the program. Discusses likely causes of the negative effects:
(1) inadequate reward system; (2) perceived
breach of faith by Congress on SES bonuses; (3) political nature of SES ap-
pointments; (4) lack of appropriate skills
of newly appointed members of the SES;
(5) inconsistency in removal of poor performance; and (6) shift away from merit
system principles. Recommends some changes
to improve SES: (1) agency flexibility in
awarding bonuses up to congressional cei-
lings; (2) rethinking of SES premises; and
(3) seeking cooperation of non-SES colleagues
by SES executives.

75. Roberts, Samuel L., and Willis R. McCabe.
    "Training Municipal Employees on the Job."
    PUBLIC MANAGEMENT, 27, 1 (January 1945),
    40-43.

Reviews a comprehensive training program
conducted in San Diego for both supervisors and employees that implemented an
agreement between the city and school
board to give their employees equal opportunities in promotion. Notes that it
is too early to determine results as
program was newly launched.

76. Rommel, Rowena Bellows. "The Making of
    Administrators." PUBLIC ADMINISTRATION
    REVIEW, 2, 2 (Spring 1942), 113-115.

Reviews the problem of securing administrative personnel for higher levels of
government, specially all-around, well-

trained administrators. Places the blame
on the government's emphasis on techni-
cians, along with the stress on specialization in the employment market. Argues
that there is need for administrative
development of employees.

77. Rosen, Bernard. "In the National Interest."
    THE BUREAUCRAT, 12, 1 (Spring 1983),
    41-43.

    Contends that: (1) unfair pillorying of
government agencies and bureaucrats will
adversely affect recruitment and retention
of competent and thereby weaken performance
of government; (2) unwarranted abuse des-
troys citizens' respect for usefulness and
quality of work by public employers and
reduces ability of public service to
perform. Argues that dealing with these
issues should be top priority for public
employee organizations--unions, professional
societies and associations. Recommends that
government bureaucrats fight back against
irresponsible criticism because they have
a record of performance that demonstrates
professionalism, justifies pride, and merits
public commendation.

78. Stanley, David. "Trying to Avoid Layoffs."
    PUBLIC ADMINISTRATION REVIEW, 37, 5
    (September-October 1977), 515-517.

    Describes briefly the public sector en-
vironment with respect to layoffs caused
by budget cutbacks. Presents some alternatives to avoid layoffs: early squeeze on
the capital projects; delay in new construction starts; cancellation of other
projects; freeze on a wide variety of expenditures; fiscal adjustments ("manipula-
tions"); and a mixture of confrontations,
accommodations, plays to the press, and ap-
peals to the state capitals and Washington.

79. Staufenberger, Richard A. "The Profession-
    alization of Police: Efforts and Obs-
    tacles." PUBLIC ADMINISTRATION REVIEW,
    37, 6 (November-December 1977), 678-685.

    Analyzes selected indicators of police
improvement. Observes specifically the selection procedures, training and conduct
standards, and higher education as positive
efforts towards police improvement. Holds,
nevertheless, that there remain several
areas in need of change. Concludes by
recognizing degrees of success in the
profession and by predicting an optimis-
tic future.

80. Stockard, James G. "A Training Strategy
    for Decentralized Organization." PUBLIC
    PERSONNEL MANAGEMENT, 2, 3 (May-June
    1973), 200 -204.

    Recognizes the need for a training
strategy for decentralized organizations.
Endorses the use of a network of Employee
Development Centers (EDC) to solve problems
on employee training and development. Believes that the EDC plan deals with the
various continuing needs for training and
development such as instructional methods,
training content, delivery system, testing
and counseling dimension, upward mobility,
systematic approach, state of educational
technology, professionally managed function,
and an "integrated, organizationally coor-
dinated management function."

81. Stone, Daniel B. "The Critical Mass." THE
    BUREAUCRAT, 12, 2 (Summer 1983),39-43.

    Describes how the Animal and Plant
Health Inspection Service of the U.S. Department of Agriculture established senior
management Preparation Program for its
middle level managers. Outlines key lessons learned during development of the
program to constitute guidelines for

evaluating managerial and executive development programs.

82. Taylor, William J. Jr. "Military Profes-
    sionals in Changing Times." PUBLIC
    ADMINISTRATION REVIEW, 37, 6 (November-
    December 1977), 633-641.

    Analyzes the impact of societal change
    and technology on the military profession:
    anti-militarism movement in the mid-1960s;
    gradual emergence of "worker democracy;"
    amilitarism of the 1970s; demise of mi-
    litary conscription; increased and greater
    specialization which runs counter to the
    traditional concept of generalist officer;
    unionization of the military; high pro-
    ductivity of the officer education system;
    and pressures to reduce military costs.
    Raises some issue areas that constitute
    future challenges to maintenance of mili-
    tary professional expertise: recruitment and
    retention of best educated men and women;
    fragmentation of the military profession
    caused by trends in specialization and
    unionization; and commensurateness of mili-
    military authority in national security
    decision making with military operational
    responsibilities.

83. Theony, A. Robert. "Promoting Academic/
    Practitioner Interaction: The Memphis
    Experience." PUBLIC ADMINISTRATION RE-
    VIEW, 37, 6 (November-December 1977),
    590-594.

    Reviews a project where academicians and
    practitioners join in an effort to develop and
    evaluate patterns of interaction which could
    provide avenues to improved urban management
    education. Notes several benefits resulting
    from the project. Also notes that curriculum
    changes have occurred, demand for intern
    service increased, and academics and univ-
    ersities have been accepted as valuable
    resources for local governments.

84. Townsend, James R. "Planning for Replace-
    ment of Key People." PUBLIC MANAGEMENT,
    33, 1 (January 1951), 31-32.

    Acknowledges the importance of training re-
    placements for key positions. Proposes
    several methods, one of which is the
    adoption of the in-service program offered
    by the Institute for Training of Municipal
    Administration conducted by the Interna-
    tional City Management Association; other
    approaches include intensive training of
    rank and file employees, and recruitment
    from other cities' managers.

85. Uhlman, Frank W. "Training, the Conspi-
    racy Against Employees." PUBLIC PERSON-
    NEL MANAGEMENT, 2, 5 (September-October
    1983), 342-344.

    Views training workshops as anathema to
    employees. Points out the difficulty in
    measuring effectiveness of supervisors who
    have attended seminars. Suggests that or-
    ganizations develop a training guide based
    on needs, and adopt one that has shown
    results rather than use it "as the panacea
    for all the ills of the organization."

86. Villanueva, A.B. "In-Service Training: An
    American County Government's Experience."
    PUBLIC PERSONNEL MANAGEMENT, 2, 5
    (September-October 1983), 332-335.

    Evaluates the results of an in-service
    program conducted for supervisors of the
    Clark County in Nevada from 1967-69. Ad-
    judges it a success based on excellent se-
    minar ratings--courses were relevant to their
    area of work and the discussion method of
    instruction proved effective.

87. Weckler, J.E., and Theo E. Hall. "Training
    Police in Interracial Relations." PUB-
    LIC MANAGEMENT, 26, 7 (July 1944), 198-202.

Discusses methods and tactics to be
used by the police force in the proper
handling of situations involving minority
groups. Suggests that a well-trained police force can be knowledgeable in civil
rights laws, background of minority groups
and areas in which they live, and the methods
of preventing clashes and disorder as well as
attitudes of the minority groups.

88. Zeina, Yoram. "Is External Management Train-
    ing Effective for Organizational Change?"
    PUBLIC PERSONNEL MANAGEMENT, 2, 6
    (November-December 1973), 400-407.

Views external management training as an
ineffective tool in organizational change.
Emphasizes that managerial behavioral change
can be brought about by internal training
activities. Suggests a systematic approach
in training field to cope with specific
problem of behavioral changes. Concludes
that internal training can be helpful if
it is based on needs, managerial and
employee participation, in-house training
conducted by experienced staff, and cons-
tant evaluation.

2. ECOLOGY OF PUBLIC ORGANIZATIONS

A. Political Economy and
Citizen Participation

89. Abney, Glenn, and Thomas P. Lauth. "The
Tasks of State Administrators: Manage-
ment or External Relations." AMERICAN
REVIEW OF PUBLIC ADMINISTRATION, 16, 2/3
(Summer/Fall 1983), 171-184.

Investigates relative importance of management and external relations to state
agency heads. Discusses some of the causes
and consequences of the patterns identified.
Concludes that the more agency heads engage
in external relations with political actors
the less likely they are to use professional
values and judgments in program development.

90. Alexander, Ernest R. "Goal Setting and Growth
in an Uncertain World: A Case Study of a
Local Community Organization." PUBLIC
ADMINISTRATION REVIEW, 36, 2 (March-
April 1976), 182-191.

Analyzes the genesis and development of a
local community organization to reveal the
relationship between goal setting during
planning and goal displacement in implementation. Discusses that participative planning
needs an equal consideration of ends and
means. Warns that goal setting alone becomes
a self defeating process.

91. Austin, David M. "Resident Participation:

Political Mobilization and Organizational
Co-optation?" PUBLIC ADMINISTRATION RE-
VIEW, 32 (Special Issue 1972), 409-420.

Reports on the relation between participation experience and continuing issue
of citizen involvement and citizen action in
a society that is democratic and conten-
tious. Studies the Community Action Program
experience to aid in the further development
of CAP's by community action agencies.

92. Bercal, Thomas E. "Calls for Police As-
    sistance: Consumer Demands for Govern-
    mental Service." AMERICAN BEHAVIORAL
    SCIENTIST, 13, 5/6(May-June/July-
    August 1970), 681-691.

Views metropolitan policy departments
as service agencies which are involved in
dispensing a wide and diversified variety of
services, both to the individual and society. Observes that responsibilities of the
police executive encompass the delivery of
services in response to a wide variety
of societal "needs," which may be outside
the realm of law enforcement.

93. Bishop, George T. "What Must My Interest
    in Politics Be If I Just Told You I Don't
    Know." PUBLIC OPINION QUARTERLY, 48, 2
    (Summer 1984), 510-519.

Formulates that how much people think
they follow what's going on in government
and public affairs depends on the context
in which they are asked the question.
Finds that if asked immediately after
difficult questions about what they know
of their congressman's record, they are much
less likely to think they pay attention to
public affairs than if they are asked,
first, how interested they are in such
matters. Shows that two independent experiments demonstrate that this context
effect cannot be eliminated, or significantly

reduced, by interposing a buffer of questions
on unrelated topics between the items that
are known to affect one another. Discusses
the psychological significance of these
findings and their implications for survey
research.

94. Bomer, Joseph. "Effective Public Management."
    HARVARD BUSINESS REVIEW, 55, 2 (March-
    April, 1977), 131-140.

    Contends that public management is not
    just different in degree from corporate
    management but different in quality. Dis-
    cusses important implications for public
    managers as they view their jobs, for cor-
    porate managers seeking to develop good
    relationships with government, and for
    management educators.

95. Boone, Richard W. "Reflections on Citizen
    Participation and the Economic Opportu-
    nity Act. PUBLIC ADMINISTRATION REVIEW,
    32 (Special Issue 1972), 444-456.

    Investigates the impact of the Economic
    Opportunity Act on participation by the
    poor. Needs to be viewed with an unders-
    tanding of current forces of poor citizen
    participation which requires examining
    forces that generated prior actions.

96. Brouillete, John R. "The Department of
    Public Works: Adaptation to Disaster
    Demands." AMERICAN BEHAVIORAL SCIEN-
    TIST, 13, 3 (January-February 1970),
    369-379.

    Studies the DPW's disaster responses.
    Finds that DPW would function in times
    of disasters with a high degree of ef-
    fectiveness because it possesses great
    capabilities in utilizing material and
    personnel resources. Concludes that the
    DPW becomes an integral part of any

community   response   to   a   natural   disaster.

97. Brudney, Jeffrey and Robert England. "Toward
    a Definition of the Co-Production Con-
    cept." PUBLIC ADMINISTRATION REVIEW,
    43, 1 (January-February 1983), 59-65.

    Defines co-production as the critical
    mix of activities that service agents and
    citizens contribute to production of pub-
    lic services. Distinguishes three types of
    co-production: individual, group, and col-
    lective.

98. Chambliss, William J. ON THE TAKE: FROM
    PETTY CROOKS TO PRESIDENTS. Blooming-
    ton: Indiana University Press, 1978.
    269 p.

    Studies and analyzes from the bottom-up
    a system of racketeering, pay-offs, and
    political empire building. Delineates the
    roles of presidents, vice-presidents, sen-
    ators, governors, and racketeers who are
    implicated in a ubiquitous systemof pay-
    offs and favors, backscratching, stealing,
    campaign contributions, and personal ag-
    grandizement. Blames capitalism and the
    organizational politics for the systematic
    organization of illegal activities. Dec-
    lares that the people in the crime net-
    work were simply acting within both the
    logic and values of American political eco-
    nomy. Proposes either a revolutionary change
    in the political economy to stop crime
    networks, and absent this alternative, a
    decriminalization of illegal activities to
    eliminate or reduce the magnitude and
    change the character of crime networks.

99. Chatman, Linwood, and David M. Jackson.
    "Citizen Participation--An Exercise in
    Futility: An Action Program for ASPA."
    PUBLIC ADMINISTRATION REVIEW, 32, 3 (May-
    June 1972), 199-201.

Calls on ASPA to make a stand and influence local government to open up to
participation by minority groups. Proposes
that ASPA should recruit minority group
people for ASPA membership, create strong
ASPA community outreach, and use minority-
owned businesses.

100. Collinge, F.B. "A Projective Technique
    for Political Behavior." AMERICAN BEH-
    AVIORAL SCIENTIST, 5, 6 (March 1961),
    3-7.

Applies psychological theory in analyzing political behavior. Uses photos in the
1960 presidential campaign (administered
as "projective tests") in exciting a wealth
of free fantasy in people, which can enrich
political psychology.

101. Dixon, John. "How Can Public Participation
    Become Real?" PUBLIC ADMINISTRATION RE-
    VIEW, 35, 1 (January-February 1975),
    69-70.

Feels that the way to increase participation is by first defining the community involved, and developing trust in the
citizens' desires.

102. Dolbeare, Kenneth and Phillip Hammond. "The
    Political Party Basis of Attitudes Toward
    the Supreme Court." PUBLIC OPINION QUAR-
    TERLY, 32, 1 (Spring 1968), 16-30.

Explores public attitudes toward the
Supreme Court based on surveys by Gallup,
Michigan & Berkeley Survey Research Centers, and Wisconsin Survey Research Laboratory in 1966. Relates perceptions of
the Supreme Court to political party
identification. Suggests that basic political factors are powerful determinants
of support for, or antipathy toward, the
court. Appears to be not so much awe or

reverence, or even non-partisan neutrality, that supports the court, but rather the fact that one's political party controls the White House!

103. Dworak, Robert J. "Economizing in Public Organizations." PUBLIC ADMINISTRATION REVIEW, 35, 2 (March-April 1975), 158-165.

Examines the question of enhancing efficiency, effectiveness and economy in terms of macro-organizational behavior. Combines and operationalizes efficiency, effectiveness, and economy in the concept of "economizing." Proposes means of implementing economizing in the form of four market mechanisms which may be introduced into public organizations: flexibility, delegation of authority, cost assignment techniques, and task acquisition systems.

104. Elliot, Clarence H. "Municipal Responsibility for Cultural Activities." PUBLIC MANAGEMENT, 35, 10 (October 1953), 218-221.

Recognizes the need for cultural opportunities in the community as a means to attract high quality workers and maintain satisfied citizens. Discusses the role of city government in encouraging participation through endorsements and active cooperation with various groups: stresses the significance of the city manager in streamlining activities and coordinating projects to meet the aesthetic needs of the citizens.

105. Fessler, Donald R. FACILITATING COMMUNITY CHANGE: A BASIC GUIDE." La Jolla, CA: University Associates, 1976. 146 p.

Assumes that a much larger and more representative number of citizens need to be involved in the decision-making process before changes can be brought about to

solve community problems. Emphasizes the
need for citizens to understand group
process before they can energize interest
in bringing about change through cooperative community effort.

106. Friedrich, Carl J. THE PATHOLOGY OF POLITICS.
New York: Harper & Row, 1972. 287 p.

Discusses the interrelationships between
violence, betrayal, corruption, secrecy and
propaganda in politics. Analyzes the func-
tionality of violence in settlement of disputes in the international system, the implications of treason, and the consequences
of the pervasiveness of corruption in the
political system. Relates secrecy and propaganda to the previously mentioned political phenomena. Concludes that politics
needs all these dubious practices: it
cannot be managed without violence, betrayal, corruption, secrecy and propaganda.

107. Grossman, Howard, and Robert A. Cox. "Coor-
dination: Teamwork in a Small Community."
PUBLIC ADMINISTRATION REVIEW, 23, 1
(March 1963), 35-39.

Illustrates how a small community was
able to coordinate the efforts of county,
state and federal agencies and voluntary
citizen groups to solve community problems.
Identifies some of the significant ingre-
dients of successful coordination through a
case study.

108. Guttman, Daniel and Barry Willner. THE
SHADOW GOVERNMENT. New York: Pantheon
Books, 1976. 354 p.

Analyzes the extent and function of delegation of governmental responsibilities
and decision making by the Executive
Branch through contracts, grants, subsidies, and consultancy studies. Places

the blame on Congress which has not insisted
that the Executive Branch develop a reason-
able expertise of its own to fulfill its
authorized missions. Underscores the influence of consulting industry officials in
suggesting, shaping, and even implementing
much governmental policy in both its nar-
rowest and broadest sense. Refers to this
contract-consulting bureaucracy as "shadow
government."

Declares that a combination of the
abdication of its responsibilities by the
Executive Branch and the assertiveness of
the firms themselves insinuates them so-
lidly into the governmental process. Illustrates the impact of this "shadow government" through several case studies. In-
sists the need for dismantling of this
shadow government to insure an accountable
governmental structure and to prevent the
government from abdicating in favor of
special interest groups. Assigns the responsibility to Congress as the most appropriate branch of government in asserting
governmental supremacy over the shadow
government.

109. Harman, Douglas B. "Can Planners Find Hap-
     piness in a Political World?" PUBLIC
     ADMINISTRATION REVIEW, 30, 4 (July-
     August 1970), 449-453.

     Discusses that planners have begun to
realize the political nature of their
work and that they have developed political skills to be effective. Makes this
conclusion after reviewing three books.

110. International City Management Association.
     "The City Manager's Relation to the
     Public." PUBLIC MANAGEMENT, 28, 7 (July
     1946), 199-204.

     Details the what, how, and why of the
city manager's public relations program.

Enumerates activities as: affiliation with
local organizations, radio programs, municipal "open house" for the public, survey
of public attitudes, training in cour-
tesy for all employees, participative
administration, extension of municipal
services as need arises, efficient and
courteous service at low cost, use of
media, prompt action on complaints, and
responsiveness to suggestions.

111. Johnson, Bert W. "Sustaining Citizen Inte-
     rest in City Government." PUBLIC MAN-
     AGEMENT, 33, 7 (July 1951), 146-147.

     Advocates a program of action to main-
tain the citizens' interest and understanding of city government. Lists a de-
dicated organizational workforce, team work,
participation in budget proposals, improvement of first impressions through
planning and coordination of zoning and
utilities installation, distribution of
attractive and readable pamphlets on municipal services, selective personnel program, and the use of public utilities to
keep citizenry informed of government
activities.

112. Kauffman, Kris and Alice Shorett. "A Perspec-
     tive on Public Involvement in Water
     Management Decision Making." PUBLIC
     ADMINISTRATION REVIEW, 37, 5 (September-
     October 1977), 467-471.

     Recognizes water use policies as having
tremendous impact on its citizenry. Suggests
that water program administrators consider
a more democratic approach toward involving
the people whom they serve. Proposes techniques of involvement such as: formal hearings, workshops, radio, television, advisory committees, and mediation. Concludes that by allowing greater participation, the water resources administrator is
properly executing his/her roles as a public
servant.

113. Levy, Sidney J. "The Public Image of Gov-
      ernment Agencies." PUBLIC ADMINISTRA-
      TION REVIEW,   23, 1 (March 1963), 25-29.

      Argues that government agencies cannot do
      much to improve public recognition of their
      accomplishments. Interprets findings that
      Americans want to believe their government
      is bureaucratic, lazy, and authoritarian.
      Emphasizes that they want to be able to
      criticize this authority.

114. Lieske, Joel A. "In Quest of the Manpower
      Grail: Politics, Planning and Pluralism."
      PUBLIC ADMINISTRATION REVIEW,   36, 3
      (May-June 1976), 327-333.

      Reviews several books on manpower.
      Demonstrates how manpower programs have
      attempted to bridge the dislocations of
      the nation's economic policies and the
      inadequacies of its social welfare prog-
      rams.

115. Lucy, William. "A Public Employee View of
      Management." PUBLIC MANAGEMENT, 55, 7
      (July 1973), 8-9.

      Voices concern over prevailing negative
      attitudes of taxpayers toward political
      system. Suggests that a working partner-
      ship between public employees and public
      management can be forged to overcome
      these views and to resolve conflicting
      issues existing between both camps.

116. Marsh, Burton W.   "Solving the Automobile
      Parking Problem." PUBLIC MANAGEMENT,
      23, 1 (January 1941), 10-14.

      Summarizes findings and recommendations
      of three-year study of the problem of
      parking and terminal facilities. Considers
      the following factors: parking time req-
      uirements, loading and unloading of mer-

chandise, variations in demand for parking
in different parts of the business
district, public's willingness to pay for
parking space, influence of parking lots
on traffic flow and street use in the
area, motorists' willingness to walk from
parking lots to destinations, and adequacy
of mass transportation facilities.

117. Marver, James. CONSULTANTS CAN HELP. Lexing-
     ton, Mass.: Lexington Books, 1979. 225 p.

     Inquires into some issues involving the
use of outside experts. Examines the
substantive and political functions that
outside experts serve. Provides detailed
information about the use of consultants
by the Office of Child Development in
two specific demonstration programs. Identifies some sample expert products, along
with several related characteristics. Includes the communication of the expertise,
its intended uses, the reasons for seeking outsiders, and the functions to be
served by the products. Investigates the
satisfaction of clients over some products
and dissatisfaction over others. Discusses
the legal and administrative constraints
on contracting procedures and the rules
and ways of circumventing them. Recommends some ways to improve consultant
contract services.

118. Maxwell, Thomas F. "Citizens--the Key to
     Good Government." PUBLIC MANAGEMENT,
     36, 8 (August 1954), 173-177.

     Advises city managers that citizen par-
ticipation in municipal affairs is the
only way the community can achieve and retain good government. Encourages citizen
participation through a good public relations program, suggestion boxes and opinion
polls, complaint procedures, public reporting, public relations training for city
employees, public hearings especially in

controversial groups, and appointment of citizen advisory committees.

119. McEachern, A.W., and Al-Arayed Jawad. "Discerning the Public Interest." AD-MINISTRATION & SOCIETY, 15, 4 (February 1984), 493-553.

    Examines and proposes means which can discern the values, preferences, and interest of individual citizens: (1) have "public service" as primary objective of government employees who act as ombudsmen for citizens; (2) annual national survey on citizen satisfaction to provide public guidance for national priorities; and (3)special surveys before passing legislation or implementing projects that would change social or environmental conditions of the community. Urges the need for good people in government and empirically sound instrumentalities that will accomplish public interest objectives.

120. Mikesell, John L. "Administration and the Public Revenue System: A View of Tax Administration." PUBLIC ADMINISTRATION RE-VIEW, 34, 6 (November-December 1974), 615-624.

    Illustrates the need for public agencies to effectively raise revenues. Focuses on the administration of tax systems.

121. Newhouse, Margaret Locke. "Citizen Orientations Toward Local Government: Structure, Determinants, and Behavioral Consequences." Ph.D. Dissertation, University of California at Los Angeles, 1975. 437 p.

    Focuses on the structure, determinants, and behavioral consequences of citizen orientation toward local government. Uses four kinds of participant behavior in predicting effects of orientation on proba-

bility of participation--voting, particular-
ized contacting, campaign and civic group
activity, and non-violent protest. Discusses following implications of research:
(1) transfer of power and resources from
federal to local government will increase
citizens' involvement and political participation; (2) performance of local government
in line with heightened citizen expectations will increase citizen satisfaction
with government policy and processes;
(3) specific evaluations can be affected by
relatively short-term policies; (4) cognitive
and normative orientations appear to be primarily a consequence of early socialization
and inherited personality characteristics
and less affected by current experiences
and environments; and (5) different policy
options that could be used to achieve
desired patterns of citizen participation
are reduction of costs and increasing
expected benefits associated with different kinds of behavior.

122. Olsen, John B. "Applying Business Manage-
     ment Skills to Local Governmental Ope-
     rations." PUBLIC ADMINISTRATION REVIEW,
     39, 3 (May-June 1979), 282-289.

     Presents the case study of 'ComPAC',the
     Committee for Progressive Allegheny County,
     which was formed by executive officers of
     corporations in the area to aid local gov-
     ernment. Makes several statements about the
     involvement of business in government.

123. Preble, John F. "Anticipating Change: Futu-
     ristic Methods in the Public Sector."
     AMERICAN REVIEW OF PUBLIC ADMINISTRATION,
     16, 2/3 (Summer/Fall 1983), 139-150.

     Proposes borrowing from the private
     sector planning methods and tools to monitor
     and anticipate changes in public attitudes and
     sentiments. Provides examples demonstrating
     applicability of futuristic methodologies

and orientations ofthe public sector.

124. Riethmayer, Leo C.   "Relations   of   the   City
       Manager with   Pressure   Groups."   PUBLIC
       MANAGEMENT,   36, 1 (January 1954),   2-5.

       Supports   the   role   of   the   professional
       city managers in   emphasizing   the   public
       interest as they perform   their   important
       responsibilities, in spite   of   opposition
       from   interest groups. Cautions city man-
       agers   that   self-styled leaders of special
       interest   groups   are   merely speaking for
       themselves and not for the whole membership.

125. Rinehart,   Jeffrey C. , and   E. Lee Bernick.
       "Political Attitudes and Behavior Patterns
       of Federal   Civil   Servants." PUBLIC AD-
       MINISTRATION   REVIEW,   35, 6 (November-
       December   1975),   603-611.

       Examines the impact of the establishment of
       a Commission on Political Activity of Gov-
       ernment Personnel by Congress to determine
       the effect of   laws restricting the voluntary
       political activities   of   federal   employees.
       Finds that a majority of employees would
       not   participate   if   the   restrictions   were
       removed. Recommends that   serious   consi-
       deration   should   be   given   to   repealing
       unnecessary   restrictions.

126. Roderick, Sue Schock.   "The White House Con-
       ferences on Aging: Their Implications for
       Social   Change."   D.P.A.   Dissertation,
       University of Southern California, 1984.
       223 p.

       Provides   an   in-depth   historical   review
       and   analysis of the White House Conferences
       on Aging. Discusses the impact of the growth
       of   older people   and   the projections for
       the   future   in light of social   issues,
       changes in public policy for the elderly, and
       their   effects   on   the   political   process

itself. Concludes that the "gray lobby,"
including older persons themselves, controls
the senior movement's political power and
influence which has continued to accelerate
over the past 50 years. Finds that the WHCoA
have provided a significant role in formu-
lating and nurturing this acceleration.

127. Rosener, Judy B.   "Citizenship Participation:
        Can We Measure Its Effectiveness?" PUBLIC
        ADMINISTRATION REVIEW, 38, 5 (September-
        October 1978),   457-463.

        Points out that citizen participation
demands continue to grow, but little agreement exists among and between citizens
and administrators as to their goals and
objectives. Laments that little is known
about the "effectiveness" of participation.
Suggests that the use of evaluation research methodology which forces articula-
tion of heretofore "hidden values" and
assumptions, can produce an acceptable
framework for both the conceptualization
and measurement of citizen participation
effectiveness.

128. Rosenthal, Albert H. "The Ombudsman-
        Swedish Grievance Man." PUBLIC ADMINIS-
        TRATION REVIEW, 24, 4 (December 1964),
        226-230.

        Describes the positive aspects and be-
nefits of the Ombudsman in Swedish system
to its citizens. Provides each person with
a systematic method of redress in his
dealings with the government bureaucracy
at all levels.

129. Rowat, Donald C. "Ombudsman for North
        America." PUBLIC ADMINISTRATION REVIEW,
        24, 4 (December 1964),   230-233.

        Claims that ombudsman in North America
would function as a watchman over the total

administrative operation at all levels of
the government. Notes that finely tuned
instruments for the early detection of
procedural and substantive irregularities in
the treatment of citizens could result.

130. Schuck, Peter H. "Public Interest Groups
     and the Policy Process." PUBLIC ADMINIS-
     TRATION REVIEW,37, 2 (March-April 1977),
     132-140.

     Provides an overview of American public
     interest groups. Observes the increasing
     role of the public interest group in the pol-
     icy making process and suggests that fur-
     ther involvement of groups into agencies
     should, in part, be reimbursed for the
     costs of their participation under certain
     circumstances.

131. Stipak, Brian. "Citizen Satisfaction with
     Urban Services: Potential Misuse as a
     Performance Indicator." PUBLIC ADMINISTRA-
     TION REVIEW, 39, 1 (January-February
     1979), 46-52.

     Reports on the problems involved in
     using sample surveys of citizens. Cautions
     that potential problems arise because policy
     makers can misinterpret information received
     in the survey. Attributes this danger to two
     problems: (1) citizen responses to satisfac-
     tion may not reflect service performance;
     and (2) analyzing subjective indicators
     may be difficult. Recommends that policy
     makers use survey data for purposes
     other than performance evaluation.

132. Woolpert, Elton D. "Bringing City Employees
     and Citizens Together." PUBLIC MANAGE-
     MENT, 22, 4 (April 1940), 106-110.

     Explores how citizens can participate in
     local government activities and how public
     employees can join in the nongovernmental

enterprises.   Aims   at   improving   municipal
public   relations   and   consolidating   civic
resources   of   the   community.   Suggests eras-
ing   distinction   between   "public"   or
"private"   contributions to the common welfare,
forming advisory   boards or   committees, and
participating by city officials in   community
life, and   coordination   of   community   resources.

133. Zukin, Cliff, and   Robin   Snyder.   "Passive
     Learning: When   the Media   Environment   is
     the   Message."   PUBLIC OPINION QUARTERLY,
     48, 3   (Fall 1983),   629-638.

     Investigates the   phenomenon   of   "passive
     learning" or   how   people   may   acquire   in-
     formation about   the mass   media   despite
     lacking the motivation to do so.   Claims a
     unique   data   source   allows   us to overcome
     the "situation   effect" that generally
     makes the study of   this phenomenon dif-
     ficult. Says that saturation   conditions
     commonly occur because exposure to political
     programming is virtually universal.   Compares
     two   groups receiving different   media   mes-
     sages over two elections, with   interest con-
     trolled. Finds   that   those   who   had   no
     interest in an election,   but   who   lived   in
     a media-rich environment, were 40 percentage
     points more likely to   have   acquired   in-
     formation than   their   uninterested   cohorts
     living in a media-poor environment.

     B.   Budgetary Strategies and Constraints

134. Bailey, John J., and   Robert J. O'Connor.
     "Operationalizing   Incrementalism   Measur-
     ing   the   Muddles."   PUBLIC ADMINISTRATION
     REVIEW, 35, 1   (January-February 1975),
     60-66.

     States   that   incrementalism   has   been
     employed   as a general   concept to   describe

policy making but several difficulties have
arisen in its application to budgeting.
Examines several works to illustrate the problems encountered when the distinction between
process and output is not observed.

135. Balloun, James, and John F. Maloney. "Beating
     the Cost Service Squeeze: The Project
     Team Approach to Cost Improvement." PUBLIC
     ADMINISTRATION REVIEW, 32, 5 (September-
     October 1972), 531-538.

     Describes how to get action and to ge-
     nerate tangible cost-effectiveness benefits
     in public agencies. Uses an actual case
     in explaining how the results were obtained.

136. Berg, Bruce. "Public Choice, Pluralism, and
     Scarcity: Implications for Bureaucratic
     Behavior." ADMINISTRATION & SOCIETY,
     16, 1 (May 1984), 71-82.

     Discusses why presence of societal
     scarcity has modified ability of pluralism
     and public choice to explain societal
     events and, in particular, bureaucratic
     behavior. States that ability of these
     two approaches decreases in explaining
     societal events in the absence of so-
     cietal growth. Examines the implications
     of this phenomenon in explaining bureaucra-
     tic behavior. Concludes that these approaches
     in predicting bureaucratic behavior are not
     successful during times of scarcity,
     shrinkage, and decline.

137. Borrego, Espiridion A. "A Study of Ef-
     ficiency in a Public Organization."
     Ph.D. Dissertation, University of South-
     ern California, 1981. 139 p.

     Explores organizational efficiency of one
     city, using Katz and Kahn's organizational
     slack as a measure of organizational effi-
     ciency, in examining financial transactions

of Monterey Park, California. Finds, by
comparing published budget to the city's
working documents, a consistent pattern of
overestimating expenditures or underspending
in the categories of salaries, employee benefits, and supplies and services. Discovers the picture of the financial condition
reported in published budget as quite different from the picture in working documents.
Indicates that accumulation of excess sur-
plus as protection for possible future
revenue cutbacks places an excess burden
on citizens in terms of purchasing power
and non-production of additional services.
Cautions against use of initiative process
by citizens as a tax-cutting method which
may result in further accumulation of
surpluses.

138. Botner, Stanley B. "Action-Forcing Budgeting:
     The Fourth Stage?" AMERICAN REVIEW OF
     PUBLIC ADMINISTRATION, 15, 3 (Fall 1982),
     23-27.

     Postulates that the United States has en-
     tered a new stage of budgeting which req-
     uires public entities to justify their ap-
     propriations, the continuation of their
     programs, and their very existence to an
     unprecedented extent. Bestows appropriate
     title to this stage as action-forcing, integ-
     rated phase of budgeting.

139. _____. "Revenue Limitation--Missouri Style."
     PUBLIC BUDGETING & FINANCE, 3, 3 (Winter
     1983),   23-27.

     Studies the amendment to the Missouri State
     Constitution limiting revenues and govern-
     mental expenditures through the November 4,
     1980 initiative. Makes a case for the re-
     examination of the entire initiative process
     due to its increasing use and misuse, and
     the resulting encroachment on representative
     government. Concludes that constitutional
     processes should not be subject to the whims

of a small minority rallied around su-
perficial and potentially damaging proposals.

140. Blum, James L. "The Congressional Budget
     Process." THE BUREAUCRAT, 12, 4 (Winter
     1984), 14-16.

     Reviews the 1983-1984 congressional
     budget process under the Congressional Budget
     Act of 1974 in relation to attaining balanced
     budgeting. Declares that 1983 and 1984 are
     not good years for the budget process.
     Sees FY 1986 as having the best chance of
     making a significant change in projected de-
     ficit levels. Looks for a strong political
     consensus for the process to produce a
     significant change in budget policies.

141. Caiden, Naomi. "Guidelines to Federal Budget
     Reform." PUBLIC BUDGETING & FINANCE, 3, 3
     (Winter 1983), 4-22.

     Contends that budget reform is not a pa-
     nacea for problems arising from fundamen-
     tal differences in political outlook, in-
     consistent revenue and expenditure policies
     and results of pressure group politics; but
     that it is shaped by political choices and
     development of consensus on ground rules
     of financial decision making. Discusses
     some federal shortcomings: "uncontrollability"
     of majority of federal expenditures, insta-
     bility of budget numbers, fragmentation of
     accounts, and repetitiveness of procedures.
     Summarizes some proposal clusters: time
     frame, volatility, program control, and in-
     tegration.

     States that budget reforms will inevitably
     be judged not by their theoretical be-
     nefits or rationality, but by their im-
     pacts on the power struggle and their proba-
     ble effects on budget allocations.

142. Carey, Stephen W. "The Effects of Congres-

sional Sub-Committee Confidence on Appropriations of Governmental Agencies: An
Examination of the Records of One Appropriations Sub-Committee and Four Agencies." Ph.D. Dissertation, Howard
University, 1981. 264 p.

Investigates the role which confidence
played in determining increased or dec-
reased appropriations by sub-committees for
agencies they appropriate for. Observes
that confidence is not proportionally related
to increases or decreases in budgets of several agencies; that in many cases, perceived
lack of confidence in agency resulted in
increased appropriation; that confidence is
based on agency integrity, fund specification, task accomplishment, and degree of
favorable or unfavorable oversight operations.

143. Carroll, Michael A. "The Impact of General
Revenue Sharing on the Urban Planning
Process: An Initial Assessment." PUBLIC
ADMINISTRATION REVIEW, 35, 2 (March-
April 1975), 143-150.

Argues that urban planning as a function of local government, and urban planners as professionals in public service,
need to recognize that general and special
revenue sharing represent long term directions in intergovernmental relations and
fiscal policy. Suggests that these trends
will require increased adaptability, improved linkages with the political process,
greater managerial and operational skills,
strengthened budgetary and fiscal capaci-
ties, and heightened sensitivity to public
interest priorities.

144. Connelly, Michael D. "Budgeting and Policy
Analysts in Missouri." Ph.D. Dissertation, University of Missouri, 1981.
584 p.

Studies the roles, activities and in-

fluence of the executive analysts in the Missouri Division of Budget and Planning on the
Missouri budgetary and planning processes.
Relates these three elements to external
factors--state culture, finances, politics;
and internal factors--leadership, organizational structure, and communications. Inquires into the interactions of the analysts
with other major participants--the governor,
legislature, and executive departments. Discovers that even during executive-legislative
political battles resulting in "weakened"
positions for the analysts, they remained important figures in Missouri policy making, often finding their policy recommendations accepted.

145. Exley, Charles M. "A Comparative Analysis of
     Selected Alternatives for Allocation of
     Resources for Recreation Services by
     Local Government." Ph.D. Dissertation,
     Pennsylvania State University, 1977.
     282 p.

     Endeavors to provide some insights and
     understandings regarding the various al-
     ternatives for allocation of resources, as
     demonstrated through the distribution of
     services, specifically the delivery of
     recreation and park services. Analyzes the
     decision making process for allocation of
     resources for recreation services by local
     government. Delimits the study to the
     selected alternatives of Equity, Demand, and
     Social Problem Amelioration.

146. Gosling, James J. "The Wisconsin Budgetary
     Process: A Study of Participant In-
     fluence and Choice." Ph.D. Disserta-
     tion, University of Wisconsin-Madison,
     1980. 250 p.

     Describes and evaluates the pattern of ins-
     titutional relationships among budget partici-
     pants in the Wisconsin budgetary process.
     Focuses on the requests and recommenda-

tions made on each decision item considered
in the budgetary process. Finds that the
decision rules employed by institutional
budget participants varied as the characteristics of the budgetary decisions before
them differed: (1) for the legislative
budget deliberations, the individual characteristics of the budget items under consider-
ation--relative policy significance and
cost, and extent to which they affect local
units of government--emerged as key factors
influencing budgetary choice. Contrasts this
behavior to that of budget reviewers in the
executive stage of budget deliberations, who
appeared to be less influenced by the individual characteristics of decision items,
and more influenced by agency level
characteristics--appointing authority--
agency head relationship and the agency's
relative acquisitiveness in seeking new
funds.

147. Hale, George E. "Executive Leadership Versus
     Budgetary Behavior." ADMINISTRATION &
     SOCIETY, 9, 2 (August 1977), 169-190.

     Underscores existing studies which under-
estimate the barriers to using the budgetary
process as a mechanism for "steering," that
is, determining the goals and direction of
public organizations. Explains the apparent-
ly infinite adaptability of public administrators to changes in processes and priorities,
under two successive and sharply contrasting
chief executives from Delaware. Examines
how public administrators adapted budget
preparation to take advantage of each governor's priorities. Looks at how budget
examiners respond to changing executive priorities and how this may undermine executive
leadership. Investigates alterations in
legislative behavior which follows shifts in
executive preferences and agency actions.
Contains, finally, an assessment of how numerous actions steadily erode executive
leadership.

148. Hale, George E., and Scott R. Douglas. "The
     Politics of Budget Execution: Financial
     Manipulation in State and Local Govern-
     ments." ADMINISTRATION & SOCIETY, 9, 3
     (November 1977), 367-378.

     Notes that until recently, political scien-
     tists focused on the approval of budget req-
     uests and ignored budget execution. Counters
     the budgeting literature's almost single-
     minded concentration on legislative action.
     Reviews existing studies which touch on
     budget execution in state and local govern-
     ments. Identifies five major techniques of
     budgetary adjustment: (1) accounting le-
     gerdemain; (2) conservative special fund
     revenue estimates; (3) transfers; (4) repro-
     gramming; and (5) juggling of special
     funds. Concludes that additional research
     on budget execution is necessary before
     developing more effective theories about
     the steering of government institutions.

149. Hulpke, John F., and Donald A. Watne.
     "Budgeting Behavior: If, When, and How
     Selected School Districts Hide Money."
     PUBLIC ADMINISTRATION REVIEW, 36, 6
     (November-December 1976), 667-674.

     Reviews some popularly held views about
     public budget-making behavior, and proposes
     that these views be systematically tested.
     Touches on one test, finding income under-
     estimated and expenses over-estimated in
     24 San Francisco Bay area suburban school
     districts.

150. Kuespert, Edward F. "Limitations on Moving
     Ahead, While Cutting Back." PUBLIC BUD-
     GETING & FINANCE, 3, 2 (Summer 1983),
     79-82.

     Centers on the Food and Drug Adminis-
     tration's handicaps posed by budget limit-
     ations. Suggests that improved services
     may result through flexibility in identi-

fying new priorities and objectives, reprogramming scarce resources, and operating
within the budget.

151. Levine, Charles. "More on Cutback Manage-
      ment: Hard Questions for Hard Times." PUB-
      LIC ADMINISTRATION REVIEW, 39, 2 (March-
      April 1979), 179-181.

      Explores the development of a methodology
      for cutback management by investigating
      the major steps in the cutback process
      through strategic choices.

152. Levine, Charles H., Irene S. Rubin, and
      George G. Wolohojean. "Managing Orga-
      nizational Retrenchment: Preconditions,
      Deficiencies, and Adaptations in the
      Public Sector." ADMINISTRATION &
      SOCIETY, 14, 1 (May 1982), 101-136.

      Presents preconditions necessary for
      managing a contraction. Examines the cons-
      traints operative in the public sector
      which exclude or limit the availability of
      the prerequisites to public managers in
      effectively managing retrenchment. Demons-
      trates how a public organization without
      these prerequisites behaves under condi-
      tions of fiscal stress by using a multi-
      state model of public sector contraction
      that includes several political dimensions
      as well as organizational factors. Takes
      several of the model's components from the
      experience of New York City's government
      since its fiscal crisis of 1973-1974. Makes
      conclusion that retrenchment forces public
      organizations into a position of exces-
      sive oversight which stifles initiative and
      encourages errors. Projects that, over
      the long run, retrenchment may make pub-
      lic organizations even less effective and
      less capable of dealing with their problems.

153. Lucy, William. "Social Planning and Bud-

geting."   PUBLIC   MANAGEMENT,   65, 4
(April 1983), 13-16.

Presents the case for a Social Development
Commission (SDC) in social planning which can
provide   an   educational   aspect, a   buffering
aspect, and an   advisory role.   Finds   that
effectiveness of SDC depends on credibility
of appointees. Notes that credibility   in
budget making depends on participants' establishing   a   reputation   for   being   believable
(accurate),   trustworthy   (will not lie),   and
objective   (will attempt   to   balance   diverse
considerations).

154. McCaffery, Jerry.   "Revenue Budgeting: Dade
     County   Tries   a   Decremental   Approach."
     PUBLIC   ADMINISTRATION   REVIEW,   41,
     Special Issue   (January 1981),   179-188.

     Views revenue budgeting as giving emphasis
to most value   for   least   cost.   Focuses   on
cost growth retardation in relation to revenue constraints.   Describes decremental
budgeting   process   as   weighing service needs
against total money available, and   selecting
budget proposals that maximize savings and
minimize service level and community impact.
Provides   mechanism   for   oversight of   line
operations.

155. McTighe, John J.   "Management   Strategies
     to Deal with Shrinking Resources."
     PUBLIC   ADMINISTRATION REVIEW,   39, 1
     (January-February 1979),   86-90.

     Attempts   to   provide   further   guidance   to
managers confronted with shrinking   revenues
and cutback management.   Provides   a set   of
strategies for   managing   under   declining
conditions.

156. Menzel, Donald C.   "Federal Fiscal Influences
     on   State Agency Behavior."   INTERNATIONAL
     JOURNAL   OF PUBLIC ADMINISTRATION, 3, 3

(1981),   261-282.

Concentrates on increasing interdependence and dynamic federal arrangement between federal, state and local governments which has received little systematic, empirical study. Adds that few studies currently exist which analyze the influence that agencies at one level of government have on agencies at another level of government. Fills this knowledge gap by reporting findings that delineate how units in a large state natural resources agency in West Virginia respond to changing levels and conditions of dependency on federal resources over an eighteen-year period (1961-1978).

157. Ogden, Daniel M. Jr. "Beyond Zero-Based Budgeting." PUBLIC ADMINISTRATION RE-VIEW, 38, 6 (November-December 1978), 528-529.

Manifests that the most practical budgeting system for most managers is a formalized combination of incremental and zero based analysis.

158. Patton, Carl Vernon. "Budgeting Under Crisis: The Confederacy as a Poor Country." ADMINISTRATIVE SCIENCE QUARTERLY, 20, 3 September 1975), 355-370.

Studies the budgetary process of the Confederate government, an aspect of the Confederacy generally ignored by Civil War historians. Finds that the budgetary process of the Confederacy resembled that employed by contemporary poor countries. Shows, by using Wildavsky's budgeting model, that the Confederacy's budgetary process should have been conflict-laden, as indeed it was. Discovers that the Confederacy budget process was repetitive in terms of both requests and appropriations, and since it lacked predictability, participants could not take their bearing from it. Adds to our general knowledge of an important period in American history, and describes how a budgetary process similar to the U.S. Federal model operated under extreme pressure. Gives an insight into the kinds of problems experienced by governments undergoing periods of development while experiencing extreme financial crisis.

159. Pitsvada, Bernard T. "Flexibility in Federal Budget Execution." PUBLIC BUDGETING & FINANCE, 3, 2 (Summer 1983),83-101.

Relates budget control and budget flexibility during budget execution phase. Argues that budget execution lies at the heart of improving governmental performance and public perception of performance in government. Analyzes techniques for flexibility in: object classification, appropriation structure, contingency appropriations, emergency provisions, transfer authority, and reprogramming authority.

160. Plyman, Jeffrey, and Lyndon Perkins, "Fitness Monitoring." PUBLIC MANAGEMENT, 65, 8 (August 1983), 6-9.

Defends argument that a progressive organization cannot "continue to sit on the sidelines and simply watch health care become an ever growing budget item." Proposes a wellness program to convert preventive health into gains for the municipality. Includes: general testing for all employees, intensive testing for all employees, and reinforcing lifestyle changes.

161. Presthus, Robert. "Decline of the Generalist Myth." PUBLIC ADMINISTRATION REVIEW, 24, 4 (December 1964), 211-216.

Challenges going conceptions of the generalist administration by citing British observers and personal research into the

activities of the British European Airways.
Finds the inadequacies of generalists in
making the sophisticated fiscal decisions
required in a modern industrial state.

162. Rosenthal, Albert H. "Intergovernmental
Relations: Insights and Outlooks." PUBLIC
ADMINISTRATION REVIEW, 28, 1 (January-
February 1968), 3-9.

Deals with the grant-in-aid programs
in a symposium article. Enumerates salient
impediments and approaches to improvements.
Blames federal requirements for the impediments.

163. Scott, Paul, and Robert J. McDonald.
"Local Policy Management Needs: The Fe-
deral Response." PUBLIC ADMINISTRATION
REVIEW, 35 (Special Issue 1975), 786-794.

Refers to the need for a major revision
in federal urban policy. Concentrates on federal actions to be considered in the formation of a new policy structure, pointing to
block grants as a step in the right
direction.

164. Sherwood, Frank P. "What is Behind the
City's Budget?" PUBLIC MANAGEMENT,
36, 4 (April 1954), 78-80.

Contends that previous year's expenditures
are not a good guide to current year's needs--
decisions must be based on thorough management
analysis and work measurement. Recommends a
more sophisticated use of the budget as a
device of executive control to substantially
improve administrative operations of government.

165. Swierczek, F.W., P.N. Rigos and G.W.
Robertson. "Factors in the Successful
Implementation of a Budget Innovation: A

Case Study of Pinellas County, Florida."
AMERICAN REVIEW OF PUBLIC ADMINISTRATION,
16, 1 (Spring 1982), 37-53.

Highlights some features of the implementation process which contributed to the
success of a budget innovation: combining
cost-center accounting approach of performance
budgeting and program-service concerns of program budgeting. Denotes these features as
important in the implementation process:
(1) support and active involvement of top
government officials; (2) training of people
implementing innovation; (3) participation of
relevant managers and unit personnel; and
(4) consensus on the need for planning and
monitoring the process.

166. Thurow, Lester. "Equity Versus Efficiency in
     Law Enforcement." PUBLIC POLICY, 18, 4
     (Summer 1970), 451-462.

Articulates that the interest in police efficiency without a discussion of equity is
misplaced since society has not made enough
equity decisions even to be efficient. Resolves that the use of benefit-cost analysis
requires establishing an explicit set of
equity constraints.

167. Usher, Charles, and Gary C. Cornia. "Goal-
     Setting and Performance Assessment in
     Municipal Budgeting." PUBLIC ADMINISTRA-
     TION REVIEW, 41, 2 (March-April 1981),
     229-235.

Examines budgets and budget manuals of
123 large American cities to determine incorporation of performance assessment into
municipal budgeting. Finds, among others,
that most cities require workload indicators
to be submitted with agency budget requests.
Laments that the availability of performance
data does not guarantee the use of the data.
Raises some critical issues for future
research concerning: (1) reasons for under-

taking program analysis and evaluation;
(2) actual implementation of productivity
measurement systems; (3) environmental pressures identification; and (4) degree to
which analysis actually improves performance
or changes in resource allocation.

168. Vanderbilt, Dean H. "Budgeting in Local Gov-
ernment: Where Are We Now?" PUBLIC ADMIN-
ISTRATION REVIEW, 37, 5 (September-
October 1977), 538-542.

Covers the current "state-of-the-art" budgeting methods and speculates as to the future of both zero-base and target budgeting.
Recognizes that many features of performance budgeting and PPB systems were not
practical for local governments. Argues, however, that ZBB and target budgeting respond to difficult economic constraints by
requiring re-examination of current service
levels and accommodating the use of performance and program analyses when possible or feasible.

169. Waldron, Ronald, and John Altemose. "De-
termining and Defending Personnel Needs in
Criminal Justice Organizations." PUBLIC
ADMINISTRATION REVIEW, 39, 4 (July-
August 1979), 385-389.

Contends that the atmosphere of rising
taxes, runaway inflation, and forecasting
of personnel needs is important in any
political climate. Discusses several empirical methods of personnel forecasting that
can be objectively defended as logical,
sound and used within the framework of
a ZBB-based budgeting system.

C.   Technology and Office Modernization

170. Alexander, John B.   "The New Mental Battle-
         field: Beam Me Up, Spock." MILITARY RE-
         VIEW,   60, 12   (December 1980),   47-54.

         Explores paranormal research that mani-
      pulates human behavior through use of psy-
      chological weapons effecting sight, sound,
      smell, temperature, electromagnetic energy or
      sensory deprivation.   Believes that the
      Soviets have more advanced parapsychological
      (psychotronics or bio-energetics) research
      than the United States.   Stresses need for
      more coordinated research and providing
      leaders with a basic understanding of
      weapons systems of all kinds in the future.

171. Bledsoe, Ralph C.   "Technology and Govern-
         ment Management." THE BUREAUCRAT, 12, 4
         (Winter 1984), 29-34.

         Raises two questions: When has there not
      been a "technological age?" When has the
      "entire social system" not been "controlled
      by scientists and engineers?" Answers
      "never" to both questions. Claims that
      assessment of impacts of technology on gov-
      ernment management in the United States req-
      uires more analysis of continuing changes
      of ˙ tools, techniques, vocabulary, problems,
      and decisions which public managers have to
      master.

         Asserts that in addition to knowledge
      of POSDCORB, behavioral science and human
      relations skills, managers must also know
      how to use automated data processing, man-
      agement information systems, office automa-
      tion, and related systems and management
      analysis; and must possess a basic un-
      derstanding of computer applications, data
      base management, teleprocessing, and nu-
      merous other fast-developing technologies.

172. Calbos, Dennis P. "Information System Im-
     plementation: PPBS at New South Univ-
     ersity." D.P.A. Dissertation, University
     of Georgia, 1984. 168 p.

     Investigates problems associated with the
implementation of computer-based information
systems as experienced by NSU, a traditional
institution. Identifies major implementation
problems: inability to develop operational
definitions of the organizational objectives;
personality and territorial conflicts; preoc-
cupation with more pressing concerns; inadequate foundation for computer-based information systems; and absence of supportive
environmental organizations. Recommends that
the organization: take its information
system goals seriously, assume a thoughtful
planning perspective on information system-
building, develop a selective strategy
for installing information systems, recognize existence of political subtleties and
pockets of resistance, focus on system-
building as an incremental process and
develop an implementation strategy appropriate to the stage and understanding of top
management.

173. Danziger, James N. "Computer Technology and
     the Local Budgetary System." SOUTHERN RE-
     VIEW OF PUBLIC ADMINISTRATION, 1, 3
     (December 1977), 279-292.

     Explores the effects and implications
of applying computer technology to the
local budgetary system. Construes the notion
of budgetary systems as both planning and management of financial resources, and also the
control of these resources. Interprets data
generated by the URBIS research project,an
extensive study of computer technology in
the United States municipal and county
governments. Concludes that given the
needs and centrality of the budgetary system
to the local government, capabilities match
between that system and computer technology. Predicts that the finance-related

functions would be the most extensively au-
tomated among all local government functions
as confirmed in a recent empirical analysis.

174. Desai, Uday, and Michael M. Crow. "Failures
     of Power and Intelligence: Use of
     Scientific-Technical Information in Gov-
     ernment Decision Making." ADMINISTRATION
     & SOCIETY, 15, 2 (August 1983), 185-206.

     Studies the Coalcon project, first federal
     attempt to demonstrate a synthetic fossil
     energy technology. Determines that the
     major R&D decision in energy policy was
     based on the inadequate use of available, re-
     levant technical information. Alleges that
     the nature of the decision, the power set-
     ting, and the consequences of the crisis
     situation on the agency operations resulted
     in its neglect.

175. Galonis, Peter E. "A Study of the Impact
     of Computers on County Government in the
     State of Pennsylvania." Ph.D. Disserta-
     tion, University of New York at Bingham-
     ton, 1977. 147 p.

     Reports on the influence and impact that
     computers are having on county government in
     the State of Pennsylvania. Accesses the
     social and psychological implications of com-
     puter technology and to what extent this
     technology is affecting the functions and
     operations of county government. Studies
     the impact of computerization on the organi-
     zation, decision making, authority and
     control, and job content of lower levels
     of governmental activities.

176. Hughes, Arthur. "Robotics: Effect on Japa-
     nese and American Labor and a Practical
     Application in the New York City Depart-
     ment of Sanitation." PUBLIC PRODUCTIVITY
     REVIEW, 7, 2 (June 1983), 112-121.

Reviews the study by New York City
Department of Sanitation which explored
possibilities of introducing robotics
(Trallfa robot) in its vehicle painting
shop. Views robots as man amplifiers and
not as man supplanters. Recognizes that
whether robotry is the end of human mi-
sery or the beginning of a new plateau
of human suffering would seem to depend
on how it is handled from the start.

177. King, John L., and Kenneth L. Kraemer.
     "Changing Data Processing Organization."
     THE BUREAUCRAT, 12, 2 (Summer 1983),
     21-27.

Focuses on the question of how computer
and information technology will develop in
the next decade, and specifically, how
small computers will fit into the existing
pattern of data processing organization in
government settings. Addresses likely impact
of these changes toward decentralization.
Considers what managers ought to know to
be better able to assess, and cope with,
these processes and the conflicts that
attend them. Concludes that new decentralized technology of mini and microcompu-
ters will require new arrangements for control within individual government agencies,
and new kinds of information exchanges among
agencies.

178. Knight, Fred. "Local Government Technology:
     The View from 2078." PUBLIC MANAGEMENT,
     60, 7 (July 1978), 6-11.

Looks at the actual work performed by municipal employees and the tools that were used
to carry out those tasks as a key influence
which affected local government administration during the period. Opens up an avenue
of inquiry that would inevitably lead to the
examination of ways in which technology affected municipal services. Identifies three
of the principal management challenges which

city and county administrators had to overcome: (1) lack of technological options;
(2) attitudes prevailing within the municipal organizations; and (3) broadening
perspective of the managers themselves on
how to creatively deploy technology. Ends on
a positive note that attitudes and commitment of managers toward improving the quality
of municipal services and the municipal work
place are paramount to understanding how
technology was harnessed to meet city and
county problems.

179. LaPorte, Todd A. "The Context of Technology
     Assessment: A Changing Perspective for
     Public Organization." PUBLIC ADMINISTRA-
     TION REVIEW, 31, 1 (January-February
     1971), 63-73.

     Assumes technological development as a
     major source of political and cultural
     change. Calls for a changed perspective
     of technology and the application of ex-
     panded and more difficult criteria to the
     systems analysis of technological development.

180. Macy, John W. Jr. "Executive Preparation for
     Continuing Change." PUBLIC ADMINISTRATION
     REVIEW, 29,5 (September-October 1969),
     501-503.

     Concerns ways in which managers must change
     in order to keep up with technological
     changes, especially in the area of developing
     programs to meet the needs of future
     technological developments yet to occur.

181. Menzel, Donald C. "Intergovernmental Support
     of Technological Innovation in Local
     Government." ADMINISTRATION & SOCIETY,
     10, 3 (November 1978), 317-334.

     Examines the influence that governmental
     support has on the adoption of new tech-
     nologies within and among four areas of

local government: fire protection, traffic
control, solid waste management, and air
pollution control. Reports on interviews
conducted with more than 80 program managers
in 20 cities throughout the United States.
Keynotes the respondents' perceptions of the
influences that cause higher level officials
to adopt new technological decisions:
funds, rules, technical assistance, and
attitudes of high level officials. Gives
emphasis on two findings that emerged:
(1) intergovernmental influences do not impact in a uniform fashion on local decisions to innovate; and (2) such influences
are often minimized by local circumstances.
Explores the policy implications of these
findings.

182. Michael, Donald N. "Technology and the Human
     Environment." PUBLIC ADMINISTRATION RE-
     VIEW, 28, 1 (January-February 1968),
     57-60.

     Involves social technology and the study of
     the social impacts of new technologies. An-
     ticipates the need of social inventions
     to combat the effects of technological in-
     ventions.

183. Owen, Sam Jr. "Training and Orientation for
     Computer Usage." PUBLIC MANAGEMENT, 55, 8
     (August 1973), 13-14.

     Provides insights into the procedures used
     in management, user, and technician train-
     ing in information systems. Discusses sys-
     tem analysis, system design, and system im-
     plementation.

184. Press, Frank. "Science and Technology in
     the Service of Cities." PUBLIC MANAGE-
     MENT, 60, 7(July 1978), 16-18.

     Contemplates the likelihood that bureau-
     cracy is on the threshold of a major new

dimension in local government--a serious application of science and technology to urban
problems. Focuses on the role of the Intergovernmental Science, Engineering and Technology Advising Panel (ISETAP) as by no
means the only avenue by which local governments can avail themselves of the benefits of science and technology. Avers that
ISETAPS' real value depends largely upon
what state and local governments are able to
do in terms of creating a positive, proactive
environment for innovation, and in developing sound strategies and programs for their
presentation to the federal research and
development community.

185. Rafferty, Robert R. "The Military Manager
      Versus the Computer." MILITARY REVIEW,
      53, 3 (March 1973), 72-82.

      Brings to the attention of the military
functional manager some non-technical,
lessons-learned type guidance that may be encountered in dealing with ADP. Provides
some pointers to managers to help their understanding of ADP.

186. Weddle, Peter D. "The Soldier-Machine
      Connection." MILITARY REVIEW, 62, 1
      (January 1980), 60-68.

      Charges that the military services do not
conduct adequate early analysis in the process
of developing and acquiring weapons systems.
Declares that this results in the failure to
effectively integrate equipment and the
people who use it. Makes some recommendations to improve the process.

187. William, Gordon L., and Allan R. Young.
      "Manpower Planning: A Markov Chain Appli-
      cation." PUBLIC PERSONNEL MANAGEMENT,
      2, 2 (March-April 1973), 133-144.

      Discusses the concepts and benefits of man-

power planning. Considers certain controlla-
ble and non-controllable factors, such as:
firm's future growth, its objectives,
sales and production forecast, changes in
economic, social and political conditions.
Demonstrates a theoretical application of
Markov process to arrive at a simplified
prediction of manpower requirements and
workforce composition.

            D. Administrative Ethics

188. Barton, Allen H. "A Diagnosis of Bureaucratic
        Maladies." AMERICAN BEHAVIORAL SCIENTIST,
        22, 5 (May-June 1979), 483-492.

        Analyzes the causes of bureaucratic mala-
    dies. Points out the characteristics of the
    structure of bureaucracy, its surrounding
    political system, and interrelationships
    among these characteristics which have to
    be changed to cure the maladies. Suggests
    some approaches to improve performance
    measures and better communication among bu-
    reaucrats and the people they serve. Creates
    means for the elected representatives to
    oversee performance. Proposes more market-
    like conditions to counter the weakness in
    reward-penalty bureaucracy by representation
    of the needs of broader sections of the
    public.

189. Beckman, Norman, and Clyde Christofferson.
        "Reducing WFA: The Newest Public Admin-
        istration." THE BUREAUCRAT, 12, 3 (Fall
        1983), 6-9.

        Reports on recent federal and state ini-
    tiatives to work together in reducing
    waste, fraud and abuse in jointly funded
    or administered programs, primarily in the
    human services and labor fields. Aims at

restoring public confidence in federal-state
programs and government's ability to manage
them.

190. Benson, George C.S. POLITICAL CORRUPTION
     IN AMERICA. Mass.: Lexington Books,
     1978. 339 p.

     Defines the methods and techniques of
     corruption. Outlines the forms of corruption
     at different levels of the government at
     different periods. Lists reasons for cor-
     ruption advanced by academicians and politi-
     cal scientists. Recommends concerted ef-
     forts of media, educational and religious
     institutions in emphasizing each indivi-
     dual's   social   and   moral   responsibili-
     ties, and strict enforcement of laws
     in the conduct of the affairs of the nation.

191. Brady, F. Neil. "Ethical Theory for the
     Public Administrator: The Management of
     Competing Interests." AMERICAN REVIEW OF
     PUBLIC ADMINISTRATION, 15, 2 (Summer
     1981), 119-126.

     Provides a basic account of the two
     current main movements in ethical theory.:
     Rawl's Kantianism and classical utili-
     tarianism. Examines their application to
     one of the fundamental processes with
     the public administrators' life--the manage-
     ment of competing interests. Suggests that a
     clear understanding of these basic ap-
     proaches is important if one's ethical think-
     ing is to be consistent and justified
     and not arbitrary and changeable. Defines
     ethical theory simply as careful, systematic
     thinking about what the administrator ought
     to do. Warns that without a framework for
     approaching the issue of managing competing
     interests, the administrator will flounder
     in expediencies.

192. Brown, David. "The Managerial Ethics and Pro-

ductivity Improvement." PUBLIC PRODUCTI-
VITY REVIEW, 7, 3 (September 1983),
223-250.

Discusses erosion of managerial ethics and
its effect on productivity. States that the
failure of American managers, public and
private, to require a sufficient level of
productivity either of themselves or of
others is one of the reasons for low productivity. Relates the difficulty of government work to the fact that "not only has it
to be well done, but also that the public
has to be convinced that it is being well
done." Defines managerial ethics as a
"need to do better." Views managing as
more than presiding or keeping everyone
happy but as a passion and an obsession
which involves an "ethos" for acting
responsibly.

193. Buchanan, Bruce II. "Red Tape and the Service
     Ethic: Some Unexpected Differences Between
     Public and Private Managers." ADMINISTRA-
     TION & SOCIETY, 6, 4 (February 1975),
     423-444.

     Contributes to the growing body of compa-
     rative data on business and government
     organizations. Subjects two rather prevalent
     assumptions about public organizations and
     public servants to a preliminary empirical
     test. Tests assumptions concerning the pro-
     minence of administrative red tape in public
     agency operations and the suspected existence
     of a service ethic, a special kind of in-
     volvement with duty among public servants.

194. Bush, Malcolm, and Andrew C. Gordon.
     "Client Choice and Bureaucratic Accounta-
     bility: Possibilities for Responsiveness
     in a Social Welfare Bureaucracy." JOURNAL
     OF SOCIAL ISSUES, 34, 4 (1978), 22-43.

     Poses increasing concern about the effec-
     tiveness and the cost of social welfare

services. Discusses two strategies which
might improve the relationship between the
expected and the actual outcome of encounters
with social service bureaucracies: client-
choice, and bureaucratic accounting procedures. Illustrates the issues of the
conditions necessary for authentic choice--
limits of choice and the corruptibility of
choice--in the field of child welfare. Includes a description of factors which thwart
effective accounting and contains some suggestions for improving the process.

195. Caiden, Naomi. "Shortchanging the Public."
     PUBLIC ADMINISTRATION REVIEW, 39, 3
     (May-June 1979), 294-298.

     Reviews books dealing with public sector
corruption: political corruption, corruption
and reform in land-use building regulation,
and police corruption. Shows that corruption is highly probable because of the sensitivity of the decisions themselves and the
need for discretion by officials. Concludes
that controls and sanctions to reduce opportunities for corruption will always be necessary, but will be helpless in a society
which fosters and protects corrupt values.

196. Cohen, Richard M., and Jules Witcover.
     A HEARTBEAT AWAY. New York: The Viking
     Press, 1974. 379 p.

     Recounts the chain of events that sparked
the investigation into Vice President Spiro
T. Agnew's activities, particularly pay-off
charges in his political life. Delivers an
absorbing analysis and clarifying observations on Agnew's last days. Questions the
disposition of the case--"Has justice
been served?"

197. Dempsey, Charles L. "Managerial Accountabi-
     lity and Responsibility." THE BUREAUCRAT,
     12, 4 (Winter 1984), 17-23.

Discusses reasons for reemergence of critical management concepts of accountability,
responsibility and internal controls. Suggests how these can be used most effectively
through teamwork, responsibility, and accountability.

198. Douglas, Paul H. ETHICS IN GOVERNMENT. West-
port, CT: Greenwood Press, 1952. 114 p.

Analyzes political and moral standards of
Americans, focusing on the ethical problems of
administrators and legislators. Urges a need
for moral regeneration which will develop a
loathing for the shoddy and the corrupt as
well as a deep desire for integrity. Pres-
cribes a code of ethics declaring certain acts
as improper and imposing penalties for the
corrupt and the corrupted.

199. Flynn, John M. "Internal Control Reform."
THE BUREAUCRAT, 12, 3 (Fall 1983),
11-18.

Supports thesis that internal control
reform in government offers an effective general strategy for minimizing fraud, waste
and abuse in government. Assesses internal
control environment in a comprehensive manner. Considers methods for monitoring and
evaluating the operation of controls to en-
sure maintenance of the system.

200. Foster, Gregory D. "Law, Morality, and the
Public Servant." PUBLIC ADMINISTRATION
REVIEW, 41, 1 (January-February 1981),
29-34.

Argues that there is a negative correla-
tion between laws and moral behavior--as laws
increase, morals decline. Contends that it
creates an inability to judge right versus
wrong but views things as legal or illegal.
Asserts that public service must convince
the public that it can make moral judgments

if it is to succeed in the future.

201. Friedman, Robert S., Bernard Klein, and
     John H. Romani. "Administrative Agencies
     and the Publics They Serve." PUBLIC
     ADMINISTRATION REVIEW, 26, 3 (September
     1966), 192-204.

     Reports the results of interviews with 96
     officials in 11 agencies atFederal, State,
     and local levels as to their perceptions of
     their agency's role. Finds that most felt
     they served particular groups, not the gene-
     ral public.

202. Gardiner, John A., and David J. Olsen, eds.
     THEFT OF THE CITY. Bloomington: Indiana
     University Press, 1974. 432 p.

     Consists of readings on corruption in Ame-
     rican cities. States that corruption is not
     confined to municipal jurisdictions but oc-
     curs throughout the American political sys-
     tem. Explains the patterns of corruption
     and the environmental setting that leads to
     it. Discusses the targets of corruption,
     its causes and consequences, as well as the
     costs and benefits of corruption.

203. Gardiner, John A., and Theodore R. Lyman.
     DECISIONS FOR SALE. New York: Praeger
     Publishers, Praeger Special Studies,
     1978. 432 p.

     Defines corruption as "payments offered in
     return for specific actions which have been
     or will be taken by public officials." Sug-
     gests that the occurrence of this ubiquitous
     practice lies in the opportunities for it--
     high volume flow of funds from local govern-
     ments to local firms. Focuses on corruption
     in land-use and building regulations. Cites
     various examples and conducts in-depth case
     studies of community experiences with cor-
     ruption and corruption control. Prescribes

applications (theoretical and practical) in
reducing corruption.

204. Haefele, Edwin T. "Urban Transports: Who
     Decides." PUBLIC ADMINISTRATION REVIEW,
     25, 3 (September 1965), 234-239.

     Postulates that the future of the city is
     one of ethics: what is the good life for man
     and what are the institutions most conducive
     to realizing the good life. Raises the
     issue of who decides.

205. Hart, David K. "The Honorable Bureaucrat
     Among Philistines." ADMINISTRATION &
     SOCIETY, 15, 1 (May 1983), 43-48.

     Contends that argument of using analytical
     philosophy as working philosophy of public
     administration is premature. Argues that ne-
     cessary foundation for public administra-
     tion education is ability to do moral philoso-
     phy which is indispensable to the correct
     exercise of discretionary powers of public
     administration. Supports this argument on
     the primary loyalty of public administrators
     to the "American regime values," rather
     than to elected officials.

206. Hartwig, Richard. "Ethics and Organization
     Structure." THE BUREAUCRAT, 9, 4 (Win-
     ter 1980-1981), 48-56.

     Points out that in recent years, the laws
     of supply and demand have pushed up the
     stock of ethical behavior which is evi-
     dently in short supply in the public and
     private sectors alike. Stresses renewed in-
     terest in training programs geared to help-
     ing public employees deal with on-the-job
     value or ethical conflict situations.
     Explores some possibilities and limitations
     of training programs of this nature. Claims
     that ethical conflicts are frequently built
     into the structure of organizations. Re-

commends that if this is the case, serious
consideration should be given to ethical or
value problems when organizations are first
designed or when they are reorganized. Cautions that ethical training programs may be
only marginally valuable.

207. Henning, Daniel H. "Forest Personnel: Pro-
     fessional and Environmental Education."
     PUBLIC PERSONNEL MANAGEMENT, 2, 6
     (November-December 1973), 429-434.

     Views the need for education in the area
of values, people and environment for forest
personnel management as necessary. Suggests a
professional education dealing with humani-
ties, social science or people management as
relevant to a forest administrator.

208. Highsaw, Robert B. "The Southern Governor--
     Challenge to the Strong Executive Theme."
     PUBLIC ADMINISTRATION REVIEW, 19, 1
     (Winter 1959), 7-11.

     Claims that private interests often are
served ahead of the public interest by
the strong Southern governor when his
administrative practices are unchecked by
the legislature and public. Discusses two
emerging checks on irresponsible executive
action: (1) professionalization within the
career service; and (2) close relations between program administrators and their counterparts in other units of government, with
standards and guidance from the federal
government.

209. Hildreth, W. Bartley. "Applying Professional
     Disclosure Standards to Productivity Finan-
     cial Analysis." PUBLIC PRODUCTIVITY RE-
     VIEW, 7, 3(September 1983), 269-287.

     Recommends a professional code of ethics
for public finance officers who serve as
gatekeepers of financing records. Presents

six criteria to be incorporated into this
Code: relevance, materiality, meaningful-
ness, reliability, neutrality, and compara-
bility. Concludes that the use of these
criteria can serve "what is best for the
public interest."

210. International City Management Association.
"A Post-Watergate Code of Ethics." PUBLIC
MANAGEMENT, 57, 6 (June 1975), 7-12.

Presents transcript of questions and
answers before a panel of local officials
and one Federal official. Focuses on the
current status of ethical conduct in the
public service. Describes how the ICMA Code
of Ethics helps the individual practitioners.
Looks at future trends of either improvement
cr an erosion in the ethics of public service.

211. Johnson, Gary R. "The Image of the Administrator." PUBLIC PERSONNEL MANAGEMENT,
2, 6 (November-December 1973), 418-423.

States that the image of an administrator
is determined by his job performance.
Attempts to dissuade us from stereotyping
administrators based on their job functions. Believes that a successful administrator should possess trait of flexibility in
dealing with situations and in decision
making, possess correct information in his
field of responsibility and desirable traits
of honesty and public morality--all of which
will impact on his image as an administrator.

212. Kusserow, Richard P. "Fighting Fraud, Waste,
and Abuse." THE BUREAUCRAT, 12, 3 (Fall
1983) 19-23.

Examines the role of the Office of
Inspector General (OIG) in fighting fraud,
waste and abuse in the Department of
Human and Health Services. Concludes that
for every dollar spent in operating the

OIG, the department gets back between $14 and
$17. Justifies the OIG's role in restoring
the trust that exists between taxpayers and
their government.

213. Lasky, Victor.   IT DIDN'T START WITH THE WA-
     TERGATE. New York: The Dial Press, 1977.
     478 p.

     Opines that the Watergate scandal which
rocked the nation in 1974 is only a small
issue of a larger perspective--that of hy-
pocrisy. Believes that "political transgres-
sion" has been and is a way of life in
the political circles. Reveals startling
facts about the well-accomplished use and
abuse of political power in the FDR, LBJ,
and JFK administrations, all of which were
played down by the media. Presents evidence that Nixon was "hounded out of the
Office by the rampaging media," which often-
times over-stretched its role as a do-gooder
for the American public.

214. Manning, Bayless. FEDERAL CONFLICT OF IN-
     TEREST LAW. Cambridge, Mass.: Harvard
     University Press, 1964. 285 p.

     Concerns federal law and practices regu-
lating actual or potential conflicts between
the public obligations and the private economic interests of government employees in the
executive branch. Includes extensive analysis of the law which took effect in 1963.

215. Martin, James W. "Administrative Dangers in
     the Enlarged Highway Program." PUBLIC AD-
     MINISTRATION REVIEW, 19, 3 (Summer 1959),
     164-172.

     Surveys the impact of the increase in high-
way construction. Finds that it strained
state highway administration at many
points. Lists widespread weaknesses: (1) inadequate preparation of top officials for

administration; (2) underemphasis on long-range planning and budgeting; and (3) serious management breakdown in states traditionally practicing a high degree of political patronage. Notes that administrative controls have been strengthened as the enlarged program has developed.

216. Marx, Fritz Morstein. "Ethics and Local Administration." PUBLIC MANAGEMENT, 34, 10 (October 1952), 219-222.

Presents the Code of Public Ethics in Arlington County, Virginia done by the Citizens Commission on Ethics on Government. Covers elective and appointive officials and regular staff. Expresses itself in the form of a guideline. Suggests improvements to make government practices foolproof. Concludes that the codes' standards can be raised by people when they apply a higher standard most of the time.

217. Miles, Rufus E. Jr. "Administrative Adaptability to Political Change." PUBLIC ADMINISTRATION REVIEW, 25, 3 (September 1965), 221-225.

Declares that loyalty is the single, most important factor in the adaptability of the career bureaucracy to political leadership. Asks what if adaptation is impossible. Answers and defines why he feels that administrative loyalty has deteriorated and how adaptability can be made "operational."

218. _____. "Non-Subservient Civil Servants." PUBLIC ADMINISTRATION REVIEW, 30, 6 (November-December 1970), 620.

Argues strongly in editorial for civil servants who are loyal and yet have the public's interest at heart and are intelligently developing their philosophy.

219. Pearson, Drew, and Jack Anderson. THE CASE
     AGAINST CONGRESS. New York: Simon &
     Schuster, 1968. 473 p.

     Provides detailed accounts of misuses of
authority in the Capitol Hill. Exposes the
unscrupulous tactics of senators and congressmen who enrich themselves at the expense of
the American public. Describes flagrant
practices ranging from junket trips, nepo-
tism, political pay-offs from lobbyists,
retainer contracts with corporations, extra-
vagant parties and gifts, among others. Presents profiles of a few honest and conscien-
tious congressmen in the flock. Advocates
reforms to restore ethical standards in
Congress in a ten-point proposal.

220. Peters,Charles, and Taylor Branch, eds.
     BLOWING THE WHISTLE. New York: Praeger
     Publishing, 1972. 298 p.

     Compiles a series of readings on
whistle-blowing. Provides insights into the
workings of government administrative agencies, the ordeals and consequences of
whistle blowers within the ranks. Believes
that more protection should be given to
whistle blowers, particularly in jobs.
Suggests that support be given to future
whistle blowers who have the courage to ex-
pose the malaise existing in the government
and in the industry.

221. Quinn, Thomas A. "California Conflict of In-
     terest Laws: Building an Ethical Structure
     in Government." Ph.D. Dissertation, Clare-
     mont Graduate School, 1979. 303 p.

     Evaluates the impact of the California
Political Reform Act of 1974 requiring detailed disclosure of financial interests by
elected and appointed officials, and self-
disqualification from participation in making
decisions where they have a financial
interest. Suggests that despite administra-

tive difficulties, public disclosure of financial interests is achieving its goal, but
self-disqualification from decision making is
largely unenforceable. Concludes that this
Act does place public officials on notice
that ethical norms exist and that financial
disclosure is a powerful deterrent against
official misconduct.

222. Rohr, John A. "Ethics for the Senior Executive Service." ADMINISTRATION & SOCIETY,
12, 3 (August 1980), 203-216.

Notes that the Senior Executive Service
(SES), the showcase of the Civil Service Reform Act, has been caught up in controversies on the degree to which it will "pol-
iticize" the higher reaches of the career
civil service. Argues that the creation of
the SES represents a formal recognition of the
higher civil service as an institution of
government with significant normative consequences for those who hold these positions.
Cites that among these consequences is the
extent to which SES personnel should welcome
or resist political pressures. Develops a method of integrating ethical aspects of this
question into management training programs
which would have three parts: oath of office,
institutional literacy, and presidential
politics.

223. _____. "The Problem of Professional
Ethics." THE BUREAUCRAT, 11, 2 (Summer
1982), 47-50.

Keynotes that professional codes and
statements of ethics often engender cynicism
and division. Attributes this situation to
frequent self-serving statements which em-
barrass the progressives and delight their
critics. Explains why professional statements tend to be self-serving, and examines the ethics of public administration
in the light of this explanation. Hopes to
illuminate an aspect of professionalism that

should be of particular interest to the public administration community.

224. Sherwood, Frank P. "Professional Ethics."
     PUBLIC MANAGEMENT, 57, 6 (June 1975),
     13-14.

     Discusses possible learning from Watergate
that should demand most careful thought:
(1) principal culprits in the Watergate were
public office holders who were professional
people but were not career government types;
(2) tendency of codes to be unrealistic,
setting outer boundaries for   behavior.
Reveals the tremendous importance of in-
formation--both in terms of disclosure and of
secrecy--to the moral dimensions of administrative life, through the Watergate
scenario.

225. Sikula, Andrew F.   "The Values and Value
     Systems of Governmental Executives." PUB-
     LIC PERSONNEL MANAGEMENT, 2, 1 (January-
     February 1973), 16-22.

     Analyzes the values and the value sys-
tems of different levels of employees in
various governmental organizations. Suggests that this value survey can be used effectively to match individual attributes to a
prototype job or position, to meet institutional needs, and to design a financial and
non-financial compensation package for government employees and executive groups.

226. Staats, Elmer B. "The Challenge of Public
     Service."   PUBLIC PERSONNEL MANAGEMENT,
     2, 5 (September-October 1973), 358-361.

     Presents the challenge of public service
as "discovery that men serve themselves only
as they serve others." Sees the need of
government in having as many people as possible with the kind of vision required
to solve the complicated problems that

arise in our society. Concludes that personnel management is a key to a productive workforce and effective public service.

227. Swiss, James E. "Accountability and Effici-
    ency: The Problem." ADMINISTRATION & SO-
    CIETY, 15, 1 (May 1983), 75-96.

    Views accountability process as a
    simple feedback model: setting standards,
    comparison of activities against those stan-
    dards, and imposition of sanctions if acti-
    vities fall below standards. Emphasizes a
    combination of surrogate monitoring and di-
    rect sanctions to improve accountability me-
    chanisms for efficiency. Sees lack of con-
    sumer information as single greatest draw-
    back in most proposed accountability systems.

228. Thompson, Dennis F. "Moral Responsibility
    of Public Officials: The Problem of Many
    Hands." AMERICAN POLITICAL SCIENCE REVIEW,
    74, 4 (December 1980), 905-916.

    Explains the difficulty of ascribing moral
    responsibility to any official because many
    different officials contribute in many ways
    to decisions and policies in the modern
    state. Comments that the usual responses
    to this problem--based on concepts of
    hierarchical and collective responsibi-
    lity--distort the notion of responsibility.
    Promotes the idea of personal responsibility,
    based on causal and volitional criteria, as
    constituting a better approach to the
    problem of ascribing responsibility to
    public officials.

229. Totten, Michael W. "US Army Psychological
    Operations and the Army Reserve." MILITARY
    REVIEW, 63, 12 (December 1983), 48-65.

    Analyzes the deterioration of the Army's
    psychological operations (PSYOP), now mainly

found in the Army Reserve. Blames this development on various problems: command structure,   training insensitivity,   obsolete and
inadequate equipment,   organizational complexity, and absence of professional standards.
Calls for urgent solution of PSYOP problems
to alleviate dangers of an amateurish or bad
PSYOP.

230. Tretten, Rudie W.   MORALITY IN GOVERNMENT.
     Boston: Allyn and Bacon, 1977. 109 p.

     Presents a detailed, in-depth look at
ethical behavior or morality in government
as influenced by several factors: money,
lobbying,   graft,   and   power.   Portrays
through brief vignettes   a person in
political life faced with a choice of
how to act in particular situations.
Defines ethical behavior or morality as the
sum total of decisions centering around
questions of right and wrong. Raises issue
of "Is honest government possible?"

231. Wise, David. THE POLITICS OF LYING. New
     York: Random House, 1973. 415 p.

     Directs attention to blatant facts of
government deception and its damaging effects
on public trust and confidence. Discusses
the role of the press in political institutions. Emphasizes the urgent need to
bridge the widening gap between the political institution and the public. Urges
the President of the United States to ini-
tiate steps in bringing about and sustaining a new atmosphere of trust and candor.

232. Woodard, J. David. "Ethics and the City Man-
     ager." THE BUREAUCRAT, 13, 1 (Spring
     1984), 53-57.

     Analyzes city manager's observance of code
of ethics in complying with requests from
elective political overseers. Concludes

that the city management code of ethics
is no longer useful and is verbose, vague and
impractical in daily applications. Admits
that observance of code of ethics should be
tempered with political reality. Recommends
some reforms to make the 1920's Code of
Ethics suit the management environment of the
1980's.

E. Management Philosophy: Issues
and Prospects for the Future

233. Bingman, Charles F. "Changes in Public Organization." THE BUREAUCRAT, 12, 4
(Winter 1984), 24-28.

Predicts the next fifteen years to be tough
and demanding for the people who govern, and
marked by negotiation and realignment in domestic programs. Calls for greater private
sector contracting with appropriate planning of actions and understanding of these
consequences.

234. Brenneman, D. Sanders, and Lee D. Kittredge. "Matching Management Systems to
Organizational Realities of Large State
Agencies." PUBLIC PRODUCTIVITY REVIEW,
7, 4 (December 1983), 354-377.

Analyzes the application of PBS/MBO by
North Carolina Department of Human Resources. Finds that major barriers to effective
use of the system are: (1) lack of investment
in effective information systems; and
(2)need to coordinate multiple purposes
for planning activities. Makes following
recommendations to improve management:
(1) understanding the complex nature of
the organization; (2) matching systems with
capability; and (3) identifying necessary in-
vestments.

235. Brianas, James G. "A Challenge to Modern Man-
         agement." PUBLIC   PERSONNEL   MANAGEMENT,
         2, 4 (July-August 1973),   290-298.

         Focuses on the concept of humanization in
     the working environment as a means for
     establishing a sound organizational climate.
     Presents the managerial matrix as a method-
     ology for identifying existing organiza-
     tional climates and defining the direction
     for change. Defines Behavioral Technology
     as a melding together of man the technical
     being and man the human being in the working
     environment. Emphasizes that both beh-
     avioral and technological (hard) sciences
     should provide for man's full participation
     both as a human and as a technical resource.

236. Cleveland, Harlan. "How Do You Get Every-
         body in on the Act and Still Get Some
         Action?" PUBLIC MANAGEMENT,   57, 6
         (June 1975), 3-6.

         Examines the new demand for openness and
     participation in the governmental process,
     which some have seized upon as a remedy for
     what they believe to be our ailment and the
     results. Declares this new demand as one
     of the symptoms for the current low prestige
     of the public service.

         Believes that the benefits of openness and
     wide participation are flawed by: (1) apathy
     and non-participation; (2) muscle-binding
     legalisms; (3) processes which polarize two
     adversary sides; (4)an excess of voting and
     parliamentary procedure; (5) the nay-saying
     power of procedural objections; and (6) the
     encouragement of mediocrity.

237. Copeland, Richard. "Why Throw Out Your Valua-
         ble Resources." PUBLIC MANAGEMENT,
         65, 5/6 (May/June 1983), 10-11.

         Advocates utilizing a city manager who
     has been fired due to a change in the politi-

cal philosophy, social aims, and goals of
both city council and manager during the
remaining tenure. Creates this opportunity
by giving him a consultant position through
the remainder of his employment agreement
with no loss in salary or fringe benefits.

238. Dahl, Robert A. "The Science of Public
     Administration: Three Problems." PUBLIC
     ADMINISTRATION REVIEW, 7, 1 (Winter
     1947), 1-11.

     Concludes that no science of public admin-
     istration is possible unless: (1) the place
     of normative values is made clear; (2) the
     nature of man in the area of public adminis-
     tration is better understood and his con-
     duct is more predictable; and (3) there is
     a body of comparative studies from which to
     discover principles and generalities that
     transcend national boundaries and peculiar
     historical experiences.

239. Galnoor, Itzhat. "Government Secrecy: Ex-
     changes, Intermediaries and Middlemen."
     PUBLIC ADMINISTRATION REVIEW, 35, 1
     (January-February 1975), 32-43.

     States that secrecy in public affairs is
     needed in order to protect a public in-
     terest which is judged to be more im-
     portant than other public interests. Discus-
     ses the context of government activities
     related to domestic affairs; the impor-
     tant public interests to be protected which
     are usually the efficiency of the gov-
     erning process; and the privacy of indivi-
     duals, groups and organizations.

240. Golembiewski, Robert T. "Professionaliza-
     tion, Performance, and Protectionism: A
     Contingency View." PUBLIC PRODUCTIVITY
     REVIEW, 7, 3 (September 1983), 251-268.

     Presents the case for professionalization

in the public service as a powerful motiva-
tor, but cautions that it might exacerbate
"protectionism." Sees protectionism as a
predictable consequence of professionalism
that requires limiting. Focuses on how to
maximize performance-related outcomes of
professionalization while minimizing
protectionism-related consequences.

241. Granger, Clinton E.   "Studies in Conflict."
     MILITARY REVIEW,   64, 6 (June 1984),
     58-67.

     Comments that the rate of change being ex-
perienced today is unsurpassed in history,
that far more changes are taking place now
than ever before. Urges that if we are to
maintain peace, it will be only through a
system that identifies trends and produces
accurate projections of the future.

242. Harmon, Michael M.   "Social Equity and Organi-
     zational Man: Motivation and Organiza-
     tional Democracy." PUBLIC ADMINISTRATION
     REVIEW,   34, 1 (January-February 1974),
     11-18.

     Critiques John Rawls' A THEORY OF JUS-
TICE by contrasting social equity to utili-
tarianism. Proposes that concept of social
equity suggests an unequivocal commitment to
internal organizational democracy rather
than contingent upon empirical evidence.
Demonstrates that organizational democracy
leads to greater productivity, efficiency,
or even organizational loyalty.

243. Keating, Wm. Thomas.   "On Managing Ignorance."
     PUBLIC ADMINISTRATION REVIEW,   35, 6
     (November-December 1975),   593-597.

     Explores the governing and administer-
ing of programs that control environmental issues. Enjoins the development of
new modes of politics and administration--

ones based upon sophisticated management of
appalling ignorance and substantial uncer-
tainty--if we are to have any hope of sur-
viving the "environmental crisis."

244. Kramer, Fred A. "Public Accountability and
     Organizational Humanism." PUBLIC PERSONNEL
     MANAGEMENT, 3, 5 (September-October
     1974), 385-391.

     Contends that the concepts implied by orga-
nizational humanism--the drive toward greater
democracy within organizations--will not alter
the current accountability patterns between
Congress and the federal bureaucracy. Discusses some of the trends in budget
politics--engendered by increased use of systemic planning and analysis in the federal
government--and the general movement away
from line-item budgets toward a more
program-budget-oriented system. Concludes
that the types of organizations that would
benefit from organizational humanism would
not be significantly less accountable than
existing professionally-oriented, traditionally organized government agencies.

245. Newland, Chester. "Federal Government Manage-
     ment Trends." THE BUREAUCRAT, 12, 4
     (Winter 1984), 3-13.

     Attempts to appraise defects and strengths
in federal management, identifying patterns
of trends and needed changes. Assesses management developments in six areas: policy
management and implementation, finance and
budget, procurement and property, information
and communications, personnel, and evaluation
and audits. Critiques relevant public administration concepts and notes the most
crucial issue--decline in values of public
service and civic duty.

246. Platt, C. Spencer. "Humanizing Public Ad-
     ministration." PUBLIC ADMINISTRATION RE-

VIEW,   7, 3   (Summer 1947),   193-199.

Reviews better ways for public agencies to increase their productivity by organizing and managing human activity. Proposes that public agency managers can make their agencies more effective through the use of human relations skills. Urges that the methods and skills needed are simple tools of analysis and appraisal that must be teachable to managers and their assistants of average competence. Stresses need for experimentation and demonstration in the work places, not in the laboratory.

247. Richter, Anders. "The Existentialist Executive." PUBLIC ADMINISTRATION REVIEW, 30, 4 (July-August 1970), 415-422.

Claims a pervasive relevance of philosophical existentialism to public administration. Argues that the primary tenet is the freedom to choose. Discusses the activist behaviors of choice: intentionality, objectivity, risk-taking, and authenticity.

248. Rosenthal, S., and E. Levine. "Case Management and Policy Implementation." PUBLIC POLICY, 28, 4 (Fall 1980), 381-413.

Looks at a class of service organizations which spend much of their resources processing and managing "cases." Defines case management and describes its particular importance in government. Illustrates usefulness of case management in exploring how public policy may become articulated through the management of individual cases. Draws implications for policy formulation, program design, management, evaluation, and the conduct of applied research in this field.

249. Rushin, Emmet R. "A New Frontier for Employee Management Cooperation in Government." PUBLIC ADMINISTRATION REVIEW,

3, 2 (Spring 1943), 158-163.

Reviews the Victory Council formed in
W.W. II in an effort to create employee-
management participation. Feels there are
certain aspects of the council that would
be worthwhile for peace time utilization.

250. Sayre, Wallace S. "Trends of a Decade in Ad-
       ministrative Values." PUBLIC ADMINISTRA-
       TION REVIEW, 11, 1 (Winter 1951), 1-9.

Discusses the changing trends in administrative values of the 1940's as related
to the changing interpretations placed on
the concept of the role of science in administration. Notes the emerging emphasis upon
the fuller values of democratic administra-
tion--that morale in administration depends
upon a vital participation in the definition
of purpose by those who are affected by it
as citizens and as civil servants. Foresees
the values to be contributed to public administration by other social sciences as one of
the brightest features of the coming decade of
the 1950's.

251. Sigelman, Lee, H.B. Milward, J.M. Shepard,
       and M. Dumler. "Organizational Responses
       to Affirmative Action: 'Elephant Burial
       Grounds' Revisited." ADMINISTRATION &
       SOCIETY, 16, 1 (May 1984), 27-40.

Tests the "elephant burial grounds" hypothesis of Milward and Swanson: that tendency will emerge to stock minority and female employees in "elephant burial grounds"--
posts that are highly visible to those outside the organization (perfect for public
relations purposes) but are isolated from
the core activities of the organization.
Finds, through analysis of both CUPA Compensation Survey (College and University Personnel Association), little support for the contention that organizations isolate women and
minorities in positions away from core activi-

ties (management and   control) of the organization.

252. Smith, Michael P. "Barriers to Organizational
     Democracy in Public Administration: Democ-
     ratizing Working Life in Public Organiza-
     tions." ADMINISTRATION & SOClETY, 8, 3
     (November 1976), 275-317.

        Explores the forms that organizational de-
     mocracy might   take in   public administra-
     tion.   Argues that organizational democracy
     need not be incompatible with principles of
     representative democracy. Enumerates barriers
     to   work democratization in public bureau-
     cracy: (1) prevailing political arrangements;
     (2) needs, habits, and interests of organiza-
     tional elites; (3) folk ways and organiza-
     tional ideologies found in public bureau-
     cracies;   (4) bureaucratic socialization and
     reward system; and   (5) competitive impact of
     alternative "change models."

        Discerns, despite these obstacles, po-
     tential opportunities for structural change
     that may be unique to public as against
     large scale private organizations. Sug-
     gests that a change strategy, fostering or-
     ganizational democracy by accretion or en-
     croaching control, has some likelihood of
     long-run success.

253. Tedesco, Ted. "The Future City Manager Build-
     ing on Good Ideas We Have Now." PUBLIC
     MANAGEMENT, 60, 7 (July 1978), 9-11.

        Maintains that a good way to learn about
     the future is to learn what others are doing
     each day in other cities, about the same
     issues they are dealing with today. Discus-
     ses experience with California Innovation
     Group and Urban Technology System where the
     same questions are asked often by different
     municipalities trying to solve a   prob-
     lem. Notes that the results of each city's
     research could benefit subsequent searches

both from the question format and the responses. Describes the teleconferencing system
which would provide managers with instant
communication, questioning, and answers to
specific problems.

254. Walker, Donald C. "When the Tough Get Going,
     the Going Gets Tough: The Myth of the
     Muscle Administration." PUBLIC ADMINISTRA-
     TION REVIEW, 36, 4 (July-August 1976),
     439-445.

     Discusses the problems associated with
muscle administration. Claims that not
only does it create false heroes and real
tyrants, but that it also fails to provide
alternative solutions or suggestions. Expresses preference for a "metabolic administration" in place of the dictatorship style
of administration. Defines the former
concept as a humanistic approach that implies a relationship between the administrator and the people that is mutually ad-
vantageous.

255. Wedin, Wayne D. "Technology and the Future
     of Local Government." PUBLIC MANAGEMENT,
     60, 7 (July 1978), 2-5.

     Speculates that we may see radical changes
in the communication field. Points out that
where each house could become a network,
newspapers could be printed in one's own living room, and the innermost workings of local
government exposed on a daily and continuous
basis to the public. Talks about the alternative futures that are before us and suggests that we are going to have to extend
our horizons much farther out into the future
to adequately manage at the local level.

                    F. Organization Design:
          Pyramids, Adhocracy, and Quality Circles

256. Baber, Walter F. "Reform for Principle
       and Profit." THE BUREAUCRAT, 13, 2
       (Summer 1984), 33-37.

       Focuses on government reorganization as
    one of the major political reforms. Concludes
    that the goal of strategic reorganization is
    institutionalizing behavioral and programma-
    tic flexibility and allowing administrative
    factors to respond to, and participate in ,
    processes of political change.

257. Blachly, Frederick F., and Mirian E. Oatman.
       "Sabotage of the Administrative Process."
       PUBLIC ADMINISTRATION REVIEW, 6, 3
       (Summer 1946), 213-227.

       Analyzes the Administrative Procedures Act
    and shows its probable effects on federal
    administration. Follows the brief sketch of
    the established system with a discussion of
    the principal changes contained in the new
    law on: organization and relationships, proce-
    dure, changes in forms of action, judicial
    review of administrative action, and en-
    forcement. Concludes that these changes are
    destructive and malicious policies to confuse
    and impede administration, weaken important
    government controls, and add to incomes of
    lawyers who sponsored it through the American
    Bar Association.

258. Chisholm, Rupert. "Quality of Working Life:
       Critical Issues for the 80s." PUBLIC PRO-
       DUCTIVITY REVIEW, 7, 1 (March 1983),
       10-25.

       Offers the QWL approach as a powerful means
    for public sector organizations in dealing
    with conflicting environmental forces: lagging
    productivity, citizen demands for responsive
    public organizations, and changing employee

values/expectations. Clarifies QWL concept
and reviews costs and benefits from previous
QWL reports. Analyzes the durability and
diffusion of organizational changes resulting from QWL efforts.

259. Coleman, Charles. "Personnel: The Changing
     Function." PUBLIC PERSONNEL MANAGEMENT,
     12, 3 (May-June 1983), 186-194.

     Analyzes the importance and influence of
     personnel function in organizations. In-
     cludes activities concerning labor rela-
     tions, safety, benefits, and services.
     Emphasizes the shifts in personnel function--
     from "trash can" to matters concerning em-
     ployment, salary administration, and person-
     nel development. Attributes the increasing
     influence of personnel on organizational
     decision process (e.g., organizational struc-
     ture, staffing) to environmental changes.

260. Denhardt, Robert B., and Jan Perkins. "The
     Coming Death of Administrative Man." PUB-
     LIC ADMINISTRATION REVIEW, 36, 4 (July-
     August 1976), 376-384.

     States that feminists are developing alter-
     native models of organization which depart
     from the rational model of administration.
     Asks how these new patterns may affect the
     way individuals think about and consequently
     behave in complex organizations. Describes
     the concept of administrative man and then
     focuses on alternative theories of organiza-
     tion developed in the women's movement.

261. Foster, John L., and Judson H. Jones.
     "Rule Orientation and Bureaucratic Re-
     form." AMERICAN JOURNAL OF POLITICAL
     SCIENCE, 22, 2 (May 1978), 348-362.

     Notes that scholars, popular writers, and
     the general public often assume that large
     organizations produce the petty bureaucrat

syndrome. Reviews a wide range of academic
literature pertaining to the bureaucratic rule
orientation phenomenon. Tests a number of hypotheses using the Atlanta Model Cities Program as data base.   Finds organizational
structure as having a negligible relationship
with   bureaucrats' attitudes, contrary to expectations. Views respondents' career orientation as the best explanation for rule
orientation. Seeks some preliminary explanations for organization members becoming
rigidly committed to formal rules and lines
of authority.

262. Fagin, Robert F.   "The 95 Percent Solution."
     THE BUREAUCRAT, 13, 1 (Spring 1984),   3-5.

     Decries   the move from the in-house re-
viewer in   the federal sector to the public
inspector   general with independent means.
Points out that managers and auditors are no
longer attempting to solve a problem in the
organization jointly, but that dynamics of interaction becomes defending against some
attack from Congress about how poorly the
programs are being managed. Recommends making
the inspector general an internal auditor with
significant independence within this framework. Concludes that goal of managers and
auditors should be to improve the delivery
of government products and services.

263. Ferguson, Kathy E.   "Bureaucracy and Public
     Life: The Femininization of Polity." AD-
     MINISTRATION & SOCIETY, 15, 3 (November
     1983),   295-322.

     Opposes modern trend toward bureaucrati-
zation and seeks a nonhierarchical understanding of collective action. Explains and defends this posture by showing that an anti-
hierarchical, antibureaucratic stance is central to a consistent feminine analysis.
Views femininity as a political, rather than
a biological, category. Maintains that femininization is the structural complement of

domination. Concludes that the possibilities
for human liberation rests on the elimina-
tion of all dominance-subordinate relations.

264. Gardner, Neely. "The Non-Hierarchical Organi-
        zation of the Future: Theory Versus
        Reality." PUBLIC ADMINISTRATION REVIEW,
        36, 5 (September-October 1976), 591-598.

        Speculates about the future organiza-
    tion, visualizing the setting in which it
    would operate. Conceptualizes an organis-
    mic structure which avoids many of the
    dysfunctions described in much of the litera-
    ture. Reflects the key concept that most
    work is best done in small groups which
    should be temporary, semi-autonomous, self-
    accountable, flexible, interdependent, mo-
    dular, participative and democratic, and
    changing and learning.

265. Gawthrop, Louis. PUBLIC SECTOR MANAGEMENT,
        SYSTEMS, AND ETHICS. Bloomington: Indiana
        University Press, 1984. 184 p.

        Poses a two-fold challenge facing public
    sector organizations today: (1) perception
    of public management function within the
    context of a system's framework; and
    (2) maintenance and enhancement of an ethical
    perspective as preeminent purpose of public
    management. Talks in terms of developing
    public sector systems management through:
    (1) understanding of basic components of
    general systems theory; (2) understanding of
    different directions that systems manage-
    ment may take; (3) application of systems
    management in the framework of a new organi-
    zation design; (4) collateral accomplishment
    of new organization design with the develop-
    ment of a new sense of purpose; and (5) en-
    hancement and maintenance of a creative
    ethics. Explores the basic premise that the
    notions of management, systems, and ethics
    must be viewed collectively as an integrated
    metasystem to achieve fundamental change

in the public sector   organizations in the
United States.

266. Gregg, James   M.H., and   Robert F. Diegelman.
     "Red Tape on Trial: Elements of a
     Successful Effort to Cut Burdensome Federal
     Reporting Requirements." PUBLIC ADMINIS-
     TRATION REVIEW, 37, 2 (March-April 1977),
     171-176.

     Uses the U.S. Law Enforcement Assistance
     Administration to illustrate successful red
     tape-cutting. Gives a brief overview of the
     paperwork problem of the LEAA. Examines the
     approach taken and the evidence of theef-
     fectiveness of the actions taken.

267. Hagebak, Beaumont R. "The Forgiveness
     Factor: Taking the Risk Out of Efforts to
     Integrate Human Services." PUBLIC ADMIN-
     ISTRATION REVIEW, 42, 1 (January-February
     1982), 72-76.

     Contends that due to budget cuts it is ne-
     cessary for many agencies to redesign their
     organizations and integrate many autonomous
     agencies into one. Asserts that this action
     requires some risk-taking by individuals.
     Suggests that to alleviate the risk, indivi-
     duals must take action permission and uti-
     lize forgiveness factor for action taken.
     Offers five key protections in utilizing for-
     giveness factor: (1) solid professional
     reputation; (2) local support; (3) grounding
     of activities at community level; (4) im-
     plementation of integration in thoughtful in-
     cremental steps; and (5) awareness of long-
     range large scale implications in implementing
     integration.

268. Hanks, Dale E. "From Peas to Stringbeans."
     THE BUREAUCRAT, 12, 2 (Summer 1983),
     33-38.

     Distinguishes between the environment and

pressures between the academe and regular
government agencies. Concludes that both are
bureaucracies although minimal or subtle
differences may exist concerning pressures,
turbulence, and satisfactions. Observes
greater freedom and less strife in the academe, but more ambiguity in role and
mission.

269. Hassler, John F. "Improving Administrative
     Organization." PUBLIC MANAGEMENT, 31, 5
     (May 1949), 130-133.

     Relates the changes in the administrative
structure of Oakland City due to adoption of recommendations made by Public
Administration Service in 1947-1948. Indicates eradication of problems in complex
organizational structure, personnel classification and compensation plans, new sources
of revenues, and inability to meet the
growing city's needs for services due to
charter limitations.

270. Helfand, Gary. "The Applicability of Japa-
     nese Management Techniques in the American
     Public Sector: Some Cultural Considera-
     tions." PUBLIC PRODUCTIVITY REVIEW,
     7, 2 (June 1983), 105-111.

     Contrasts three major cultural traits in
Japanese and American societies as critical in
applying Theory Z techniques in America's public sector: spiritualism, population, and
individual's job performance. Concludes
that quality circles, consensus documents, and
other forms of consensus-based decision making
can be copied, to some degree, by U.S. public
sector organizations. Predicts that the potential of Japanese management techniques
for productivity improvement will fall
short unless the American public servant
experiences the same sense of loyalty,
commitment and communal spirit that is
instilled in the Japanese worker through
his society's socialization process.

271. Mazmanian, Daniel A., and Lee Mordecai.
     "Tradition be Damned! The Army Corps of
     Engineers is Changing." PUBLIC ADMINIS-
     TRATION REVIEW, 35, 2 (March-April 1975),
     166-172.

        Posits that bureaucratic theory has as-
     sumed a life cycle parallel to bureau-
     cracies, and they become stagnant and con-
     servative with age. Looks at the US Army
     Corps of Engineers which has been charac-
     terized as such, and reveals that changes
     are occurring in the Corps. Raises ques-
     tions about conservatism of the Corps and
     about bureaucratic theory.

272. McGill, Michael E., and Leland M. Wooten.
     "Management in the Third Sector." PUBLIC
     ADMINISTRATION REVIEW, 35, 5 (September-
     October 1975), 444-455.

        Defines the Third Sector as organizations
     that do not conform to traditional assump-
     tions about public and private entities.
     Attempts to identify some new directions in
     management theory and practice relating to the
     emergence of third sector organizations as im-
     portant entities in our post-industrial
     society.

273. Miller, David R. "New Challenges, New Insti-
     tutions." PUBLIC ADMINISTRATION REVIEW,
     33, 3 (May-June 1973), 236-242.

        Discusses the formation of state depart-
     ments of transportation as a response to the
     new challenge of transportation planning in-
     sisted upon by the federal government.
     Notes the major shift in the role of the
     state in transportation planning by giving
     increasing attention to urban transporta-
     tion problems.

274. Paine, Thomas O. "Space Age Management and
     City Administration." PUBLIC ADMINIS-

TRATION REVIEW, 29, 6 (November-December 1969), 654-658.

Examines significant similarities and differences between NASA and cities. Identifies comparable management problems. Classifies optimum approaches to these problems on a "spectrum of management" scale. Calls attention to the fact that NASA and urban institutions each requires appropriate institutional architecture for successful problem solving within complex environments.

275. Pope, H.G. "New Agencies in City Government." PUBLIC MANAGEMENT, 36, 6 (June 1954), 122-125.

Explores integration of new activities with existing municipal governments instead of creating special districts and authorities. Postulates that the relation of a new agency to an existing municipal government is to make agency responsible and responsive to municipality's citizens, facilitate program implementation, and strengthen framework of local government.

276. Roll, Joyce, and David Roll. "The Potential for Application of Quality Circles in the American Public Sector." PUBLIC PRODUCTIVITY REVIEW, 7, 1 (March 1983), 122-142.

Concludes that the Quality Circle Model can and should be attempted in the public sector. Points to administrative ability and strong administrative support as prerequisites for success. Cites selection of a consultant with proven track record as one of the predictors of success in the implementation process.

277. Saroff, Jerome R. "Is Mobility Enough for the Temporary Society? Some Observations Based Upon the Experience of the

Federal Executive Institute." PUBLIC AD-
MINISTRATION REVIEW, 34, 5 (September-
October 1974), 480-486.

Investigates case of high mobility. Finds
that the existing institutional equilibrium
tends to be reinforced when mobility is the
primary means employed to seek temporariness.
Suggests that while mobility may be a significant piece of an organizational strategy designed to create the Temporary Society, other
approaches must be tried along with it.

278. Wilson, John. "Army Readiness Planning."
     MILITARY REVIEW, 64, 7 (July 1984),
     60-73.

Sustains the need to develop a military
force capable of meeting all of the commit-
ments that are placed upon it. Describes
how the military planners of the early
years of this century faced numerous difficulties in trying to put together an appropriate organization. Claims that many of the
problems that existed then are still around
today.

279. Young, John D. "Implementation: Key to Re-
     form." THE BUREAUCRAT, 12, 1 (Spring
     1983), 35-40.

Recommends a set of essential understandings to be mastered in the design phase of a
major federal program or administrative
reform. Argues that soundness of a proposed reform is inextricably tied to whether or not idea can be implemented in the
real world of public management. Lists the
following design conditions: (1) historical
evolution of the program or administrative
reform; (2) current status of descriptive and normative theory; (3) institutional setting and project environment;
(4) clear definition or specification of
proposed changes; and (5) interactive
nature of these understandings.

3. INDIVIDUAL BEHAVIOR

A. Motivation and Productivity

280. Ammons, David N. "Peer Participation in Local Government Employee Appraisal." ADMINIS-TRATION & SOCIETY, 16, 2 (August 1984), 239-256.

Remarks that despite the importance of employee performance appraisal and the generally low regard in which the process is held in local government, there has been little municipal experimentation with peer appraisal, a technique demonstrated elsewhere to be reliable and valid. Reviews previous research on peer rating, and enumerates common reasons for hesitancy in adoption of peer rating. Examines the validity of some of the principal reasons for hesitancy in the light of the experience of a city which adopted a peer-supplemented system for recognizing outstanding employees. Discovers some evidence, after analysis of 1,452 appraisals, of reliability and validity of peer assessments. Indicates that outstanding employees under peer-supplemented method may even possess stronger evaluation ratings from their supervisors.

281. Ammons, David N., and Joseph King. "Productivity Improvement in Local Government: Its Place Among Competing Priorities." PUBLIC ADMINISTRATION REVIEW, 43, 2 (March-April 1983), 113-120.

Presents the results of a survey of 298

chief administrators on importance and incentives needed for productivity improvement
efforts in local government. Reveals that
productivity improvement must compete with
other pressing issues and does not generally
enjoy top priority. Lists the following
priorities for local governments: (1) fiscal
crisis; (2) capital improvement; (3) economic development; (4) productivity improvement; (5) public safety; (6) relationships
with community; (7) relationships with employees; and (8) relationships with
other governments. Declares that stronger
incentives are necessary to promote administrative initiative in productivity
improvement.

282. Bailey, Stephen. "Improving Federal Gov-
     ernance." PUBLIC ADMINISTRATION REVIEW,
     40, 6(November-December 1980), 548-553.

     Makes suggestions on how the Federal Gov-
ernment can be improved by reorganizing
the Executive Office, strengthening party
leadership in Congress, involving the national committees in rewarding congressional party loyalty and regaining the constitutional integrity of the Executive Branch.
Contends that these can be more impor-
tantas guarantors of the public interest
than any amount of detailed tinkering with
the structures and processes of the bureaucracy.

283. Balk, Walter E. "Toward a Government Produc-
     tivity Ethic." PUBLIC ADMINISTRATION
     REVIEW, 38, 1(January-February 1978),
     46-50.

     Suggests four major areas of emphasis
which apply to Federal, State and local
levels: measurement complexities, determi-
nation of efficiency, employee involvement,
and outside influences.

284. _____. "Why Don't Public Administrators
Take Productivity Seriously?" PUBLIC PER-
SONNEL MANAGEMENT, 3, 4 (July-August
1974), 328-324.

Inquires into some of the unique aspects of
government productivity which have to do with
motivations of managers, controls, political,and social factors. Discusses conditions which could serve as impetus for the
formulation of policies in order to start a
major productivity effort throughout government. Highlights three realities:
(1) motivating productivity in the public
sector is markedly different than it is in industry; (2) improvement will be evolutio-
nary and exploratory rather than the result of
quick fixes; and (3) motivating improvement,
along with finding solutions, is largely in
the hands of policy making managers and
employee associations rather than in those
of technical experts.

285. Barbour, George P., and Stanley M. Walfron.
"Productivity Measurement in Police Crime
Control." PUBLIC MANAGEMENT, 55, 4
(April 1973), 16-19.

Studies approaches in measuring crime control. Uses indicators such as crime rates,
clearance rates, arrests per police department employee, and population served per
police employee. Concludes that data analysis of the actual productivity measurement indicator is needed but that no
guarantee in productivity improvement can be
made.

286. Becker, Theodore, and Peter R. Meyers.
"Empathy and Bravado: Interviewing Reluc-
tant Bureaucrats." PUBLIC OPINION QUAR-
TERLY, 38, 4(Winter 1974-1975), 605-613.

Applies supportive (ego-building) and as-
sertive (ego-threatening) tactics in interviews among reluctant bureaucrats. Confirms

that bureaucrats' reactions to supportive tactics were almost predictably good since they
tend to enhance the bureaucrats' self-impor-
tance. Considers three factors whatever
tactics are used: (1) reward incentives
for bureaucrats; (2) element of surprise
in obtaining information; and (3) interview setting.

287. Bernstein, Samuel J., and Leon Reinharth.
      "Management, the Public Organization and
      Productivity: Some Factors to Consider."
      PUBLIC PERSONNEL MANAGEMENT, 2, 4
      (July-August 1973), 261-266.

      Analyzes some operational problems involved
      in increasing productivity in the public
      sector. Identifies four basic organization
      components that play important roles in in-
      dividual and organizational productivity.
      Appraises problems which include: (1) un-
      qualified candidates for upper and middle-
      level management positions; (2) the indivi-
      dual's productivity; (3) struggle between
      management-introduced productivity norms and
      informal groupings in the organization; and
      (4) the coordination between levels of
      agencies and bureaucracy. Suggests incen-
      tives, job-enrichment programs, and inter-
      nal organizational improvement efforts.

288. Best, Fred. "Preferences on Work-Life Sched-
      uling and Work Leisure Trade-Offs."
      MONTHLY LABOR REVIEW, 10, 1 (June 1978),
      31-37.

      Presents findings of exploratory survey
      of public employees. Indicates that workers
      may be willing to exchange earnings for
      more free time and that they favor increased
      flexibility in the timing of education, work,
      and leisure.

289. Beutel, Allen Edwin. "Determinants of Em-
      ployee's Job Performance at Selected

Federal Government Installations." Ph.D. Dissertation, University of Southern California, 1976. 317 p.

Concerns the efficiency of the largest selected single employer in the United States--the Federal Government--as it is affected by performance appraisal, a potentially valuable management tool. Focuses on performance appraisal systems in six selected U.S. Navy installations. Seeks to determine whether these systems incorporate some key behavioral science findings bearing on the performance appraisal systems, and are consistent with CSC guidelines. Yields large discrepancies between selected organizations' appraisal systems and CSC guidelines. Believes that further experimentation involving policy compliance and incorporation of behavioral science and MBO techniques in existing performance appraisal systems would assist in increasing productivity and efficiency, while aiding employees in achieving a more meaningful life by moving towards self-fulfillment.

290. Bouchard, Gerald R. "Fringe Benefits for Municipal Administrators." PUBLIC MANAGEMENT, 55, 10 (October 1973), 10-13.

Compares the differences in fringe benefits accruing to public employees and municipal executives. Feels that more incentives should be given to municipal executives to enable them to carry their social responsibilities seriously and to fulfill their social needs as well. Reminds us that private and public sectors are competing for leadership talents and that the former provides executive benefits which the public sector has neglected.

291. Brown, Karen, and Philip Coulter. "Subjective and Objective Measures of Police Service Delivery." PUBLIC ADMINISTRATION REVIEW,

43, 1 (January-February 1983), 50-58.

Applies objective and subjective measurements in police service delivery. Determines
empirical relationships between subjective
and objective police service through use
of a citizen satisfaction model. Finds citizens' satisfaction with police protection
is related to specific aspects of police
performance: response time; police treatment of people, and perceived equity of
police service.

292. Bryant, Stephen, and Robert Joyce. "Fede-
    ral Productivity Lessons." THE BUREAU-
    CRAT, 13, 1(Spring 1984), 42-47.

    Raises the question: "Are there ex-
cellent public agencies?" Reviews OPM's
(Office of Personnel Management) exemplary
practices program which attempts to
spread managerial improvements from successful federal organizations to others.
Lists a variety of techniques used, ranging
from employee involvement in quality circles,to automating personnel operations,
to rewarding employees with monetary incentives. Draws on eight factors that contribute to successful productivity improvement
programs: (1) outside pressures to improve
overall performance; (2) autonomy of senior
managers to carry out improvement programs;
(3) results-orientation; (4) use of prototype
or models tailored to the work units;
(5) analytical staff knowledgeable about
new approach; (6) previous training of employees on new processes; and (7) impact on
operations; and (8) feedback.

293. Burkhead, Jesse, and Patrick J. Hennigan.
    "Productivity Analysis: Search for Defini-
    tion and Order." PUBLIC ADMINISTRATION
    REVIEW, 38, 1(January-February 1978),
    34-40.

    Reviews the economic characteristics of

public sector output, attempts to clarify
the field of productivity improvement and
taxonomize productivity approaches.

294. Clary, Thomas C. "Motivation Through Positive
     Stroking." PUBLIC PERSONNEL MANAGEMENT,
     2, 2 (March-April 1973), 113-117.

     Asserts that positive stroking is helpful
     to employees and to the organization, mo-
     tivates employees, increases productivity
     levels, and leads to a positive and happier
     lifestyle.

295. Coplinger, James L. "The Future of Fringe Be-
     nefits." PUBLIC MANAGEMENT, 55, 10
     (October 1973), 18-21.

     Claims that the public employee is ex-
     tremely interested in his work and can be
     motivated by factors intrinsic to the work
     itself. Argues that the public administra-
     tor must attempt to offer those fringe
     benefits that motivate without releasing
     ultimate control over the organization and
     without spending an undue amount of money on
     them. Lists areas of fringe benefits that can
     increase productive workers: educational
     assistance, counselling, improved work
     areas, participatory management, flexible job
     assignments, flexible work schedules, insu-
     rance, professional or union activities, and
     family involvement.

296. Costello, John M., and Sang M. Lee. "Needs
     Fulfillment and Job Satisfaction of Profes-
     sionals." PUBLIC PERSONNEL MANAGEMENT,
     3, 5 (September-October 1974), 454-461.

     Involves personal goal satisfaction
     and analysis of the individuals and their
     perceived importance. Decries the relative-
     ly little concrete research concerning
     the relationship of the employee's degree
     of needs fulfillment and/or need deficiency

to job satisfaction. Alleges that the individual's perceived importance of needs has
often been ignored in the study of job satisfaction. Analyzes the relationship between
needs fulfillment and job satisfaction
among professional employees in a publicly-
owned utility firm, the City Public Service Board of San Antonio.

297. Crane, Edgar G. "The State Environment for
     Productivity Improvement: The Case for
     an Open Systems Approach." D.P.A. Dis-
     sertation, State University of New York
     at Albany, 1977. 436 p.

     Constructs a model which has implications
for action, research and training requirements for successful productivity approaches. Urges that central to these
requirements is the need for a better
understanding of conditions, perceptions and
exchanges supportive of productivity
coalitions. Concludes that the critical factor in determining the creation and survival
of contemporary productivity efforts is not
active opposition but the creation and
maintenance of supportive coalitions which
permit the selection of politically and tech-
nically realistic approaches.

298. Decotiis, Allen R., and Gerard S. Gryski.
     "Role Orientations and Job Satisfaction in
     a Public Bureaucracy." SOUTHERN REVIEW OF
     PUBLIC ADMINISTRATION, 5, 1 (Spring
     1981), 22-33.

     Investigates selected factors found to be
related to job satisfaction among the state of
Georgia Merit System Personnel. Supports the
plausibility of a two-tiered approach to the
analysis of job satisfaction, with the
strongest and most direct influences coming from the role orientation measures.
Analyzes how satisfaction is affected by organizational variables of participation, bureaucratic regulation, and organization posi-

tion. Finds that background variables (with
the exception of organization position) is
significantly related to the study's measure
of job satisfaction.

299. Eaton, Joseph W. "Role Expectations: The
     Social Worker Looks in the Mirror." PUB-
     LIC ADMINISTRATION REVIEW, 23, 3 (Sep-
     tember 1963), 170-175.

     Presents findings on social workers in
the veterans administration. Demonstrates
that while social workers expressed a
preference for giving direct service to
clients, they also showed an inclination toward upward mobility that would remove them
from direct service. Indicates strong identification with their own field.

300. Ewell, Julian J. "High Morale in Combat."
     MILITARY REVIEW, 62, 6 (June 1982),
     19-33.

     Looks back on the difficulties encountered
in the Vietnam battlefield. Recalls measures
taken to ease the impact of these difficulties on unit morale, which allowed command
to concentrate more fully on its main
mission.

301. Fosler, R. Scott. "State and Local Government
     Productivity and the Private Sector."
     PUBLIC ADMINISTRATION REVIEW, 38, 1
     (January-February 1978), 22-27.

     Approaches productivity from three dif-
ferent perceptions of economic activity:
economy, pluralistic economy, and a holistic
economy. Provides different definitions of
productivity for each perception. Discusses
their relationship between government and
business under economic perceptions and
how the two should interact to improve productivity.

302. Gabris, G., and W. Giles. "Improving Produc-
     tivity and Performance Appraisal through
     the Use of   Non-Economic Incentives." PUB-
     LIC PRODUCTIVITY   REVIEW, 7, 2 (June
     1983), 173-189.

     Finds that   many   lower-level   and non-
     managerial employees reject a   variable
     compensation program   (VCP) to enhance pro-
     ductivity. Signifies that   non-economic in-
     centives   would   increase   productivity:
     good management   practices, job enrichment,
     and professional skill   development. Sees
     productivity also as a subjective issue which
     requires   placing of more stress on people
     issues connected with   public   sector   pro-
     ductivity.

303. Garcia, Richard L.   "A Study   of   Sick-Time
     Usage by   White Collar Employees   in the
     Public Sector."   D.P.A. Dissertation,
     University of Southern   California, 1982.
     221 p.

     Reports the findings of   research   con-
     ducted on 644 white collar employees of
     the   City   of   Los Angeles.   Matches actual
     sick-time usage against   personal, job and
     attitudinal characteristics. Investigates
     employee   perceptions of   the   effects and
     implications of various control   strategies
     designed to reduce sick-time use.   Finds
     relationships   between   sick-time   usage,
     age, sex, race, education, marital status,
     time with the City,   and   job   level   of   em-
     ployees. Reveals feelings of employees on
     absenteeism control   strategies   that   reward
     work better than penalties.

304. Gawthrop, Louis   C.   BUREAUCRATIC BEHAVIOR IN
     THE   EXECUTIVE BRANCH: AN ANALYSIS OF ORGA-
     NIZATION   CHANGE.   New York: Free Press,
     1969.   276 p.

     Inquires into how bureaucratic behavior in
     the executive branch of the   federal   govern-

ment is conditioned to respond to the inevitable demands for change. Develops the inquiry within the context of some well-established propositions borrowed from the literature on large, complex, profit-motivated, product-producing, private corporations. Uses the comparison in focusing on some of the most salient characteristics of governmental bureaucracy. Covers controlling conflict, decision making, organizational loyalty, and organizational change.

305. Goldberg, Joel A. "Putting Productivity to Work." THE BUREAUCRAT, 12, 2 (Summer 1983), 12-15.

Summarizes some papers presented at the second national public sector productivity conference (March 24-25) 1983. Concludes that success of the conference indicates interest in, and concern for, productivity improvements in the public sector. Predicts a secure future for productivity improvement efforts in the public sector despite and because of budget cuts and limited resources. Dispels misconceptions that public sector managers care little about operational efficiency and effectiveness.

306. Goode, Leon F. Jr., and David H. Meier. "Productivity Measurement for Thinkers." THE BUREAUCRAT, 10, 1 (Spring 1981), 30-42.

Discusses the unique productivity measurement system at the U.S. Army Training and Doctrine Command Systems Analysis Activity. Points out that since the process measures performance, it also motivates behavior. Emphasizes quality of output with quality assessment by peer group.

307. Gotbaum, Victor, and Edward Handman. "A Conversation with Victor Gotbaum." PUBLIC ADMINISTRATION REVIEW, 38, 1 (January-February 1978), 19-21.

Provides taped interview with Victor
Gotbaum, Chief spokesman for municipal
unions of New York. Gives a good idea on
labor's opinion of productivity programs.

308. Greiner, J.M. "Motivating Improved Produc-
     tivity: Three Promising Approaches." PUB-
     LIC MANAGEMENT, 61, 10 (October 1979),
     2-19.

     Focuses on productivity improvement ef-
     forts by local governments to enhance motiva-
     tion of their personnel. Regrets that al-
     though more than sixty cents from every
     dollar of local government's operating expen-
     ses go toward employee salaries and bene-
     fits, many feel that government service is not
     conducive to maximum employee efficiency or
     effectiveness. Charges that government per-
     sonnel policies and civil service systems are
     frequently accused of stifling incentive
     and ignoring excellence. Warns that this
     can lead to alienation, frustration, poor
     morale and low productivity.

309. Hale, Thomas M. "Military Retirement Pay:
     A Time of Crisis." MILITARY REVIEW,
     63, 8 (August 1983), 52-59.

     Explores the undergoing review of the
     military retirement pay system. Provides
     background on what is happening, tracing the
     system's evolution. Compares it with other
     systems involving dangerous or stressful work
     and considers likely impact of recent
     changes. Concludes that timing is right for
     a major study in relation to the recruitment
     and retention of the desired force.

310. Hatry, Harry P. "Issues in Productivity
     Measurement for Local Governments." PUBLIC
     ADMINISTRATION REVIEW, 32, 6 (November-
     December 1972), 776-784.

     Manifests that measurement leads to increased

productivity. Cites specific uses of local
government productivity measurement so
that their current status is known. Illustrates some of the major issues in productivity measurement by presenting two
examples on solid waste collection and
police crime control.

311. _____. "The Status of Productivity Meas-
urement in the Public Sector." PUBLIC
ADMINISTRATION REVIEW, 38, 1 (January-
February 1978),28-33.

Defines and discusses the current status of
productivity measurement. Includes discus-
sions on output/input ratios, effectiveness-
measurement procedures, comprehensive measurement systems, federal output indicators,
and state budget officials' rating of effective and efficient measurements. Provides
examples of application of work standards
in Phoenix, Arizona.

312. Hayes, Frederick O. "City and County Productivity Programs." PUBLIC ADMINISTRATION
REVIEW, 38, 1 (January-February 1978),
15-18.

Analyzes eight local programs taken from a
study which was funded by the Ford Foundation
and the National Center for Productivity
and Quality of Working Life.

313. Hayward, Nancy. "The Productivity Challenge." PUBLIC ADMINISTRATION REVIEW,
36, 5 (September-October 1976), 544-550.

Defines public sector productivity as
efficiency with which resources are consumed
in the effective delivery of public services, implying not only quantity, but also
quality. Presents the productivity efforts
of Washington State in illustrating the
variety of techniques and approaches to
improve governmental productivity. Out-

lines improvement strategy for productivity
and the sources of gains in technology.
Concludes that the bottom line commitment of every official--federal, state
and local--in better managing public resources, particularly, human resources.

314. Hayward, Nancy, and George Kuper. "The
     National Economy and Productivity in Gov-
     ernment." PUBLIC ADMINISTRATION REVIEW,
     38, 1 (January-February 1978), 2-4.

     Points to the gains made in productivity.
     Contends that different levels of government
     affect each other causing local governments
     to put productivity at a low priority level
     in program design and implementation.

315. Herrick, John S. "Work Motives of Female
     Executives." PUBLIC PERSONNEL MANAGEMENT,
     2, 5 (September-October 1973), 380-387.

     Studies the work motives of female
     executives in private industry and federal
     levels. Reveals that there seem to be
     few differences between the perceptions
     of male and female executives with regard
     to their jobs: personal satisfaction first
     before income, or in Maslow's term, "self-
     actualization needs.

316. Hill, David Barton. "The Content and Beh-
     avioral Implication of Popular Evalua-
     tions of Government." Ph.D. Disserta-
     tion, Florida State University, 1975.
     159 p.

     Examines the origins and implications of
     declining positive evaluation of government
     and politics. Enumerates the following find-
     ings: (1) distrust of leaders in general,
     which does not stem primarily from distrust
     of any specific leader or leaders; (2) cyni-
     cism for a level of government results,
     arising, in part, from evaluation of self-

initiated contact and unfulfilled expectations; (3) more distrustful nature of blacks
toward their leaders but more trustful of
federal government than whites; and (4) dissatisfaction of the old and the middle class,
especially the skilled workers, because of
their perception that government does not
attend to their specific and unique policy
needs. Concludes that evaluative attitudes
are poorly constrained and lack the
ideological character which would make them
a more potent threat.

317. Hill, Richard A., M.S. Halliday, and J.C.W.
      Cadoo. "Washington State Management Sys-
      tems Reviews." THE BUREAUCRAT, 13, 1
      (Spring 1984), 53-57.

      Defines management systems review as a
technique used by the Management Services Division of the Office of Financial Management
to evaluate capacity to perform. Describes
approach as a medical model--performance
failures are seen as symptoms of systems
problems. Features self-examination in rev-
ising management systems reviews. Argues
that because agency management systems are
"more alike than different," it is feasible
to develop uniform evaluation criteria on
"management systems standards" that are appropriate to virtually all agencies.

318. Holzer, Marc, ed. PRODUCTIVITY IN PUBLIC OR-
      GANIZATIONS. Port Washington, N.Y.:
      Kennikat Press, 1976. 328 p.

      Structures readings around a specific
framework for compensation and analysis.
Attempts to categorize the various concepts
developed in the literature in terms that
administrative practitioners, academics and
politicians alike might find useful.

319. Hooper, Michael. "The Motivational Bases of
      Political Behavior: A New Concept and

Measurement Procedure." PUBLIC OPINION
QUARTERLY, 47, 4 (Winter 1983), 497-515.

Draws on classic definitions of power,
authority, and persuasion. Develops the
concept of the motivational basis of political behavior. Defines and describes four
motivational bases. Presents measurement
procedure, a proximity scaling model for
empirical applications, and a theory which
specifies the conditions under which behavior motivated on the various bases will
be performed. Discusses these conditions as
having different consequences for the functioning of the political system. Avers that
the techniques and theory presented are
based on the individuals but are directed
to the prediction and explanation of system
functioning.

320. International City Management Association.
      "Employee Recognition: A Key to Motiva-
      tion." PERSONNEL JOURNAL, 60, 2
      (February 1981), 103-104.

Addresses the problem of how personnel administrators deal with employee dissatisfaction or feelings of unappreciation or
under-compensation. Proposes that employee
recognition programs can boost awareness of
the organizations, raise morale, and ultimately, increase productivity. Claims that
higher salary is not always the answer,
but that everyone's pride is boosted by a
public demonstration of appreciation.

321. _____. "Salary Increases for Municipal
      Employees." PUBLIC MANAGEMENT, 23, 11
      (November 1941), 323-328.

Brings up the issue of increased salaries
of municipal employees to meet rising costs
of living and to retain them from being lost
to the military service, federal government,
and private industry.Contends that in making
pay adjustments, differences in following fac-

tors must be considered: living costs (rural-
urban communities), climate and consumption
habits, housing, fuels, means of transportation, etc.

322. Jehring, J.J. "Participation Bonuses."
     PUBLIC ADMINISTRATION REVIEW, 36, 5
     (September-October 1976), 539-543.

     Urges the use of participation bonuses to
     give employees an incentive to participate
     in labor and supply savings for which
     they would receive compensations above
     their regular pay.

323. Katz, Ralph. "Job Longevity as a Situational
     Factor in Job Satisfaction: A Study of
     Employees in Metropolitan County and
     State Governments." ADMINISTRATIVE
     SCIENCE QUARTERLY, 23, 2 (June 1978),
     204-223.

     Investigates the relationships between
     overall job satisfaction and five tasks:
     skill variety, task identity, task signifi-
     cance, authority autonomy, and feedback from
     jobs. Shows that the strength of the re-
     lationships between job-satisfaction and
     each of the task dimensions depends on both
     the job longevity and organizational longevity
     of the sampled individuals. Analyzes sig-
     nificant correlational differences and
     discusses the implications of its find-
     ings for task design, as well as for
     managing new employees.

324. Keevey, Richard F. "State Productivity Im-
     provements: Building on Existing Struc-
     tures." PUBLIC ADMINISTRATIONREVIEW,
     40,5 (September-October 1980), 451-459.

     Examines the productivity efforts in New
     Jersey. Highlights past achievements in such
     areas as state aid administration, capital
     financing, purchasing and third party con-

tracting. Suggests that past achievements
lay a necessary foundation to facilitate and
legitimate new productivity efforts.

325. King, John Leslie. "Local Government Use
     of Information Technology: The Next
     Decade." PUBLIC ADMINISTRATION REVIEW,
     42, 1 (January-February 1982), 25-37.

     Objects to forecasts about information
technology based largely on the expectation
that advances in computing and communications hardware and soft-ware will profoundly
affect the organization and use of these
technologies. Raises a less exciting but
more realistic forecast about what will happen
with the use of information technology in
local governments in the 1980's.

326. Lamare, Judith. "Intergovernmental Finance,
     Productivity, and the Local Match
     Question: The Case of California's
     Transit Subsidy Policy." PUBLIC ADMIN-
     ISTRATION REVIEW, 41, 4 (July-August
     1981), 463-470.

     Studies the 1971-1979 requirement of 50%
match policy from local tax subsidies or
fare box revenues or both, with exemp-
tions allowed. Reports on findings of the
study: (1) association of local match
requirement with relatively higher transit
performance; and (2) necessity of local
match requirements to encourage program
productivity using indicators of efficiency
and effectiveness.

327. Layden, Dianne R. "Productivity and Produc-
     tivity Bargaining: The Environmental
     Context." PUBLIC PERSONNEL MANAGEMENT,
     9, 4 (July-August 1980), 244-257.

     Attempts to describe key aspects of the
productivity issue in government as they ref-
lect the various perspectives of the partici-

pants in the policy making process--those of
the employee, union, management, and the
public.

328. Likert, Rensis. "System 4: A Resource for Im-
     proving Public Administration." PUBLIC
     ADMINISTRATION REVIEW, 41, 6 (November-
     December 1981), 674-679.

     Suggests that system 4 enables any ad-
     ministrator in government to increase produc-
     tivity of the unit he/she is managing.
     Argues that system 4 provides a challenging
     opportunity to administrators to reduce cost
     and simultaneously improve the quality of
     service to citizens.

329. Lovell, Catherine. "Training for Productivity
     Improvement: Long Beach, California."
     SOUTHERN REVIEW OF PUBLIC ADMINISTRATION,
     2, 4 (March 1979), 458-474.

     Points out that a productivity program
     should not be an add-on but must be institu-
     tionalized with an output orientation. Lays
     the foundation of such a process on a
     system-wide training program. Defines some
     important terms: productivity, productivity
     improvement, and total performance measure-
     ment. Discusses training methods and
     identifies three strategies. Evaluates the
     Long Beach, California experience with a pre-
     diction of success.

  * Lyden, Fremont J., and Ernest Goriller. "Why
     City Managers Leave the Profession:
     Longitudinal Study in the Pacific North-
     west." Cited as Item 63 above.

330. Marcus, Philip M., and Dora Cafanga. "Con-
     trol in Modern Organizations." PUBLIC
     ADMINISTRATION REVIEW, 25, 2 (June
     1965), 121-127.

Yields fresh insights into the control
mechanisms of organizations. Argues that
control must be delegated to the lower
echelons to increase the subordinate's morale
and willingness to participate and improve
the organization's performance.

331. Mark, Jerome A. "Meanings and Measures of
     Productivity." PUBLIC ADMINISTRATION RE-
     VIEW, 32, 6 (November-December 1972),
     747-753.

     Summarizes some of the concepts of produc-
     tivity, the interpretations, and the use of
     the measures developed from these concepts.
     Includes a description of the available pro-
     ductivity data.

332. Menges, Edward D. Jr. "The Lakewood, Colo-
     rado Personnel System: Creating an Envi-
     ronment for Productivity." PUBLIC PER-
     SONNEL MANAGEMENT, 9, 4 (July-August
     1980), 257-268.

     Contends that it is the responsibility
     of management to initiate changes in
     creating an environment of productivity.
     Discusses the changes made in Lakewood, Co-
     lorado. Highlights four areas: classifica-
     tion system, base pay system for classified
     employees, recognition and treatment of man-
     agerial professional personnel, and evalua-
     tion of the reward system.

333. Miles, Rufus E. "Mobility, Stability and
     Sterility." PUBLIC ADMINISTRATION RE-
     VIEW, 23, 3 (September 1963), 199-200.

     Supports the need of personnel civil
     service systems to take into account the
     need for and the benefits of shifts in as-
     signments, not simply mobility, to keep the
     employees performing to their best ability
     without boredom. Warns that stability
     can turn into sterility.

334. Neugarten, Dail Ann. "Themes and Issues in
     Public Sector Productivity." PUBLIC PER-
     SONNEL MANAGEMENT, 9, 4 (July-August
     1980), 229-236.

     Outlines briefly the need for increased
     public sector productivity. Covers the is-
     sues of definition measurement and im-
     plementation. Lists some common held
     myths about productivity. Calls for con-
     tinued research in: developing better indic-
     ators of performance, implications of in-
     creased productivity on the budget, and
     application of behavioral science knowl-
     edge to employee productivity.

335. Peabody, Robert L. "Authority Relations in
     the Organizations." PUBLIC ADMINISTRA-
     TION REVIEW, 23, 2 (June 1963), 87-92.

     Deals with results of exploratory study
     on superior-subordinate relationships in
     three local public service organizations.
     Encourages awareness of the differences in the
     concept of authority to facilitate achieve-
     ment of organizational goals and satis-
     faction of individual needs.

336. Peitzsch, Frederick C. "Trends in Municipal
     Personnel Problems." PUBLIC MANAGEMENT,
     30, 6(June 1948), 162-166.

     Summarizes the trends in personnel prac-
     tices in 1947-1948. Provides statistical
     reports on the increase in workers and sala-
     ries, shorter working hours, longer annual
     vacation leaves, increase in overtime com-
     pensation and retirement plans, and the
     locals in employee union organizations.

337. Rainey, Hal G. "Reward Preferences Among
     Public and Private Managers: In Search
     of the Service Ethic." AMERICAN REVIEW
     OF PUBLIC ADMINISTRATION, 16, 4 (Winter
     1984), 288-302.

Compares public and private managers'
reward preferences and relates differences on
reward preference items to scores on widely-
used scales of work attitudes. Finds that
the more important incentive for public
managers is involvement in worthwhile
public or social service although financial and other extrinsic rewards are also
highly valued. Reveals similarities in responses by public and private managers.

338. Rogers, William Glenn. "Organizational Per-
     formance Evaluation in California State
     Government Agencies: A Case Study and Con-
     ceptual Analysis." Ph.D. Dissertation,
     University of Southern California, 1983.
     224 p.

Addresses the measurement of organizational
performance in the public sector, using California State government agencies as data
base. Generates evidence that different
criteria preferences are likely to be
formulated by different constituencies with
their own self-interests in mind. Suggests
that program evaluations performed from narrow cognitive perspectives can result in
inadequate representation of system-related
interests. Proffers an evaluation approach
matrix of conceptual considerations for the
development of criteria in evaluating public
programs.

339. Rosenbaum, Allen. "Federal Management: Path-
     ological Problems and Simple Cures." PS,
     15, 2 (Spring 1982), 187-193.

Sheds light on five major problems,
which if successfully resolved, would have
the effect of improving federal government
productivity: (1) need to improve the performance of routine organizational functions and production of letters, memo-
randa and reports that are part of all
program activity; (2) provision and communication of routine information to the

public, to other agencies, and within the
organizations; (3) need to staff many
activities more adequately; (4) impediment
to effective management found in the inadequate distribution and utilization of
existing staff resources; and (5) employee
motivation and the need to establish open
communication between superiors and subordinates.

340. Rosow, Jerome M. "Public Sector Pay and Bene-
     fits." PUBLIC ADMINISTRATION REVIEW,
     36,5 (September-October 1976), 538-545.

     Cites methods to control public employees'
pay and benefits in an effort to respond to
the public anger at government costs. Gives
three systems of pay fixing and identifies
basic principles and practices applicable
to public employee benefits. Hopes that
better productivity should result.

341. Ross, John P., and J. Burkhead. PRODUCTIVITY
     IN THE LOCAL GOVERNMENT SECTOR. Lexing-
     ton, Md.: D.C. Heath, 1974. 170 p.

     Feels this book serves two useful pur-
poses: (1) a report on the "state-of-the-art"
in the difficult and complex field of public
sector productivity analysis, and (2) the
model that is developed in Chapter 5 and
tested in Chapter 6 as an operationally useful contribution for academic inquiry and
local government practitioners' reference.

342. Ryan, Raymond. "The Impact of Three Years of
     Experience and a New Governor on the
     State of Washington's Productivity
     Program." PUBLIC ADMINISTRATION REVIEW,
     38,1 (January-February 1978), 12-15.

     Describes the state's productivity plan,
its implementation, and how transition of
governors affected the program. Includes a
summary of the Advisory Council's Final Re-

port and the existing status of the
program, which looked promising.

343. Schroeder, Patricia. "The Politics of Pro-
     ductivity." PUBLIC PERSONNEL MANAGEMENT,
     9, 4(July-August 1980), 236-243.

     Outlines the history of productivity im-
     provement programs. Discusses the excuses
     used in the past for the productivity
     programs that did not work. Presents plan
     (a proposed bill in Congress) which has
     three main arguments: (1) productivity program
     must be an internal system; (2) must be
     parcel of the day-to-day management of the
     workforce; and (3) incentives must be
     provided.

344. Scioli, Frank P. Jr. "Problems and Prospects
     for Policy Evaluation." PUBLIC ADMIN-
     ISTRATION REVIEW, 39, 1 (January-February
     1979), 41-45.

     Pays attention to several problems inhi-
     biting policy evaluation at the state and
     local levels: (1) starting projects that do
     not have evaluations built into them;
     (2) improper use of the data collected;
     (3) lack of trained evaluators; (4) competi-
     tion between theory and action; and (6) the
     problem of bureaucratic survival. Analy-
     zes several prospects for overcoming
     problems: (1) increased interest in evalua-
     tion from the top levels of government;
     (2) increased interest of universities in
     the science of evaluation; (3) emergence
     of training programs in policy evaluation
     research or methodology; (4) more federal
     agencies advancing productivity research and
     evaluation analysis; and (5) organizing
     activities of states to advance evaluation.

345. Swiss, James E. "Unbalanced Incentives in
     Government Productivity Systems: Misrepor-
     ting as a Case in Point." PUBLIC PRODUC-

TIVITY REVIEW,   7, 1   (March 1983),   26-37.

Examines problem of incentive imbalances
in   public   productivity   management   systems.
Attributes   imbalances   to   incremental   pattern of productivity   system   installation
in government.   Specifies misreporting as a
prime example of unbalanced systemic   incentives.   Argues that incentives for misreporting   can   harm   employee morale   and   com-
pletely   negate   beneficial   effects   of
productivity systems.   Comes   up   with   two
measures: (1)   self-consciousness   or   awareness on the part of program designers   and
individual managers as a   way of alleviating
the problem;   and   (2) remedying   neglect   of
managerial incentives as a substantial   step
toward improving government productivity.

346. Weir, Michael.   "Efficiency Measurement in
      Government."   THE BUREAUCRAT,   13, 2
      (Summer   1984),   38-42.

Emphasizes construction of useful efficiency   measures as part   of   a   productivity
program.   Notes the availability of sophisticated techniques to   cope with the measurement problems in service organizations.
Recommends acceptance of less than perfect
measurement when (1) expense of constructing
a   new one is too high;   or (2) in the absence   of   a   better   measure.

347. Zagoria, Sam.   "Productivity   Bargaining."
      PUBLIC   MANAGEMENT,   55, 7   (July 1973),
      14-16.

Charges that as governmental units grow
larger   and   larger,   the   distance   between
the   public   employer   and   the   individual
employee continues to grow.   Alleges   that
this contributes to alienation,   frustration,
and the feeling of being ignored and unap-
preciated.   Recommends implementation of a
productivity program that   requires employee involvement and   acceptance of the

fairness and soundness of the approach.
Quotes a Wisconsin governor in concluding
that the productivity program is a humanizing force in government, provides job en-
largement for those trapped in tedious positions, offers new challenges to both administrators and workers, facilitates participative management, and gives the public higher quality service at a lower
price.

B.   Creativity and Innovation

348. Crompton, John L. "Recreation Vouchers: A
      Case Study in Administrative Innovation
      and Citizen Participation." PUBLIC ADMIN-
      ISTRATION REVIEW, 43, 6 (November-
      December 1983), 537-546.

      Presents results of interview with of-
      ficials of a city in Australia who used
      vouchers issued in tax bills that could
      be returned to receive recreational serv-
      ices. Describes how the citizens choose
      where to allocate their donation and votes
      for services they feel are useful. Provides a
      degree of tax incentive allowing for the city
      not to spend funds that result from unused
      vouchers.

349. Feller, Irwin. "Managerial Response to Tech-
      nological Innovations in Public Sector
      Organizations." MANAGEMENT SCIENCE,
      26, 2 (October 1980), 1021-1030.

      Sees technological innovations as a means
      for raising productivity levels in state
      and local governments. Indicates that:
      (1) senior level bureaucrats have primary
      responsibility for decisions concerning the
      adoption of innovations; and (2) innova-
      tions adopted by state and local govern-
      ments are of two types--cost-reducing, and

service-augmenting. Explains the apparent
preference of bureaucrats for service-
augmenting innovations.

Views service-augmenting innovations as
tending to: (1) increase agency budgets to
which bureaucratic emoluments are positively correlated; (2) expand the clientele
served by the agency; and (3)obscure agency
production costs by simultaneously alter-
ing both the input mixes and the services
being provided.

Observes that federal policies designed to
foster a more rapid diffusion of technological innovations are, in part, based upon
expectations that technological innovations
will lessen the budgetary pressures upon
state and local governments. Alleges that
there may be countervailing pressures within
the adoption processes of state and
local governments which weaken the im-
plied relationship between technological
change and productivity improvement.

350. Gill, Michael Roark. "Environmental Quality
     Management in State Government: Studies in
     Administrative Improvisation." Ph.D. Dis-
     sertation, Indiana University, 1978.
     282 p.

Describes and analyzes the administration
of state environmental policies. Develops
criteria for evaluating program performance. Identifies innovations in institutional arrangements, regulatory procedures,
and public participation strategies. Finds
that a variety of innovative policies and
programs for environmental quality and resources management and new institutional arrangements have resulted in the states in
response to public demands. Identifies
principal constraints as: legislative politics, inconsistent executive leadership,
and conflicting economic development policies. Indicates that the structural
changes have occurred in a majority of

states, that public support has remained
strong for pollution control, that staff
and financial resources have improved
greatly,and that planning for environmental quality has been institutionalized
by nearly 50% over that of the 1945-1970
period.

351. Golembiewski, Robert T. "Public Sector
     Productivity and Flexible Work Hours:
     Testing 3 Points of the Common Wisdom Re:
     OD." SOUTHERN REVIEW OF PUBLIC ADMINIS-
     TRATION, 4, 3 December 1980), 324-339.

     Asserts that flexitime (flexible work
     hours) in the public sector has a very
     broad range of positive consequences for
     individuals and their organizations. Demons-
     trates positively how the behavioral the-
     ories underlying OD, which were basically
     developed in business contexts, can be ap-
     plied in the public sector. Implies that
     flexitime can avoid substantially those ins-
     titutional and historical constraints that
     complicate public sector OD.   Shows how
     "hard" productivity data support the
     usefulness of public sector flexitime
     applications.

352. Howe, Harold II. "Organization for Innova-
     tion." JOURNAL OF SOCIAL ISSUES, 21, 1
     (January 1965), 48-55.

     Presents the case of the non-profit
     Learning Institute of North Carolina (LINC),
     which is subsidized by private and/or public
     sources, to cause, encourage, and support
     innovation in public and private education.
     Discusses the problem areas, possibilities,
     and dimensions of an independent educa-
     tional body.

  353. International City Management Association.
       "The Five-Day Week in City Employment."
       PUBLIC MANAGEMENT, 22, 5 (May 1940),

131-135.

Synthesizes experiences of 14 cities with the five-day week and with monthly or annual pay for laborers. Finds that five-day week has improved employee morale. Suggests that other cities apply the plan on a test basis and consider effect on service to the public, quantity of work, extra help needed, and attitude of department heads and employees.

354. Klein, R., and Dwight M. Bissel. "A Medical Audit for City Employees." PUBLIC MANAGEMENT, 36, 2 (February 1954), 32-35.

Argues for establishment of a regular medical examination program. Talks about the experience of San Jose, California where lives of some employees were prolonged for optimum city service for a number of years.

355. LaCapra, Louis V. "Trying Out the Four-Day Work Week." PUBLIC PERSONNEL MANAGEMENT, 2, 3 (May-June 1973), 216-221.

Contains the results of an experiment in rearranging work hours in the Port Authority of New York and New Jersey. Outlines the operations of the program and the anticipated changes in productivity and morale of the staff. Observes that there was no improvement in production, goal, and service while initial improvement in morale waned early in the summer. Compares this specific experiment with those conducted by big companies. Concludes that different circumstances produce different results.

356. Levine, James P., and Theodore L. Becker. "Toward and Beyond a Theory of Supreme Court Impact." AMERICAN BEHAVIORAL SCIENTIST, 13, 4 (March-April 1970), 562-573.

Explains the limited effects of the
Supreme Court on American society: lower
court autonomy, elite unresponsiveness, and
public unawareness.   Enjoins increasing Supreme Court impact by adopting and applying new
approaches and procedures--with imagination,
flexibility, and boldness.

357. Mars, David. "Creativity and Administration."
     PUBLIC ADMINISTRATION REVIEW, 27, 3
     (September 1967), 252-256.

Undertakes to describe the special responsibility of administrators to maximize
creative behavior within their organizations. Urges that they must seek to evoke
personal creativity and lessen bureaucratic
controls.

358. McKinney, Jerome B. "Process Accountability
     and the Creative Use of Intergovernmental
     Relations." PUBLIC ADMINISTRATION REVIEW,
     41, Special Issue (January 1981), 144-150.

Distinguishes between traditional (fiscal)
and process accountability. Focuses on
process accountability as giving emphasis to
procedures and operations in carrying out
objectives. Offers an Accountability Con-
tinuum Model showing a five-range scale in
shifting from financial (fiscal) accountability to accountability for social purposes
(emerging). Discusses advantages of process
accountability: (1) reduces grant cost by
monitoring, based on agreed upon procedures
and expected outcomes; and (2) lessens
spendthrift syndrome by transforming unresponsive, costly, and rigid bureaucratic
system.

359. Miller, Glenn W., R.W. Presley, and Mark S.
     Sniderman. "Multijobholding by Firemen and
     Policemen Compared." PUBLIC PERSONNEL
     MANAGEMENT, 2, 4 (July-August 1973),
     283-390.

Analyzes the reasons for "moonlighting" by policemen and firemen. Adduces certain preconditions that contribute to this phenomenon: information, ability, and opportunity. Determines that moonlighting is an offshoot of the four-day work week.

360. Perry, James L. and Kenneth L. Kraemer. "Chief Executive Support and Innovation Adoption." ADMINISTRATION & SOCIETY, 12, 2 (August 1980), 158-177.

Uses path analysis in testing the influence of chief executive support on computing innovation outcomes in local government organizations. Presents findings concerning contrasting signs for the paths between innovation scope and the two independent variables--chief executive support, and climate favorability:(1) positive path for chief executive support suggests that his support is influential in its distribution across sub-units; (2)the negative sign between climate favorability and innovation scope suggests a constraint in the spread of cross-departmental innovation with increasing levels of elected-official and department head support of data processing.

Concludes that: (1) the path models reaffirm the importance of slack resources and professionalism in the innovation process; and (2) user involvement variable indicates that particular types of organizational processes influence the magnitude and scope of innovation adoption within an organization. Suggests that the implication of this finding is the enhancement of organizational capacity to innovate through creation of methods of client participation and adoption, design and evaluation of applications.

361. Prottas, Jeffrey. "The Impacts of Innovation: Technological Change in a Mass Transit

Authority." ADMINISTRATION & SOCIETY,
16, 1 (May 1984), 117-135.

Provides insights into the failure of
an   innovation by analyzing the experience of
the Massachusetts Bay Transportation Authority
in   using a new, technologically   advanced,
rapid transit vehicle (the Boeing Virtol
Standard Light-Rail Vehicle). Considers the
opportunities for organizational development
that innovations provide by weaving together   three threads of organizational research in the studies of innovation implementation and organizational learning.

362. Rainey, Glenn , and Lawrence Wolf.
      "Flexitime: Short-Term Benefits, Long
      Term ....?" PUBLIC ADMINISTRATION REVIEW,
      41, 1 (January-February 1981),   52-63.

Evaluates the flex-time experiment at
the Social Security Administration. Compares
findings of this study with previous
studies which generally used subjective
evaluation. Discovers that objective indicators produce mixed result with tentative signs of declining supervisor-employee
rapport. Finds unexpected rise in leave
usage which suggests that employees valued
flex-time principally for rewards obtained
away from the work site. Cautions against
some consequences arising from flex-time
implementation.

363. Roessner, J. David. "Incentives to Innovate
      in Public and Private Organizations."
      ADMINISTRATION & SOCIETY, 9, 3 (November
      1977), 341-365.

Applies the different perspectives of
economic theory, organization theory, public administration, and political science
in exploring the question of whether public organizations are inherently less innovative than private organizations. Synthesizes
existing empirical evidence to test the

predictions and explanations of the theory. Explains some of the implications of each discipline's perspective of the central question and illustrates efforts in applying these implications to public agencies.

364. Rubin, Richard S. "Flexitime: Its Implementation in the Public Sector." PUBLIC ADMINISTRATION REVIEW, 39, 3 (May-June 1979), 277-282.

Defines flexitime as flexible work schedules. Discusses the benefits, problems, and main issues that are involved in the use of flexitime by government agencies and its implications for employee relations.

365. Steinhauer, Marcia Buan. "Technology Transfer within a Government Organization: A Study of the Innovation Process in Florida's Social Services." Ph.D. Dissertation, University of Florida, 1975. 269 p.

Examines the processual dynamics of a complex organization adopting and implementing an innovative mechanism, the Client Information System (CIS), which was a departure from its own traditions. Follows the flow of the CIS in systematically analyzing the expectations, behavioral patterns, and linkage devices associated with the process of technology transfer within a complex and highly decentralized human resources organization, the Florida Department of Health and Rehabilitation Services. Reveals limited success in the transfer of the CIS technology due to the combination of dynamic factors: qualities of technology, qualities of the actors, and the transfer process. Finds absence of strong commitment from top officials which added to low legitimacy of the transfer process.

366. Stone, Donald. "Innovative Organizations

Require Innovative Managers." PUBLIC AD-
MINISTRATION REVIEW, 41, 5 (September-
October 1981), 507-513.

Explains requirements for innovative organizations: (1) development of sustained
curiosity; (2) more flexibility and unstrati-
fied structure as opposed to classical bureaucratic forms;(3) institutionalization
of search for opportunities for innovation;
and (4) recruitment, training and fostering
of distinctive breeds of executives and
managers. Deals with requirements for innovative managers: (1) insatiable curiosity;
(2) flexibility, creativity and facilita-
tion; and (3) institutionalization of
search for opportunities for innovations.
Enumerates attributes of top quality managers as: intellectual strength, ability to
synthesize, mastery of work content, "political" sensitivity and skill, leadership,
development of personnel, and integrity.

Expresses concern for the growing scarcity
of first-rate managerial talent in government due to the weak and poorly publi-
cized system of public management education, as well as the employment and promotion of mediocre and inferior public
executives.

367. Weimer,David L. "Federal Intervention in
the Process of Innovation in Local Public
Agencies: A Focus on Organizational Incentives." PUBLIC POLICY, 28, 1 (Winter
1980), 93-116.

Cautions that in the absence of federal intervention, innovation and diffusion of
innovations among local public agencies are
likely to proceed at a slower rate than the
social optimum. Presents a simple typology
which describes the various ways that information funding and technical assistance can
be combined in federal programs to encourage
innovation. Indicates that in choosing
among the federal intervention strategies,

however, it is important to consider the
organizational incentives each creates.
Warns that inadequate attention to organization incentives risks the initiation of
programs that lead to the diffusion of
inappropriate innovations.

368. Welch, Susan, and Kay Thompson. "The Impact
     of Federal Incentives on State Policy In-
     novations." AMERICAN JOURNAL OF POLITICAL
     SCIENCE, 24, 4 (November 1980), 715-729.

     Assesses the impact of federal incentives
on the diffusion rates of these policies
throughout the American states, using 57
states' public policies as basis for
analysis. Reveals that policies with federal
incentives do diffuse substantially faster
than policies that are the preserve of the
states, even when controlled for the functional area of the policy. Finds that the
speed of policy diffusion also appears to be
related to the time of the policy "invention,"
although methodological considerations
precluded a more systematic analysis of this
factor.

4. INTERGROUP AND INTRA-GROUP BEHAVIOR

A. Group Dynamics and Communication

369. Adams, Bruce, and Betsy Sherman. "Sunset
     Implementation: A Positive Partnership
     to Make Government Work." PUBLIC ADMINIS-
     TRATION REVIEW, 38, 1 (January-February
     1978), 78-81.

        Provides a brief history of the sunset
     concept and states ten basic principles
     essential to any workable sunset law.
     Discusses state and federal action in the
     area of sunset legislation. Suggests
     three key elements of a good evaluation
     process: evaluation work plan, prepara-
     tion of evaluation reports, and the eva-
     luation criteria. Opines that legislators
     and administrators need to foster an atmos-
     phere of cooperation in seeking ways to
     improve the workings of government--this in-
     cludes involving citizen participation.

370. Altman, Irwin. "Mainstreams of Research on
     Small Groups." PUBLIC ADMINISTRATION RE-
     VIEW, 23, 4 (December 1963), 203-208.

        Discusses small group behavior and how
     that knowledge may leave implications for
     the problems that beset the public exec-
     utive: areas of leadership, communication,
     and influence processes. Poses question
     on researcher's responsibility to communi-
     cate and interpret research results to line
     managers.

371. Barkdoll,   Gerald   L.   "Downside   Risk   to
     Program   Evaluations."   THE   BUREAUCRAT,
     12, 2   (Summer   1983),   16-18.

     Reports   the   results   of   research   that
suggests   evaluations can,   and do,   have negative effects on   programs and   program   managers,   such as: waste   of   resources,   demo-
tivation/disruption,   self-fulfilling prophecy,
and paired comparison.   Recommends   several
ways of   avoiding negative impacts in program
evaluation: good   technical   skills,   good
working   relationships,   and   avoiding   role
of   critic.

372. Blau,   Peter.   THE DYNAMICS OF BUREAUCRACY.
     Chicago: The   University   of   Chicago
     Press,   1955.   322 p.

     Investigates   the activities   of   lower of-
ficialdom   in   a lower setting.   Traces   the
operating adjustments which followed   the
introduction of performance records in a small
department   of   a state   agency. Examines the
relations between   colleagues,   informal
status,   and productive efficiency.   Holds
that bureaucracy   is   not   necessarily   opposed to   change;   that   this   opposition
only   occurs   chiefly   under   conditions   of
status   insecurity.

373. Brown,   David S.   "The Staff Man Looks in the
     Mirror."   PUBLIC   ADMINISTRATION   REVIEW,
     23, 1   (March)   1963),   67-73.

     Articulates   what   staff   men   say their   chief
satisfactions   and   dissatisfactions   are:
(1) how   they feel   their   work   is   seen   by
others,   measured and evaluated;   (2) how
they evaluate the importance of their work;
and   (3) how they   try to solve the problems
they   face.

374. Caldwell,   Lynton K.   "Managing the Transition
     to   Post-Modern Society."   PUBLIC ADMINIS-

TRATION REVIEW, 35, 6 (November-December 1975), 567-572.

Addresses the themes of relationships between knowledge, society, and bureaucracy in their dealings with modernity and public administration. Lists concepts of modern society as: social responsibility, organic interdependence, controlled growth, ecological necessity, selective innovation, and dynamic equilibrium. Urges social sharing of effective knowledge of trends, interactions, and synergistic effects. Concludes that effective organization and sharing of knowledge should enable public agencies to more readily achieve public goals with reduced probability of error and enable informed public to challenge administrative action.

375. Colby, William, and Peter Forbath. HONORABLE MEN: MY LIFE IN THE CIA. New York: Simon and Schuster, 1978. 493 p.

Indicts the total intelligence secrecy in CIA operations used by the President at his discretion. Declares the CIA could no longer operate within the traditions of the past. Urges that it must build public support by informing the public of its activities and accepting the public's control over them. Pays accolade to the honorable "company" of men and women in the intelligence service so that they can be better understood by their fellow Americans.

376. Davison, W. Phillips. "The Third-Person Effect in Communication." PUBLIC OPINION QUARTERLY, 47, 1 (Spring 1983), 1-15.

Sees a person exposed to a persuasive communication in the mass media as having a greater effect on others than on himself or herself. Asserts that each individual reasons: "I will not be influenced, but they (the third persons) may well be

persuaded." Claims that in some cases, a
communication leads to action not because
of its impact on those to whom it is
ostensibly directed, but because others
(third persons) think that it will have an
impact on its audience. Presents four
small experiments that tend to support this
hypothesis. Notes its complementary relationship to a number of concepts in the social
sciences. Reasons that the third-person
effect may help to explain various aspects
of social behavior, including the fear of he-
retical propaganda by religious leaders
and the fear of dissent by political
rulers. Finds that it appears to be related
to the phenomenon of censorship in general:
the censor never admits to being influenced, it is others with "more impres-
sionable minds" who will be affected.

377. Frendreis, John Philip. "Webs of Local Gov-
     ernment: Patterns of Reputation and Per-
     sonal Interaction Among Local Chief Execu-
     tives." Ph.D. Dissertation, University of
     Wisconsin, 1981. 165 p.

     Examines the form and antecedent conditions
of peer evaluation and personal communication among 1984 chief executives of American
cities. Yields four major sets of conclusions:(1) a vast amount of peer evaluation and communication informally links the
majority of chief executives; (2) process of
peer evaluation and communication is related
(e.g., tendency for frequent communication
among executives possessing reputations for
personal excellence); (3) there is little
contact between appointed and elected chief
executives (e.g., most peer evaluation and
communication appear between geographically
proximate officials occupying similar types
of positions); and (4) two mechanisms appear
to structure these behaviors--tendency for
all executives to seek information from
similar others ("decision by analogy" model),
and tendency-oriented toward management
careers to interact with other executives in

pursuit of goals relating to   their individual
professional interests.

*   Gardner, Neely, "The   Non-Hierarchical   Organi-
        zation of the   Future: Theory   versus
        Reality." Cited as   Item 265 above.

378. Goldy, Florence B.   "Program   Evaluation as
        a Problem of Organizational Interaction."
        D.P.A. Dissertation, University of Southern
        California, 1974. 190 p.

        Assesses the association between the
program evaluation outcome and the interorganizational interaction and interpersonal
relationships   among   the   actors--adminis-
trators, data collectors, and evaluators.
Analyzes evaluations conducted by the new
Program Evaluation Service at Veterans   Administration's Hospital, Brentwood,   Los
Angeles. Concludes that the administrators
were the most influential actors, that data
collectors perceived their roles as limiting and least satisfying, and that evaluators were least positive about the design and its value. Indicates that a triad
of Administrator-Data Collector-Evaluator input during the planning phase, and rene-
gotiation during operating and reporting
phase assured appropriate and accurate
data collection. Finds as more effective
for assessing program activities those
program evaluations designed as a monitoring
system not apart from other program activities. Makes conclusion that evaluation
outcome is affected by the interaction of
evaluators and organizational staff.

379. Henderson, Keith M.   "How Executives Handle
        'Hot' Questions."   AMERICAN BEHAVIORAL
        SCIENTIST, 4, 1 (September 1961), 5-7.

        Examines, through content analysis, the
practices of governmental executives in
coping with sensitive interview questions.

Finds that only 39.6% of responses ful-
filled the information seeking objectives of
the questions. Suggests further studies to
support findings and relate them to the political context in which executives operate.

380. Koontz, Ronald D., and Ira T. Kaplan. "Commu-
nication and Leadership Styles of Battalion
Commanders." MILITARY REVIEW, 63, 10
(October 1983), 11-20.

Delineates the dependence of the success of
any unit upon the quality of communication
among the commander, his staff, and subordinate commanders. Identifies behaviors that
differentiate effective and less effective
communicators by analyzing communication
patterns observed in battalion command
groups during computerized battle-
simulation exercises. Discusses the influence
of leadership styles and communication techniques to the transmission and reception of
information.

381. Murray, Michael A. "Education for Public
Administrators." PUBLIC PERSONNEL MAN-
AGEMENT, 5, 4 (July-August 1976),
239-249.

Studies client needs and marketing research on public administration education
in the United States, conducted by the
National Association of Schools of Public
Administration and Affairs (NASPAA). Finds
serious deficiencies in oral and written communication among public administration
graduates. Reveals major barrier to closing
these gaps in the virtual absence of comprehensive, yet specific and focused, information about employers and practitioners'
needs and about current and projected responses. Designs NASPAA study of client
needs and marketing research on public
administration education to produce
crucial information for public personnel
agencies, educators, trainers and

professional associations.

382. Owstrowski, John,   L.G. White, and   J.D.R.
     Cole.   "Local Government Capacity Build-
     ing." ADMINISTRATION & SOCIETY, 16, 1
     (May 1984),   3-26.

     Demonstrates use of structured group
     process techniques to enhance local legis-
     lative policy development and leadership.
     Relates three techniques to local legisla-
     tive capacity building: Nominal Group
     Technique, Delphi, and Interpretive Struc-
     tural Modelling. Illustrates techniques with
     case study in assisting a local legis-
     lative council to develop a policy-action
     strategy for several substantive local
     issues.

383. Pajir, Robert G. "Finding Selection Re-
     search Data--Federal Agencies as a
     Source." PUBLIC PERSONNEL MANAGEMENT,
     6, 6 (November-December 1977),   442-446.

     Concentrates on problems facing the re-
     searcher in the selection field based on
     federal sources.   Analyzes the federal
     government as a resource for research infor-
     mation and its limitations.   Declares that
     the overall problem is the lack of a single
     depository for all selection research which
     limits the usefulness of the search services
     as a whole. Provides a listing of the major
     selection research information sources of
     the federal government, including both
     the informal and the sophisticated search
     services.

384. Reeves,Earl J. "Making Equality of Em-
     ployment Opportunity a Reality in the
     Federal Service. " PUBLIC ADMINISTRATION
     REVIEW,   30, 1 (January-February 1970),
     43-49.

Discusses employment practices of the Federal government which have evolved gradually from positive to passive discrimination and to a positive commitment to genuine equality of opportunity under the merit system. Contends that progress in eliminating barriers is handicapped by two problems: (1) reconciling equal opportunity with merit system; and (2) problems of communication between federal agencies and minority groups, especially the black community. Cites four communication barriers: (1) suspicion felt by blacks towards all elements of the white establishment; (2) failure of managers to understand the black movement; (3) failure to utilize pipeline to the community provided by employees; and (4) sporadic nature of most attempts at communication. Concludes that the advantages of the new emphasis on equal opportunity will force a reevaluation of the whole field of personnel management.

385. Relyea, Harold C. "Opening Government to Public Scrutiny: A Decade of Federal Efforts." PUBLIC ADMINISTRATION REVIEW, 35, 1 (January-February 1975), 3-10.

Summarizes some of the achievements of the past decade in making government information more accessible through: (1) availability of information, in documentary or observable form, unless specifically exempted; (2) formal access to information in terms of timely notice of events and proper petitions for documents; (3) right of appeal or mandatory review, etc.; (4) resolution of such disputes by judicial review; and (5) intelligibility in application of the law and its effectiveness in producing desired results.

386. Rosenthal, Alan. "Administrator-Teacher Relations: Harmony or Conflict?" PUBLIC ADMINISTRATION REVIEW, 27, 2 (June 1967),

154-161.

States that school administrators are now
challenged by militant teacher organizations
demanding responsible roles in the decision
making processes of local education. Marks
significant   behavioral   patterns   in
administrator-teacher relations.

387. Savitz, Leonard.   "The Dimensions of Police
        Loyalty." AMERICAN BEHAVIORAL SCIENTIST,
        13, 5/6 (May-June/July-August 1970),
        693-704.

        Investigates the possible recipients of
        police loyalty (the public, the department,
        or fellow officers). Determines the farthest
        reaches, the limits of secrecy, and the code
        of mutual aid and assistance.

  *   Sherwood, Frank P. "Professional Ethics."
        Cited as Item 224 above.

388. Simon, Herbert A.   "A Comment on 'The Science
        of Public Administration'."   PUBLIC AD-
        MINISTRATION   REVIEW, 7, 3 (Summer
        1947), 200-203.

        Critiques Robert Dahl's article. Argues
        for a pure science of human behavior in
        government organizations by creating a
        more solid theory on the foundations of
        social psychology. Contends that public
        administration, in its "pure" aspects, cannot
        be conceived as a purely passive field,
        that accepts conclusion of psychiatrists and
        sociologists as to the "nature of human
        nature," and then applies these conclusions
        to the area of human behavior. Concludes
        that administration is itself an important
        area of human and social behavior and re-
        search in administration is research in psy-
        chology and sociology.

* Tedesco, Ted. "The Future City Manager
Building on Good Ideas We Have Now."
Cited as Item 253 above.

389. Van Straten, James G. "Health Service Support of the AirLand Battle." MILITARY
REVIEW, 63, 8 (August 1983), 45-51.

Looks at recent improvements in the
medical support provided to combat units to
accord with numerous changes in unit organization and operation. Restructures
improvements to enhance capability of medical units in providing effective health
service support and increase survivability
of combat soldiers.

* Wedin, Wayne D. "Technology and the Future of Local Government." Cited as
Item 255 above.

390. Woolpert, Elton D. "Municipal Reporting and
Publicity." PUBLIC MANAGEMENT, 22, 6
(June 1940), 173-176.

Examines the form and content of reports,
news stories, and other forms of municipal
publicity. Discusses the different and
somewhat overlapping objectives of municipal publicity. Offers suggestions for
better reporting: frankness in reporting
to the public, specific direction and
appeal, wider distribution of report,
citizen study of municipal problems,
and need for a balanced publicity
program.

B. Matrix Organizations and Relationships

391. Chadwin, Mark Lincoln. "Managing Program
     Headquarters Units: The Importance of
     Matrixing." PUBLIC ADMINISTRATION REVIEW,
     43, 4 (July-August 1983), 305-314.

     Argues that the use of matrix designs may
     be a key to effective performance for
     headquarters units of federal or state
     programs. Contends that these units con-
     front conditions--environmental, task , and
     cross-functional integrative conditions--
     that call for matrixing. Concludes that
     matrix designs provide a means for overcoming
     public sector requirements for organizational
     formalization and civil service rigidities.

392. Havelick, Franklin J. "A Labor Productivity
     Strategy for New York City Transit:
     Coming to Grips with the Monster."
     PUBLIC PRODUCTIVITY REVIEW, 7, 1 (March
     1983), 38-51.

     Analyzes the productivity problem of New
     York City's public transportation system.
     Confronts Metropolitan Transit Authority's
     (MTA) problems: inadequate management sys-
     tems, low ridership in subway routes, fede-
     ral operating subsidies, and ignoring la-
     bor relations. Calls for creation of a
     third-party mechanism--competent, unbiased,
     and resourceful--to mediate disagreements
     between labor and management, and to de-
     fine the labor productivity program.

393. McClure, Russell E., and Elder Gunter. "An
     Experiment in Employer-Employee Relations."
     PUBLIC MANAGEMENT, 26, 7 (July 1944),
     194-197.

     Studies the features and operations of
     a Wichita employees council established to
     improve employer-employee relationships.
     Allows employees to participate in person-

nel administration through the development
of a personnel manual concerned with employee welfare problems, such as service
ratings and retirement system. Proves that
its success may well indicate that its
methods could be applicable to other cities.

394. Simon, Mary Ellen. "Matrix Management at the
U.S. Consumer Product Safety Commission."
PUBLIC ADMINISTRATION REVIEW, 43, 4
(July-August 1983), 357-361.

Views matrix management as addressing multiple objectives and a permanent organization. Describes matrix management as
having dual lines of responsibility for
program outcomes. Finds increased capacity
for decision making which is achieved by
lowering the level at which decisions are
made. Gives details of CPSC matrix management
which the author feels is successful.

395. Teasley, C. III., and R.K. Ready. "Human
Service Matrix: Managerial Problems and
Prospects." PUBLIC ADMINISTRATION REVIEW,
41, 2 (March-April 1981), 261-267.

Analyzes the Florida experience relating
to matrix organizations in human services
programs. Discusses new demands on management
in matrix organizations in three key
areas: planning, conflict, and support. Explores new role demands for matrix managers
who report to two bosses, and which results in flexibility and balanced decision
making. Notes the importance of managers'
understanding the new behavior required of
them since the old rules no longer apply.
Suggests that adequate planning be done for
structural rearrangement, and that it should
be done at higher levels in the organization
to minimize challenge of change and confusion.

C. Unionism and Group Norms

396. Argyle, Nolan James. "Collective Action by
      Public School Teachers: A Study of Collec-
      tive Action as a Method of Enhancing Pro-
      fessional Status and Autonomy within Bu-
      reaucratic Organizations." Ph.D. Disserta-
      ion, Johns Hopkins University. 1977.
      235 p.

      Focuses upon the efforts of public
      school teachers in using collective ac-
      tion, particularly collective bargaining,
      to promote their professional status and
      autonomy within their work organizations.
      Examines the types of collective action
      used by public school teachers. Evaluates
      the results of the collective action to
      determine its success in promoting profes-
      sional status and economy. Analyzes the im-
      plications of such a collective action for
      school governance.

397. Berrodin, Eugene F. "Compulsory Arbitration
      in Personnel Management." PUBLIC MANAGE-
      MENT, 55, 7 (July 1973), 10-13.

      Discusses the issue of compulsory arbitra-
      tion in the regulation of employer-employee
      relationships, the reactions of employee
      groups, and statutes of various states
      covering it. Believes that it is important
      that managers assess the various claims
      made for and against arbitration, evaluate
      experiences where process has been used,
      and be prepared to cope with efforts to
      adopt it.

398. Borut, Donald, and William H. Hansell,
      Jr. "The Role of the City Manager in
      Labor Relations." PUBLIC MANAGEMENT,
      55, 7 (July 1973), 2-5.

      Discusses the nature, objective and chal-
      lenges of labor relations. Advises city

managers to abstain from bargaining process
but instead form a well-prepared team who
will keep him informed about the progress
of the contract. Suggests that this will
enable him to negotiate from a knowledgeable
position.

399. Chaison, Gary N. "The Outcomes of Multi-
Union Representation Elections Involving
Incumbents." PUBLIC PERSONNEL MANAGE-
MENT, 2, 6 (November-December 1973),
435-439.

Analyzes the victory rates for raided
versus raiding unions and the extent of
employee-voter preference for the "no-union"
choice. Finds that no union was not seen
as a viable alternative by employees voting
in a raid election. Notes that few employees were lost to unionism by raids, and
only about 5% of raided units lost to both
raider and the incumbent.

400. Elkins, R. Edison, and Martin Ragoff. "Collective Bargaining and Affirmative Action." PUBLIC MANAGEMENT, 44, 7 (July
1973), 17-19.

Recognizes the impact of Title 7 of 1964
Civil Rights Act in correcting the im-
balance in employment discrimination. Suggests that collective bargaining is the best
vehicle to determine if such discrimination
exists and to resolve the problem. Looks
at legal action (court) as a last resort.
Believes that affirmative action can result in substantial benefits to both employers and employees alike through training
and providing help in upward mobility.

401. Engel, Herbert M., and Ronald W. James.
"Negotiating for Employee Training and Development Programs: The New York State
Experience." PUBLIC PERSONNEL MANAGEMENT,
2, 2 (March-April 1973), 102-107.

Outlines the different programs designed to
meet the training needs and desires of the New
York State public employee union. Includes
skills refresher and improvement programs,
agency experimental training, high school
equivalency training (to assist those who
lack a high school education), and tuition
support for continuing employee development, among others.

* Gotbaum, Victor, and Edward Handman. "A
    Conversation with Victor Gotbaum."
    Cited as Item 307 above.

402. Hanson, John A. "Fringe Benefits in the Nego-
    tiation Process." PUBLIC MANAGEMENT,
    55, 10(October 1973), 7-9.

Emphasizes the need for the public employer
to understand the fringe benefits provided
to the employees and to use this knowledge as an effective tool in bargaining
process. Lists fringe benefits to include
insurance (medical, life, disability, ha-
zardous pay, etc.), leave with pay, retirement, severance pay, employee development,
longevity, education, incentive pay, premium
pay, and other miscellaneous benefits. Views
these benefits as costly to public employers,
hence the necessity to make the employees
aware that these are part of a total compensation package.

403. Feuille, Peter, and Gary Long. "The Public
    Administrator and Final Offer Arbitra-
    tion." PUBLIC ADMINISTRATION REVIEW,
    34, 6 (November-December 1974), 575-583.

Uses the final offer experiences in Eugene, Oregon in demonstrating that a wide
variety of final offers systems can be cons-
tructed. Presents the normative position
that each component of any final offer
system should be shaped to increase the incentive to bargain (or decrease the incentive

to arbitrate) within the boundaries of protecting the rights and interest of both
sides.

404. Imundo, Louis V. Jr. "Attitudes of Non-Union
     White Collar Federal Government Employees
     Towards Unions." PUBLIC PERSONNEL MANAGE-
     MENT, 3, 1 (January-February 1974),
     87-92.

     Describes the attitude towards unions held
     by non-postal white-collar government em-
     ployees who are not dues-paying members,
     although the sampled workers in the 30 to
     50 years of age groups are pro-union and
     are not satisfied with their present working
     conditions. Attributes non-union member-
     ship to two factors: (1) they are apprehen-
     sive of union power--believe that unions
     force people to join who do not want to, make
     trouble, and have dues and fees that are too
     high; and (2) they are able to have union
     representation without paying union dues.

405. _____. "Strikes and the Strike Issue in
     Federal Government Labor-Management Re-
     lations." PERSONNEL JOURNAL, 52, 5
     (May 1973), 381-389.

     Distinguishes the arguments for and against
     strikes in the Federal government. Proposes
     three alternatives: (1) continue to assert
     sovereignty in the face of embarrassment;
     (2) allow strikes for non-essential but not
     for essential services; and (3) decentralize
     decision-making to broaden negotiable issues
     and scope of fact-finding and arbitration.
     Suggests the third alternative as more
     acceptable.

406. _____. "Why Federal Employees Join Unions:
     A Study of AFGE." PUBLIC PERSONNEL
     MANAGEMENT, 2, 3 (May-June 1983),
     162-166.

Examines the motives of white/blue
collar workers and public/private employees in unions. Focuses on motives
ranging from psychological (protection of
rights), to economic (wage and fringe benefit increases), to social pressures.

407. Lee, Richard. "A Case Study of Organizational
Behavior of a Public School System with
Severe Management/Employee Conflict."
Ph.D. Dissertation." Pennsylvania State
University, 1978. 149 p.

Seeks to identify those factors which
created, sustained, and increased conflict
between employees and management in public
school districts of Pennsylvania. Finds
that the unwillingness of the employees to
recognize the need for compromise and their
attempt to suffer no financial loss from
striking caused the conflict periods to be
maintained longer than necessary. Concludes
that both parties lacked an adequate
understanding of the nature of collective bargaining, including bilateral decision making and the concepts of establishing and maintaining good employee/management
relationships.

408. Loevi, Francis J. Jr. "The Union Role in
Federal EEO Program." PUBLIC PERSONNEL
MANAGEMENT, 2, 3 (May-June 1973),
162-166.

Appraises the impact of Executive Order
11478 signed in 1969 on federal management
approaches for dealing with discrimination
in the work place. Believes that union cooperation is essential to enforce equal employment opportunities. Suggests that a
third party handle grievance decisions and
a prompt rendition of judicial decisions on
appealed cases be made. Believes unions
will play an active role in federal EEO
Programs.

409. Martin, David L. "Municipal Unionism." PUB-
     LIC ADMINISTRATION REVIEW, 34, 3 (May-
     June 1974), 274-279.

     Reviews five books on the unionization of
     public employees. Indicates a need for labor
     relations specialists in the future.

410. Martin, James E. "Joint Union Management Com-
     mittees: A Comparative Longitudinal Study."
     ADMINISTRATION & SOCIETY, 15, 1 (May
     1983), 49-74.

     Evaluates operation and effectiveness of
     joint union-management committees in six
     federal facilities over a four-year pe-
     riod.   Finds that committee effectiveness
     appears to be most closely related to
     the labor relations variables, particular-
     ly the labor relations climate. Recom-
     mends any future study to collect per-
     ceptual data on committee effectiveness,
     including its relationship to productivity
     and more objective measures of effec-
     tiveness. Sees this direction as providing
     a greater understanding of the potential
     impacts of joining committees on produc-
     tivity improvement.

411. Meade, Marvin. "Public Employee Unionism
     Revisited: Perspectives of the 1970's."
     PUBLIC ADMINISTRATION REVIEW, 39, 1
     (January-February 1979), 91-94.

     Reviews five books on "second generation"
     of public sector unionism which reflects
     its longer-term social significance and
     portent. Concludes that collective bar-
     gaining is to be accepted as a fact of
     life and that concerns ought to focus on
     perfecting the mechanisms, techniques, and
     tactics--the "how to"--of management-labor
     dealings in government.

412. Methe, David T., and James L. Perry. "The Im-

pact of Collective Bargaining in Local
Government Services: A Review of Research." PUBLIC ADMINISTRATION REVIEW,
40, 4 (July-August 1980), 359-371.

Synthesizes the empirical research on the
effects of collective bargaining on local
services. Develops taxonomy to compare and
evaluate the research, which is focused on
wages. Indicates that employee gains from
collective bargaining are not even distributed
across occupations and have contributed to increased municipal expenditures, and fiscal
effort. Concludes that research is lacking
in the area of the impacts of collective
bargaining on efficiency and effectiveness
of local government services.

413. Nigro, Felix A. "Managers in Government La-
     bor Relations." PUBLIC ADMINISTRATION
     REVIEW, 38, 2 (March-April 1978),
     180-184.

Addresses managers, who do not themselves
have responsibilities in the administration
of a labor relations program and not the
labor relations specialists. Reviews briefly
the growth of unionization, its constitutional
and legal status, and the diversity of unions.
Comments on the responsibilities of managers
in jurisdictions with collective bargaining
and indicates problem areas for the future.

414. Posey, Rollin B. "Recognition of Unions in
     Municipal Employment." PUBLIC MANAGEMENT,
     31, 2 (February 1949), 40-43.

Analyzes the five degrees of recognition.
Includes bargaining-for-members only, exces-
sive bargaining, maintenance of memberships,
union shop and closed shop. Compares the
merits of each. Concludes that exclusive
bargaining (collective bargaining) is the most
appropriate type of recognition of unions
that will not clash with public policy.

415. _____ . "Union Agreements in Municipal Em-
     ployment." PUBLIC MANAGEMENT, 30, 2
     (February 1948), 35-40.

     Pays attention to municipal union agree-
     ments in U.S. cities and contrasts them
     with those existing in Canada. Concludes
     that union agreements in the U.S. are in
     their infancy stage as agreements come in
     various forms and in few numbers. Alerts the
     municipal executive to become acquainted with
     union aims and method if power of employee
     organization is to be used constructively.

416. Peirce, Neal R., and Jerry Hagstrom. "Unions
     Press for Reform of the Hatch Act."
     NATIONAL JOURNAL, 9, 16 (April 1977),
     585-587.

     Discusses how public employee unions want
     to revamp the 1939 Hatch Act, which restricts
     the political activities of the federal em-
     ployees. Argues that it is time to let
     federal workers participate fully in poli-
     tical affairs, since they have won the en-
     dorsement of the Carter White House. Says
     that a bill has begun to move through the
     House, but its opponents point out that it
     could subject federal employees to undue
     pressures from their superiors.

417. Rushin, Emmett R. "A New Frontier for
     Employee-Management Cooperation in Govern-
     ment." PUBLIC ADMINISTRATION REVIEW,
     3, 2 (Spring 1943), 158-163.

     Analyzes the establishment of employee-
     management committee (or Victory Council) as
     one of the most interesting and worthwhile
     developments in public service administra-
     tion. Explains its organization and suggests
     ways to make it effective.

418. Staudohar, Paul D. "Some Implications of
     Mediation for Resolution of Bargaining

Impasses in Public Employment." PUBLIC
PERSONNEL MANAGEMENT, 2, 4 (July-August
1973), 229-304.

Examines the mediation process in the public sector. Notes that the success in
mediating depends largely on the skill and
experience of the mediator, the characteristics of the dispute, and bargaining laws.

419. Torrence, William D. "Collective Bargaining
and Labor Relations Training of State
Level Management." PUBLIC PERSONNEL
MANAGEMENT, 2, 4 (July-August 1973),
256-260.

Comments on findings in a questionnaire
study, conducted in Spring 1972, concerning
collective bargaining and meeting at the
state level management. Observes that training programs on collective bargaining and
labor relations education for both negotiating team and middle-management and supervisory levels have been in effect for approx-
mately two years. Discusses the varying mag-
nitudes of work stoppages in the states
from 1967-71. Alerts the state governments to the ever-increasing presence of
union and employee associations and their
increasing organizing activities. Suggests
that government undertake training in collective bargaining agreements to counter
this phenomenon.

420. Word, William R. "Toward More Negotiations in
the Public Sector." PUBLIC PERSONNEL
MANAGEMENT, 2, 5 (September-October
1973), 345-350.

Discusses the different negotiation procedures for negotiations in the public sector.
Involves final offer selection and mediation
combined with fact finding. Suggests an im-
passe procedure called "Proposal X" to further bilateral negotiations.

421. Wortman, Max S., and Craig E. Overton. "Com-
     pulsory Arbitration: The End of the Line
     in the Police Field?" PUBLIC PERSONNEL
     MANAGEMENT, 2, 1 (January-February 1973),
     4-8.

     Explores the implications of compulsory ar-
     bitration. Stresses the need for competent
     arbitrators. Draws experiences from the Rhode
     Island police force when they joined unions
     for the express purpose of better salary,
     terms and conditions of employment.

422. Wurf, Jerry. "The Future of Fringe Bene-
     fits: View from the Union." PUBLIC MAN-
     AGEMENT, 55, 10 (October 1973), 14-17.

     Predicts that the future for new fringe be-
     nefits and for better conditions of employment
     in the public service is not a distant
     future. Views the role of the union mem-
     bers from a dual perspective: as public
     employees who want equity in job relation-
     ships, and as taxpayers and consumers of pub-
     lic services who want efficient, effective
     government. Recognizes that public sector
     bargaining and fringe benefit demands will
     require public workers and public managers
     to get together on a reasonable and equal
     footing.

     D.   Group Conflicts and Office Politics

423. Alpern, Anita F. "One Woman's View and Exper-
     ience." THE BUREAUCRAT, 13, 3 (Fall
     1984) 25-29.

     Interprets, based on 36 years of personal
     experience, problems encountered in political
     career interface from the viewpoint of the
     careerist. Finds the interface at its lowest
     ebb. Examines some key problems: carrying
     campaign into office, strangers to government,

negative views of government, stereotypes of
bureaucracy, short-termers, careerists considered negative, different agendas, fear of
reprisal, and brain drain. Suggests some
action steps to ease the tensions and conflicts between political appointees and
career bureaucracy: training for careerists,
training for political appointees, team
building retreats, prompt action in appoint-
ments, stopping attacks on bureaucracy, and
career assistant secretaries for administration.

424. Cornelius, Loretta. "A Possible Resolution."
     THE BUREAUCRAT, 13, 3 (Fall 1984), 22-24.

     Discusses causes of tension between
political/career executives: size, time factor, stability versus change, value systems,
merit versus political selection, and conceptual differences as to spheres of responsibility. Proposes forming of cooperative part-
nerships to strive for excellence in management and executive behavior.

425. Heclo, Hugh. "A Government of Enemies?" THE
     BUREAUCRAT, 13, 3 (Fall 1984), 12-13.

     Analyzes the growing strains between poli-
tical executives and senior career staff
(SES). Lists some symptoms that public management system is not working well: getting
federal jobs after giving financial assistance to persons in high places; political executives whose tenure is shortened
by new revelations; political blacklisting
in an overseas speakers' program; proposed
lie detector tests on demand for 2.5 million
federal employees suspected of leaking
information, and so on. Presents three
approaches to encourage more constructive
working relations between political appointees and senior career staff: exhortation,
coping mechanisms, and structural reform.
Cites SES as an example and suggests a
Public Service Commission to manage the

SES   system.

426. House, Peter, and Vincent Covello. "The
     Phenomenon of the Mandarins." THE BUREAU-
     CRAT, 13, 3 (Fall 1984), 30-34.

     Lays out some basic managerial problems
     faced by a new political appointee in im-
     plementing bureaucratic change: resistance
     to change, imperfect control and coordination,
     and insufficient power and authority over
     autonomous units.

427. Lorentzen, Paul. "A Time for Action." THE
     BUREAUCRAT, 13, 3 (Fall 1984), 5-11.

     Studies the political/career executive
     interface. Discusses initial distrust and
     misunderstanding that tend to evolve into
     hostility and destructive conflict. Proposes
     institutionalization of general orientation
     programs for both political and career
     executives to provide helpful perceptions for
     effective interface dealings.   Places on
     Congress the responsibility for establishing
     a more balanced foundation for an effec-
     tive political/career interface.

428. Nalbandian, John. "The Professional Public
     Manager: Politician or Not?" THE BUREAU-
     CRAT, 9, 3 (Fall 1980), 40-43.

     Asks what the proper role of organi-
     zational politics is in administration. Re-
     opens the inquiry of the assumption of the
     inseparability of politics and adminis-
     tration--which causes rare examination of the
     role and impact of organizational politics on
     effective management. Raises the main point
     that while political solutions to organiza-
     tional conflict are appropriate under certain
     conditions, when administrative politics come
     to characterize organizational problem-
     solving, effective provision of services
     and quality of working life suffer.

* Preston, Edward. "Developing Managers: Orienting Presidential Appointees." Cited as Item 614 (infra).

429. Werling, Richard Paul. "Alternative Models of Organizational Reality: The Case of Public Law 89-306." D.P.A. Dissertation, University of Southern California, 1983. 382 p.

Examines the 20-year history of PL. 89-306 which intended to reduce Federal costs for lease or purchase of computers. Traces implementation difficulties to fundamental discrepancies among three models of organizational reality that describe behavior of three separate groups of public servants: (1) GAO and regulatory agencies, whose behavior corresponds to the "classical management" model; (2) authors of legislation and implementing procedures who function under "adversary proceedings" model; and (3) those in operating agencies, whose actions are in accord with the "organizational process" model. Shows that the "organizational process" and "adversary proceedings" models are useful predictors of implementation difficulties. Finds the classical management model useful for the first estimate of implementation results, while the "organizational process" and "adversary proceedings" models provide valuable insights for anticipating dysfunctions.

430. Zuck, Alfred M. "Education of Political Appointees." THE BUREAUCRAT, 13, 3 (Fall 1984), 15-18.

Deals with the appropriate relationship between career and political executives and with the role of the career service in the development and implementation of public policy. Recognizes that the political/career relationship is most difficult with political appointees who have had no prior public service experience and have never had the opportunity of working with career government

staff.   Concludes   that   both   career   and
political   executives   need   to   understand
and   appreciate   each   other's   role   for
continued   viability   of   the   American
governmental   system.

5. MANAGERIAL BEHAVIOR

A. Challenge of Leadership

431. Allen, Ethan R. "Institutional Leadership in Intergovernmental Administration: Challenge for the States in the 80's." D.P.A. Dissertation, University of Southern California, 1984. 153 p.

Examines the evolution of the intergovernmental system to the era of the 1980's. Pays special attention to the effect of federal action on state government. Identifies institutional leadership as an important organizational concept that has been virtually ignored in the development of modern-day federalism and in attempts to "fix" the current intergovernmental system. Defines institutional leadership as one that provides a value-based core with a long-range perspective, protecting the decision making structures of government. Avers that today's intergovernmental management labelled as "pragmatic" appears to have sacrificed the long-range view in favor of what might be called "opportunistic managerialism." Offers a model for providing institutional leadership in state-local relations developed around the hierarchy in state administration. Notes that this model deemphasizes institutional control and bargaining mechanisms. Places priority on developing learning and decisioning mechanisms which incorporate Follett's concepts of constructive conflict, revaluation and integration.

432. Bathory, Peter Dennis.   LEADERSHIP IN AMERICA:
     CONSENSUS, CORRUPTION AND CHARISMA. New
     York: Ingman, Inc., 1978.   200 p.

     Provides a common focus for the analy-
     sis of American leadership, public and
     private. Contends that the sustenance of the
     democratic values requires careful analysis
     of the nature of leadership in America, its
     limitations, and possibilities. Examines how
     four political leaders dealt with and
     confronted pressures from disparate ethnic
     groups, labor unions and business forces in
     America.

433. Bell, Wendell, Richard Hill and Charles R.
     Wright. PUBLIC LEADERSHIP. San Francisco:
     Chandler Publishing Co., 1961.   242 P.

     Selects and organizes the general method-
     ological approaches to the problems that
     have been used by different researchers.
     Discusses the five approaches to the study of
     leadership. Describes public leaders and the
     incidence of leadership among the various
     kinds of Americans. Presents evidence on the
     relative participation of men and women in
     each of four leadership roles: formal, re-
     presentational, social participants, and per-
     sonal influentials. Reviews the social clan
     and educational background of public leaders.
     Collates and expands upon several suggestions
     for future research on public leadership.

434. Bennet, David H., and David S. Bushnell.
     "Management Is An Unnatural Act." THE BU-
     REAUCRAT, 13, 1 (Spring 1984), 37-41.

     Defines an effective manager in context of
     the 1980's as one who: challenges and mo-
     tivates his subordinates, encourages new
     ideas through collaboration and participation,
     expects a high quality performance, recog-
     nizes and rewards achievement, and is action-
     oriented. Notes that organizations perform-
     ing excellently enjoy a favorable reputation;

possess a strong culture with clear, well-publicized values and goals; and demonstrates a concern for their employees and their customers.

435. Bennis, Warren G. "Where Have All the Leaders Gone?" in Patrick J. Conklin, ETHICS, LEADERSHIP AND INTERDEPENDENCE. Charlottesville, Virginia: Federal Executive Institute, U.S. Civil Service Commission, 1975. 15-49.

Contains three addresses to federal executives. Recognizes the imperatives of leadership within the public sector in a changing world. Examines the requirements needed for leaders to cope with change.

436. Benze, James G. Jr. "Presidential Management and Presidential Power: The Bureaucratic Perspective." Ph.D. Dissertation, Purdue University, 1980. 226 p.

Provides a historical and empirical examination of the bureaucracy as a countervailing force to the centrifugal forces of American politics. Pays particular attention to the Jimmy Carter administration. Focuses on the emergence and application of presidential management techniques (reorganization, staffing, manipulation of civil service personnel, PPBS, MBO, ZBB) as a dimension of presidential power. Assesses the impact of presidential management from a bureaucratic perspective. Demonstrates that modern presidents have attempted to use presidential management as a source of presidential power, i.e., as a means for increasing their control over the implementation of policy in the executive departments. Suggests that according to the perceptions and evaluations of career civil service executives, the management in the Carter administration has been unsuccessful. Lays the blame on their failure to gain control over the implementation of

policy through either:(1) presidential management techniques (external dimension of
power); or (2) political or personal skills
(internal dimension of power).

437. Blake, Robert R.,   Jane Mouton,   and   B.E.
     Dale.   "The Military Leadership Grid." THE
     BUREAUCRAT, 60,7 (July 1980), 13-26.

     Applies the managerial grid to the military
environment.   Analyzes   the   implications   of
1.1,   1.9,   9. 1,   9.9,   and   5.5 leadership
in relation to commitment to organizational
goals, influence on creativity, and resolution of conflict.

438. Bledsoe, Ralph, and   Robert F. Littlejohn.
     "Foresight for the CEO."   THE   BUREAUCRAT,
     12, 2 (Summer 1983), 19-20.

     Recognizes the difficulty of today's public
sector chief executive officer in translating
large volumes of data into information, in addressing most   critical   vital   issues, and
placing priorities on those issues. Proposes
that one way of dealing with "informational
explosion" is the creation of planning
and evaluation teams that: (1) make assessment of current status of programs; (2) examines events scheduled or likely to occur during the period; and   (3) draws up range of
options in achieving overall goals.

439. Bromage, Arthur. "The   Art   of   Management."
     PUBLIC MANAGEMENT,   65, 10 (October 1983),
     16-18.

     Describes, from his academic and politi-
cal backgrounds, the most significant techniques of the fine art of management: leadership, factgathering, utilization of technical
assistance, timing, reports, conferences,
decision-making, direction, and public relations. Concludes that by performing these
operations well, the manager   promotes   the

public interest and strengthens the   career
service of the city manager.

440. Buck, James H., and   Lawrence J. Korb.   MILI-
      TARY   LEADERSHIP.   Beverly Hills: Sage Pub-
      lications, 1981.   270 pp.

     Provides a systematic   study   of   military
leadership.   Includes historical overviews of
the concepts of leadership   as   well as   those
focusing on   the kind of leadership   exercised
in various services.   Presents insights on of-
ficership and the   various   leadership   roles
from a personal point   of view.

441. Bulgaro, Patrick.   "Bureaucrat's Guide to Sur-
      vival."   THE BUREAUCRAT,   12, 2   (Fall
      1983),   40-42.

     Contains five principles for bureaucratic
survival: (1) modesty posturing; (2) crisis
management; (3) program diversion; (4) idea
packaging; and (5) creative   coordination.
Asserts that   programs can be expanded, con-
tracted, combined,   reorganized, revitalized,
targeted, reoriented,   and reconfigured, and
if they are really good, replicated.

442. Bussey, Charles D.   "Leadership   for   the
      Army."   MILITARY REVIEW,   60, 7   (July
      1980),   69-76.

     Removes   confusion   in   the   concepts   of
leadership   and management as impersonal and
dealing largely   with things and   with   objective and quantitative   measures.   Sees leadership as a highly personal   activity that deals
with people and with considerable subjective
data.   Discusses desired leadership   climate
and the burdens of leadership.

443. Chaney, Bradford W.   "Presidential Influence
      in   Congress: The Ambivalence of Presiden-
      tial   Popularity."   Ph.D.   Dissertation,

University of Rochester, 1980. 184 p.

Uses Johnson and Nixon terms in examining
the relationship between presidential popularity and congressional support. Concludes   that   some   groups of congressmen
punish the President when his popularity
increases and support him when his popularity
decreases; that popularity varies over time
(when "honeymoon" ends,   his   congressional
coalition weakens); that popularity measured
by opinion polls is different from popularity measured by election results; and
that popularity will be sacrificed for influence.

444. Chase, Patrick. "The Elected County Execu-
     tive: A Study of Local Government Leader-
     ship." Ph.D. Dissertation, University
     of Maryland, 1980. 237 p.

     Attempts to fill a gap in county leader-
     ship research by analyzing data from a na-
     tional survey of 142 elected county execu-
     tives with a 66% response rate. Discovers
     that: (1) of county type, political par-
     tisan strength, political ambition, and
     perceived prestige, county executives had the
     most impact of leadership behavior; (2) there
     is no significant difference in leadership
     style between weak and strong political
     partisans; (3) bargaining/persuasive style
     is similar for executives with higher
     or without higher political ambitions;
     (4) degree of perceived prestige had no re-
     lationship to whether or not an executive
     practiced the bargaining/persuasive style;
     and (5) those who practiced bargaining/
     persuasive style were just as likely to have
     their policies turned down by the council
     as those who practiced the command style.

445. Chitwood, Stephen. "Can Government Learn from
     Business?" THE BUREAUCRAT, 13, 2 (Summer
     1984), 25-28.

Articulates how understanding of nature
of executive leadership in business contributes to promoting excellence in the federal
government. Examines relevance of corporate
experience in the world of political and
career civil service executives. Attributes
lack of effective executive leadership to
structural and human factors. Makes recommendations on how to achieve effective executive leadership. Concludes that if excellence
in the federal service is desired, federal
executives must understand, accept, and be
allowed to exercise executive leadership
within agencies and departments entrusted
to their care.

446. Cleveland, Harlan. "The Future Executive."
     PUBLIC ADMINISTRATION REVIEW, 32, 3 (May-
     June 1972), 247-251.

     Excerpts from a book on executive adminis-
     tration. Focuses on how one evolves into an
     executive through experience and describes
     the feeling of a public executive.

447. Fitton, Robert A. "Military Leadership and
     Values." MILITARY REVIEW, 63, 10
     (October 1983), 56-61.

     Admits that to be effective, a commander's
     personal leadership style must be based upon
     certain values that foster top perform-
     ance by subordinates. Suggests that
     these values be nurtured to produce a unit
     that will perform to its full capability on
     the battlefield.

448. Gain, Charles R., and Raymond T. Galvin.
     "Police Management: Critical Elements
     for City Manager." PUBLIC MANAGEMENT,
     55, 4 (April 1973), 12-15.

     Emphasizes that the responsibilities of
     the city manager includes police management.
     Points areas of concern for city manager

encompassing: (1) clarification of departmental goals; (2) development of system
evaluation; (3) integration of police
chief's role in community; (4) establish-
mentof a police-community relations program;
and (5) efficient utilization of management
concepts to police performance. Believes that
both police department and city manager
should work jointly to perform public
service functions.

449. Gardner, Burleigh B. "What Makes Successful
     and Unsuccessful Executives?" PUBLIC MAN-
     AGEMENT, 31, 1 (January 1949), 34-39.

     Identifies the different traits and charac-
     teristics of successful and unsuccessful
     executives. Covers achievement desires, res-
     ponses to authority, mobility drives, organi-
     zational abilities, and beliefs, among
     others. Avers that the individual's
     philosophy of life whether inarticulate or
     decisive can spell the category between
     success and failure.

450. Harris, Boyd M. "A Perspective on Leader-
     ship, Management and Command." MILITARY
     REVIEW, 64, 2 (February 1984), 48-57.

     Asserts that military leadership generates
     new discussions about the relationship bet-
     ween leadership and management. Defines army
     leadership as an influence process that
     covers command, personal leadership, organiza-
     tional leadership, management, and technical
     and tactical competence.

451. Henry, Charles T. "Urban Manager Roles in
     the 70's." PUBLIC ADMINISTRATION REVIEW,
     31, 1 (January-February 1971), 20-27.

     Outlines the key problems in Urban America,
     the probable types of remedial actions, and
     the priorities for such. Stresses possible
     urban manager involvements: (1) involvement

in   national   urban   policy   formulation;
(2) mobility   of   managers   in   policy   formulation   in other   settings through   sabba-
tical leaves,   university assignments, trans-
fers   to   federal   and   state   agencies, etc.;
(3) initiation of   local   changes;   (4) changes
at   higher   levels;   (5) advocacy of war on
domestic   ills   from   a   variety   of   vantage
points.

452. Hoy, John C.,   and   Melvin H. Bernstein.   THE
      EFFECTIVE PRESIDENT.   Pacific Palisades:
      Palisades   Publishers,   1976.   189 p.

      Contains   essays   and   commentaries   offer-
ing   varied   insights   on   the   issues   associated with effective   leadership   in   the
nation's highest office.   Takes an in-depth
at   the   meaning   and   significance,   the
problems and   prospects for Presidential
leadership   at   a   most   critical   time   in
American   history.

453. Jennings, Eugene E.   AN ANATOMY OF LEADER-
      SHIP: PRINCES, HEROES AND SUPERMEN.   New
      York: Harper   and Brothers,   1960.   256 p.

      Contemplates the types of leaders and
their   place in society. Subdivides leaders
into three categories: princes, heroes, and
supermen.   Defines,   traces   the   history   of,
and relates each   type to   modern   organizational life.   Postulates that   "ours is a
society without leaders."   Places   blame for
this on the large organization which tends
to inhibit leadership ability.

454. Jennings, M. Kent, M. Cummings, Jr., and F.P.
      Kilpatrick.   "Trusted   Leaders: Percep-
      tions of   Appointed   Federal   Officials."
      PUBLIC OPINION   QUARTERLY,   30, 3   (Fall
      1966),   368-384.

      Studies public image of   the Federal
Service based on   responses   of   four   of

nineteen publics: general employed public,
general Federal employees, high school
juniors and seniors, and college seniors.
Finds that top-ranking political appointees
(Cabinet and Cabinet-level rank) are trusted
leaders more than Congressmen and top-level
civil servants. Factors for the findings
are: non-perception of political appointees
a "politicians," non-susceptibility to
corruption, and high prestige attached to
highest strata of officialdom.

455. Jermier, John M., and Leslie J. Berkes.
     LEADER BEHAVIOR IN A POLICE COMMAND
     BUREAUCRACY. Columbus,Ohio: Ohio State
     University, College ofAdministrative
     Science, 1978. 17 p.

     Investigates the moderating effects of
     task routinization and task interdepen-
     dence on the relationship betweenleader
     behaviors and employee morale through a
     sample of police officers in a midwes-
     tern department. Shows that reported
     leader behaviors were found to be dif-
     ferently related to job satisfaction
     and organization commitment depending on
     level of task routinization and task
     interdependence.

456. Jermier, John M., L. Berkes, L. Fry, and
     S. Kerr. WORK ATTITUDES OF MUNICIPAL
     EMPLOYEES AS RELATED TO TECHNOLOGICAL
     AND LEADERSHIP PROCESSES. Columbus, Ohio:
     Ohio State University, College of Adminis-
     trative Science, 1978. 9 p.

     Reports the results of a preliminary empi-
     rical evaluation of the influence of for-
     mal, hierarchical leader behavior in a
     large police bureaucracy upon subor-
     dinates' morale. Conceptualizes this in-
     fluence at the individual level as job sa-
     tisfaction and organizational commitment.
     Relates the leadership function to poten-
     tially mitigating technological contingencies.

(Study was based on a subset of data obtained from over 800 police officers and
technical support personnel in a large mid-
western police department).

457. Johnson, Richard T. MANAGING THE WHITE
     HOUSE. New York: Harper & Row, 1974.
     270 p.

     Examines the management styles of six
Presidents, their staffing, and their assumptions about people. Raises the issue of
the managerial problem for the President
in drawing a line between allowing his
staff's interference to proceed unchecked
and restricting his aides too tightly.
Declares that the ties between the President and his top aides reveal his needs and
fears, his assumptions about people, and
why he manages them as he does. Delves
into the questions of why one President
employs rivalry and generates tension among
his staff while another President strives
to avoid conflict and promote teamwork.
Analyzes how a President manages a team of
men to provide him with information, staff
out his alternatives, and otherwise extend
his reach.

458. Lundsted, Sven. "Administrative Leadership
     and Use of Social Power." PUBLIC ADMINIS-
     TRATION REVIEW, 25, 2 (June 1965),
     156-160.

     Reports on research in social psychology
and conceptions of the exercise of social
power in contrasting leadership styles--the
authoritarian and the democratic, the permis-
sive and the coercive. Finds a "paradox"
in the assumptions of those who behave,
even though they may not advocate, the
authoritarian way. Describes the organizational cycle of coercion that illustrates
"the formidable blind spot" in administrators
who inflict this form of leadership.

459. Macy, John W. Jr.   "To Decentralize and to
       Delegate." PUBLIC ADMINISTRATION REVIEW,
       30, 4 (July-August 1970), 438-444.

       Argues that the need to decentralize
and delegate the duties of the government
in Washington to local government is ur-
gently required, not in study and research,
but in action. Describes some problems occurring in Washington-field relationships,
focusing on findings of the Oakland Task
Force: difficulty in inter-agency coordination;   complexity of application and
funding procedures; lack of decision making
power at regional level; lack of prior
consultation with local officials; inef-
ficient and incompleteness of basic management information; inadequate evaluation
procedures; and lack of geographical uni-
formity among regions. Presents some recommendations directed towards change and
reducing hostilities in Washington-field
relationships.

460. Makieliski, S.J. Jr. "The Preconditions
       to Effective Public Administration."
       PUBLIC ADMINISTRATION REVIEW, 27, 2
       (June 1967), 148-153.

       Discusses the basic preconditions to ef-
fective administration that determine the
success of public policy and administration. Describes the major solutions to
an absence of administrative preconditions
such as: education, administrative elitism,
and more flexible attitude toward the
practice and methods of modern administration.

461. Margolis, Lawrence S. "The Presidency Un-
       chained?... Executive Agreements and
       Presidential Power in Foreign Policy."
       Ph.D. Dissertation, University of Michigan,
       1984. 253 p.

       Focuses on the issue regarding the
use by presidents of executive agreements

to avoid the senate and its treaty process.
Examines all executive agreements and treaties
from the beginning of the nation until 1979.
Explores potential policy making. Demonstrates that presidents do use executive agreements to avoid the senate. Emphasizes
presidential dominance in foreign policy
making due to judicial interpretation of
these agreements as treaties and thus can
use them without hindrance from the judiciary. Argues that Congress, as second
potential barrier, has a weakened control
over funding due to congressional willingness to give president more flexibility
and non-return of unspent funds by bureaucratic departments. Concludes that congressional involvement in foreign policy
making as an equal is a mistake, but a presidency unrestricted is frightening.

462. Markoff, Helene S. "The Federal Women's
      Program." PUBLIC ADMINISTRATION REVIEW,
      32, 2 (March-April 1972), 144-151.

      Contains description and history of the
Federal Women's Program which is designed to
assure equal opportunity for women in practice as well as policy. Describes the
essence of the program as an action program
to enhance employment and advancement opportunities for women in the federal government. Presents the objectives of the
FWP: (1) creating legal, regulatory and
administrative framework for equal opportunity for women; (2) bringing practice
in closer accord with merit principles; and
(3) encouraging competitiveness of women in
examinations for federal employment and
training programs. Concludes that FWP does
not advocate a separatist society but to
prevent waste of womanpower.

463. Mathewson, Kent. "Governing Megacentropolis:
      The Leader." PUBLIC ADMINISTRATION RE-
      VIEW, 30, 5 (September-October 1970),
      506-512.

Pictures a new type of emerging leader--
one with regional responsibilities rather
than one with central city orientations--to
meet the needs of growing cities as they
interact with surrounding areas.

464. Mercer, Gordon E., and William Waugh. "Public
     Executives: Actualization and Conflict
     Approaches." INTERNATIONAL JOURNAL OF
     PUBLIC ADMINISTRATION, 3, 3 (1981),
     313-330.

     Represents a test of Maslow's hypothesis
     that the management styles of self-
     actualized executives differ from those of
     less self-actualized executives, drawn from
     among executives of seven state governments.
     Reveals that the correlation of levels of ac-
     tualization and executive behavior showed
     that the more self-actualized executives
     were more willing to lobby for their
     decisional preferences than to simply accept
     decisions from superiors.

465. Meyer, Edward C. "Leadership: Return to
     Basics." MILITARY REVIEW, 60, 7 (July
     1980), 4-9.

     Distinguishes between leadership and
     management in the military context. Ar-
     gues that military techniques are required
     as a consequence of the size and com-
     plexity of today's army. Specifies three
     basic qualities for a strong personal
     leader: character, knowledge, and applica-
     tion where he must foster the soldier's
     individual growth.

466. Price, Don K. "Listening In at the Manager's
     Conference." PUBLIC MANAGEMENT, 28, 7
     (July 1964), 194-197.

     Gives the highlights of the 32nd Annual
     Conference of the International City Manage-
     ment Association held in Quebec and Montreal

on June 16-21, 1946. Provides insights into
the breadth and scope of city managers' concerns and responsibilities and the challenges
posed by problems of management and society.

467. Rogers, Gordon L. "The Leader as a Teacher."
     MILITARY REVIEW, 63, 7 (July 1983), 2-13.

     Cites recent developments associated
with leadership and considers the significance of the leader's role in educating
those under his or her supervision. Recognizes renewed interest in leadership
within the Army with increased realization
of leader's duty to teach his subordinates.
Carries the message that to develop and
revitalize maximum effectiveness of leaders,
learning must be facilitated on the job in
operational units.

468. Savage, Paul L., and Richard A. Gabriel.
     "Turning away from Managerialism: The
     Environment of Military Leadership."
     MILITARY REVIEW, 60, 7 (July 1980),
     55-64.

     Remarks on four environmental factors
as institutional supports for good leadership: (1) small-size officer corps;
(2) assignment stability; (3) code of values;
and (4) special calling. Postulates that
absence of these supports may account for
the difficulty of the officer corps in ge-
nerating, developing, and exercising quality
leadership. Charges that today's Army
lacks all four environmental supports.

469. Shelby, Larry W. and Robert H. McKenzie.
     "Bridging the Leadership and Management
     Gap." MILITARY REVIEW, 62, 1 (January
     1982), 52-59.

     Attempts to reach the middle ground in
the leadership versus management conflict.
Considers aspects of both sides in brid-

ging the gap to achieve the goal of
high-performing units. States that "the
keystone of a bridge between the two concepts may be that sacrifice has an
honored place in leadership but not in
management."

470. Sherwood, Frank P. "The American Public Exec-
     utive in the Third Century." PUBLIC AD-
     MINISTRATION REVIEW, 36,5 (September-
     October 1976), 586-691.

     Traces evolution of the public executive in
     the United States. Contends that as or-
     ganizations grow and become more and more
     complex, the public executive will have to
     be better prepared, able to play multiple
     roles, and be willing to exhibit his/her
     competencies.

471. Schroeder, Patricia. "Is the Bridge Washed
     Out?" THE BUREAUCRAT, 13, 3 (Fall 1984),
     19-21.

     Stresses the need for presidential
     leadership in dissipating growing tensions
     and distrust between political appointees
     and careerists. Sees hostility dissipating
     when political appointees enter political
     service with humility and when careerists
     abandon their anti-political appointee
     bias.

472. Thompson,Henry. "Sleep Loss and Its Effect
     in Combat." MILITARY REVIEW, 63, 9
     (September 1983), 14-23.

     Relates extended period of work without
     rest and sleep to degradation of perfor-
     mance. Urges development of procedures to
     permit soldiers and leaders to obtain at
     regular intervals the minimum amount of
     sleep needed to assure continued useful work.
     Recalls findings of several sleep research
     studies to support degraded performance due

to lack of sleep. Places burden on the
leader to understand the effect of sleep
loss, its symptoms and countermeasures.

473. Urwick, Lyndall F.   LEADERSHIP IN   THE TWEN-
     TIETH   CENTURY. London: Pitman Pub. Co.,
     1957. 188 p.

     Looks at leadership in   terms of per-
     sonal   attributes. Assumes that the basic
     qualities of behavior are common to all
     situations and groups in which leadership
     exists. Notes that examples from the armed
     forces   are   thought   to   be applicable to
     business and vice versa.

474. Vaughn, Thomas B.   "Leadership: A Personal
     Philosophy." MILITARY   REVIEW, 64,11
     (November 1984),   17-24.

     Contends that no single leadership philo-
     sophy will serve the needs of all because
     many factors come together in the develop-
     ment of individual outlooks. Describes
     how author's own philosophy of leadership
     has evolved over a lengthy career.

475. Wikstrom, Nelson.   "The Mayor as a Policy
     Leader in the Council-Manager Form of Gov-
     ernment: A   View from the Field." PUBLIC
     ADMINISTRATION REVIEW, 39, 3 (May-June
     1979),   270-276.

     Alleges that textbook descriptions of the
     role of the mayor in the council-manager
     form of government invariably describe the
     mayor's role in a titular and restrictive
     fashion. Debunks these descriptions which
     do not acknowledge that the mayor may play
     an aggressive policy making leadership role.
     Sets forth a variety of reasons why the
     mayor usually exercises strong policy leader-
     ship. Declares that the emergence of mayors
     as policy leaders in the council-manager
     form of government is a positive development

with implications that encompass: (1) emergence of teamwork governance; (2) the
merging of policy making and administration;
and (3) a more "democratic" council-manager
form of government.

B.   Decision Making Models and Perspectives

476. Altshuler, Alan.   "Rationality Influence in
        Public   Service."   PUBLIC   ADMINISTRATION
        REVIEW, 25, 3 (September 1965),   226-233.

        Poses three conceptions of   administrative
     rationality through which public   service
     professions may   justify   their   efforts:
     ideal of   technical expertise, general
     evaluative   rationality, and   inventive ra-
     tionality.

477. Balzer, Anthony   J.   "Reflections in Muddling
        Through."   PUBLIC   ADMINISTRATION   REVIEW,
        39, 6   (November-December 1979),   537-543.

        Analyzes Charles Lindblom's "The Science
     of Muddling Through" for   its   modern   re-
     levancy as a   decision making tool.   Finds
     it can be a systematic, effective   decision
     making strategy.

478. Bowman, Ann O'Meara.   "Policy Innovation in
        Local Government."   Ph.D.   Dissertation,
        University of Florida,   1979.   245 p.

        Explores the adoption of   policy   innova-
     tions by municipalities (38 cities)   in Flo-
     rida.   Defines innovation as   a   new   policy
     that   has   experienced limited   diffusion
     throughout the population of interest,   and
     which   represents   non-incremental   change.
     Suggests that information exchange is based
     more   upon   contagion   than hierarchy,   i.e.,

cities look to neighboring communities for
cues   rather   than   to a lead city.   Associates   innovation   decisions with key attributes revolving around the policy's compa-
tibility, relevance, and political risk.   Concludes that the   politics   of the   adoption
process are vital   to understanding municipal
political innovation.   Speculates on the
likelihood of a link between innovation and
political viability.   Intimates that   to retain viable political entities, cities will
exhibit an increased reliance on innovation.

479. Cates,   Camille.   "Beyond   Muddling: Crea-
      tivity."   PUBLIC ADMINISTRATION REVIEW,
      39, 6   (November-December 1979),   527-532.

      Argues for a balance between rational and
non-rational (creative) techniques in administration.   Gives a detailed   presentation of
muddling   and   contrasts   it   to   creativity.
Likes to see a new theory   of   administration that extends the best organizational experiments and experience.

480. Cave, Cynthia Ann. "An Analysis   of   the Im-
      pact of Personnel Decisions on   Local Gov-
      ernment Labor   Costs During Economic   and
      Fiscal Expansion and   Contraction."   Ph.D.
      Dissertation,   Syracuse   University, 1980.
      438 p.

      Analyzes   the   fiscal   impact of   personnel
policies in the City of Syracuse School   District from 1968-1978.   Reports the following
results   of   the   study: (1) administrative,
managerial and clerical job   categories maintained   greatest   stability during fiscal
contractions, with   the   greatest fluctuations
occurring in   the   Service   Delivery   and
Maintenance categories; (2) direct employee
benefits were   beyond   immediate   control   of
School District officials due to automatic
pay increases built into salary schedules,
costs-of-living increases,   and payment rates
based on   flat   percentages of payroll;

(3) local government labor expenditures are
not rationally determined or based on organizational priorities but incrementally
made in response to a combination of political considerations, legislative mandates,
intergovernmental aid, and financial and
economic conditions.

481. Fox, Warren Halsey. "Uncertain Future of
      Public Management." PUBLIC PERSONNEL
      MANAGEMENT, 5, 4 (July-August 1976),
      250-254.

      Claims that societal forces will in-
      creasingly limit the discretionary author-
      ity of public managers. Foresees that
      modern management theories depending upon
      increased individual decision making freedom
      will be of decreased utility unless adjust-
      ments are made to include external and in-
      ternal constraints. Evaluates effects of
      constraining forces upon discretionary
      authority, such as: increased unionization
      of public employees, lack of resources, and
      increased politicization of public agencies.
      Calls on theories of organizational beh-
      avior to provide improved validity of
      information about discretionary authority
      in public sector management.

482. Fritscher, Lee. "Bureaucracy and Democracy:
      The Unanswered Question." PUBLIC ADMINIS-
      TRATION REVIEW, 26, 1 (March 1966),
      69-74.

      Reviews three books dealing with formal
      controls in the maintenance of democratic
      government. Questions the wisdom of con-
      tinuing the emphasis on formal controls
      since bureaucracy is a growing part of the
      governmental process. Recommends that the
      focus of future studies might be on informal
      factors which motivate bureaucrats to maintain
      democratic principles even when formal
      controls are not effective.

483. Gerhardt, Igor D. "The Commander's Deci-
      sion."   MILITARY REVIEW, 60, 8 (August
      1980), 14-17.

      Identifies the principal considerations
in determining acceptable degree of risk
in making decisions: relationship between
the mission assigned and the resources
allocated. Suggests that dialogue is the
best means of ensuring a clear understanding of the risk to be taken in
carrying out given missions.

484. Goldstein, Herman. "Police Discretion: The
      Ideal versus the Real."   PUBLIC AD-
      MINISTRATION REVIEW,   23, 3 (September
      1963), 140-148.

      Illustrates clearly the discretion
that administration has within the framework
of law enforcement administration. Manifests
that the real problem often lies in the
avoidance of the tough jobs, determining
at the policy level what goals are to be
achieved, and then furnishing the where-
withal to achieve those goals.

485. Halperin, Morton H. BUREAUCRATIC POLITICS
      AND FOREIGN POLICY. Washington, D.C.:
      The Brookings Institution, 1974. 340 p.

      Studies the decision process of the
United States government with regard to
national security. Spells out and discusses
the interests of the participants, namely,
the White House, the State Department, and
the Defense Department. Describes the manner in which policy positions are advanced
and defended in the bureaucratic arena,
before the presidential decision becomes
government action. Relates the role of
bureaucracy and the president to the implications of implementing foreign policy
decisions.

486. Jackson, Henry M. "To Forge a Strategy for
       Survival." PUBLIC ADMINISTRATION REVIEW,
       19, 3 (Summer 1959), 157-163.

       Analyzes the national policy making
   machinery. Concludes that national decision
   making has become a series of ad   hoc,
   spur of the moment crash actions, using
   the National Security Council experience.
   Sees the current practice as failing to
   produce an overall strategy adequate to the
   requirements of the cold war. Argues for a
   new and more adequate machinery for policy making under presidential leadership.

487. Jacob, Philip E.,   J. Flink, and J.
       Schuchman.   "Values and their Function
       in Decision Making." AMERICAN BEHAVIORAL
       SCIENTIST, 5 (Supplement), No. 9 (May
       1962), 5-38.

       Identifies and analyzes values which in-
   fluence public policy formulation at international and metropolitan levels of
   government. Tests applicability of different methods of behavioral analysis to
   the study of this problem. Aims at developing better understanding of factors impeding or contributing toward
   effective coordination among relatively
   autonomous governmental units in the solution of common problems.

488. Lindblom, Charles E. "Still Muddling
       Through, Not Yet Through." PUBLIC AD-
       MINISTRATION REVIEW, 39, 6 (November-
       December 1979), 517-526.

       Clarifies the meaning of incrementalism
   by distinguishing between incremental politics and incremental analysis. Breaks
   down incremental analysis into simple and
   complex, calling the latter disjointed
   incrementalism.   Points out that fragmen-
   tation of policy making and political
   interaction among many participants are

methods for curbing power and of raising
the level of information and rationality
in decision making. Concludes that social
problems can be attacked by "resultants" of
interaction rather than "decisions" arising out of anyone's understanding of the
problem--that understanding a social problem is not always necessary for its
amelioration.

489. _____. "The Science of Muddling Through."
     PUBLIC ADMINISTRATION REVIEW, 19, 2
     (Spring 1959), 79-88.

     Contrasts two methods of decision making:
rational-comprehensive (root) and successive
limited comparisons (branch). Defines and
clarifies the first method as continually
building out from the current situation,
step-by-step and by small degrees. Coins
the term "muddling through" to refer to
administrators practicing it effectively
sometimes, and sometimes not.

 * McKinley, Tina Macaluso. "One By One--Train-
    ing the Unemployed." Cited as Item 37
    above.

490. Mailick, Sydney, and Edward H. Van Ness,
     eds. CONCEPTS AND ISSUES IN ADMINISTRA-
     TIVE BEHAVIOR. Englewood Cliffs, N.J.:
     Prentice-Hall, 1962. 201 p.

     Organizes the volume of readings on the ad-
ministrative process by focusing on the
executive acting primarily as a decision
maker. Investigates the process of decision making in organization and the different
types of decision situations which confront
the executive. Examines the process by
which decisions are communicated within an
organizational context. Views the administrative organization as a political system and
looks at human interrelationships and orga-

nizational behavior.

491. Martin, Daniel Wayne. "The Utility of Tech-
     nical Advice for Government Decision
     Making." Ph.D. Dissertation, Syracuse
     University, 1979. 343 p.

     Tries to determine how technological advice
     can be more effectively used by the federal
     government in its decisions to finance tech-
     nological projects. Finds that beefing up
     congressional advice through agencies like
     the Office of Technology Assessment is mar-
     ginally useful since Congress underuses
     advice currently available. Concludes
     that beefing up agency participation and
     competition is useful in transmitting both
     technical information and the assumptions
     behind that information.

492. McGehee, Ralph W.   DEADLY DECEITS: MY 25
     YEARS IN THE CIA. New York: Sheridan
     Square Pub., 1983. 231 p.

     Reviews 25 years of covert work experien-
     ces as a CIA agent. Spurns the covert role
     of the CIA and concludes that it has never
     been a control agency. Declares that it
     shapes its intelligence to support presiden-
     tial policy and is thus subject to poli-
     tically oriented control. Recommends aboli-
     tion of CIA in efforts to create a work-
     able intelligence agency. Blames the
     Agency's difficulties on the selection of
     personnel based on personality characteristics
     rather than on recognized ability, integ-
     rity, and flexibility. Recommends life-
     time or long-term non-renewable appoint-
     ments to individuals who would provide
     independent, analytical judgment necessary
     for valid intelligence.

493. Mead, Lawrence. "Institutional Analysis for
     State and Local Government." PUBLIC ADMIN-
     ISTRATION REVIEW, 39, 1 (January-February

        1979),   26-30.

     Discusses the   need   for   institutional
analysis, one possible approach to it, and
the contribution it can make to policy analysis for state and local government. Describes
the approach as defining the administrative
and political influences on the implementation
of individual social program. Aims at working toward an administrative system which is
more effective, coherent, and accountable to
the public than the present complexity
by providing some leaders some of the
information they need.

494. Morgan, David. "Cities, Crisis and Change:
        Exploring Barriers to Problem Solving."
        PUBLIC ADMINISTRATION REVIEW, 34, 5
        (September-October 1974), 500-506.

     Raises the issue of why, despite the
enormous wealth and technical capacity of
the United States, it could not develop
the imagination, creativity, and innova-
tiveness necessary to make cities more ha-
bitable. Reviews five books dealing with an
understanding of what factors may inhibit
innovation or contribute to successful
problem solving. Demands that any reform
efforts must be in harmony with fundamental
American values. Offers the hope that decentralization and greater citizen involvement may be the ways to solve urban
problems although only incremental change may
be likely.

495. O'Leary, Vincent, and David Duffee. "Man-
        agerial Behavior and Correction Policy."
        PUBLIC ADMINISTRATION REVIEW, 31, 6
        (November-December 1971), 603-610.

     States that performance of managerial func-
tions not only has relevance to the amount
and quality of correctional production but
to a significant degree may determine

the kind of correctional programs we
shall have.

496. Pruefer, C.H. "Dual Responsibility Under
     a Head." PUBLIC ADMINISTRATION REVIEW,
     3, 1 (Winter 1943), 59-60.

     Uses the organization of the Price Admin-
     istration as an example of administrative
     duality. Discusses delayed actions caused
     by twin-headed responsibility and deci-
     sions further down the administrative
     hierarchy, although there may be one-man
     decisions at the top. Contends that
     problems may arise if the single-line of
     authority does not prevail throughout the
     organization, and that the absence of one-
     man reponsibility and decisions at the lower
     levels is a danger to administrative ef-
     ficiency. Claims that in many instances,
     speedy action is mandatory and a dual
     responsibility only slows matters down.

497. Rennagel, William Charles. "Organizational
     Responsibility to the President: The
     Military Response to the Nixon Doc-
     trine." Ph.D. Dissertation, Ohio State
     University, 1977. 228 p.

     Examines the responsiveness of the se-
     parate Armed Services to the policy
     statements of the President. Attempts
     to answer this question by analyzing
     implementation of the Nixon Doctrine by the
     Armed Services. Evaluates the correspon-
     dence between policy statement and policy
     action. Finds that in spite of the many
     stimuli which may have affected service
     behavior, the Nixon doctrine remains as a
     persuasive argument concerning organiza-
     tional responsiveness.

498. Schneider, Mark. "The 'Quality of Life'
     and Social Indicators Research." PUBLIC

ADMINISTRATION REVIEW, 36, 3 (May-June 1976), 297-305.

Investigates the use of social indicators in policy decision making systems. Analyzes the concept of "duality of life" as an instrument of comparative social indicators research. Presents both objective and subjective measures of intercity comparison of well-being. Documents the distinctiveness of these two dimensions of the quality of life. Makes some observations about objective and subjective indicators used in future social indicators research.

499. Schubert, Glendon. "A Psychometric Model of the Supreme Court." AMERICAN BEHAVIORAL SCIENTIST, 5, 2 (October 1961), 14-18.

Supports hypothesis, with the use of psychometrics, that votes of Supreme Court justices are attitudinal responses to the public policy issues raised for decision by cases. Demonstrates that Supreme Court decisions are primarily determined by the attitudes of the justices.

500. Stowe, Eric, and John Rehfuss. "Federal New Towns Policy: Muddling Through at the Local Level." PUBLIC ADMINISTRATION REVIEW, 35, 3 (May-June 1975), 222-228.

Articulates new town concept as one of pre-planned, carefully developed urban entities as opposed to urban sprawl. Presents the problems and advantages of Title VII of the Urban Growth & New Community Development Act of 1970 in dealing with the governing of "new towns."

501. Todd, Richard, J. Raymond, and T. Marton. "An Approach to Planning Organizational Transition." PUBLIC ADMINISTRATION RE-

VIEW, 37, 5 (September-October 1977),
534-538.

Views force-field analysis as a planning
technique, i.e., a way of analyzing an objective and defining those forces which facilitate or inhibit its attainment. Notes
that the force-field analysis has been successful in dealing with organizational needs
and problems.

502. Tomkin, Shelley Lynne. "OMB Budget Examiners'
     Influence." THE BUREAUCRAT, 12, 3 (Fall
     1983), 43-47.

Describes the direct and indirect influence
of OMB in the 1970's on numerous governmental decisions which affect the economic health of the country. Investigates
how budget examiners serve essentially as
information conduits and analysts who
secure and distill intelligence. Indicates
reduction of examiner influence in the 1980's
due to: more specific policy guidance, decisions made without benefit of careerist
analysis, and reactive roles of budget
examiners.

503. Ukeles, Jacob B. "Policy Analysis: Myth or
     Reality?" PUBLIC ADMINISTRATION REVIEW,
     37, 3 (May-June 1977), 223-228.

Provides an overview of policy analysis and
assesses its growth potential in the
American government. Marks the lack of a
unique methodology specifically designed
to deal with public sector policy problems. States that it is still too soon to
tell whether policy analysis is a fad or
lasting issue.

504. White, Louise G. "Improving the Goal-Setting
     Process in Local Government. PUBLIC
     ADMINISTRATION REVIEW, 42, 1 (January-
     February 1982), 77-84.

Describes some of the dimensions of the frustration which councilors are experiencing and some of the reasons for it. Examines approaches to capacity building as described in various case studies. Discusses the ability of a political body to establish goals. Analyzes the appropriateness of organizational development training models for political bodies.

505. Zinke, Robert C. "Cost-Benefit Analysis and Administrative Decision Making: A Methodological Case Study of the Relation of Social Science to Public Policy." Ph.D. Dissertation, New York University, 1984. 425 p.

Examines the nature of the relation of social science to public policy and focuses on the use of cost-benefit analysis in administrative rule-making. Hypothesizes that for all types of policies, the institutionalized use of cost-benefit-analysis approaches to rule-making in the federal executive branch makes it more objective and rational, less political, and reduces level of conflict. Suggests that the use of the cost-benefit analysis is not relevant to all types of policy arenas, and that it appears to promote the values and ways of life advocated by those who control the normative political processes under which policy issues are discussed and resolved. Concludes that the relation of social science to public policy is normative in nature.

C.   Management of Change

506. Aleshire, Robert A. "The Metropolitan Desk: A New Concept in Program Teamwork." PUBLIC ADMINISTRATION REVIEW, 26, 2 (June 1966), 87-95.

Describes Metropolitan Desk as a technique for program teamwork used by HUD to improve the effectiveness of urban development programs in metropolitan areas. Enumerates the following roles that the Metropolitan Desk plays: (1) combines a concern for inter-agency coordination at the metropolitan level with an appreciation of the complexities of intergovernmental effort;(2) provides information to state and local officials on available sources of Federal assistance; (3) serves as catalysts for conflict resolution among federal and local agencies; (4) and gives a metropolitan focus for Federal activities.

507. Aplin, John C., and Duane E. Thompson. "Feedback: Key to Survey-Based Change." PUBLIC PERSONNEL MANAGEMENT, 3, 6 (November-December 1974), 524-530.

Examines in detail the feedback process, a most vital part of an organization development and change strategy. Develops and uses a six-phase model of feedback meetings to illustrate how feedback leader skills can be improved by contracting, validity testing, problem identification and analysis, problem solving, and closure.

508. Bass, Wayne R. "The Impact of the Chief Executive Officer on an OD Effort." SOUTHERN REVIEW OF PUBLIC ADMINISTRATION, 4, 1 (September 1980), 190-210.

Illustrates the impact of the Chief Executive Officer on a major change effort in a public agency. Sees the behavior of the CEO as an important variable in the success or failure of an OD effort.

509. Bullock, Charles S.III, and Joseph Stewart, Jr. "New Programs in Old Agencies: Lessons in Organizational Change from the Office for Civil Rights." ADMIN-

ISTRATION & SOCIETY, 15, 4(February 1984), 387-412.

Offers insights into the dynamics of organizational implementation of new responsibilities. Finds that adaptability characterizes OCR's response to the new programs while regional personnel exhibit a preference to stay with earlier procedure for countering discrimination. Indicates that barriers to organizational change can be overcome and agencies can be pushed away from ossification and toward innovation.

510. Downey, Edward Hall. "Government Suggestion Systems: A Study of Administrative Process and Organizational Adaptability." D.P.A. Dissertation, State University of New York at Albany, 1975. 193 p.

Attempts to develop some formative ideas regarding the improvement of state government suggestion systems and to assist in their establishment in states where they do not already exist. Suggests ways of increasing the benefits derived from the state suggestions systems from both the process and adaptive perspectives. Draws some tentative conclusions that may be useful to state administrators in using state suggestion system as a management tool: (1) desire to make a change may be as crucial to employee's motivation to participate as is recognition and/or financial rewards; (2) supervisor does not appear to play an important role in the state suggestion system; and (3) state suggestion system is not viewed as a device that helps large organizations to change, but may be used by public managers to indicate need for large adaptive orgnizational change.

511. Eddy, William B., and Robert J. Saunders. "Applied Behavioral Science in Urban Administrative Political Systems." PUBLIC ADMINISTRATION REVIEW, 32, 1 (January-

February 1972), 11-16.

Proposes methods of organization improvement in local government derived from
the applied behavioral sciences. Suggests
that in programs to apply organization development and other behavioral science
methods in public organizations, potential
conflicts between behavioral science models
and realities of administrative systems
imbedded in political processes need to be
identified and understood.

512. Giblin, Edward J. "Organization Develop-
     ment: Public Sector Theory and Prac-
     tice." PUBLIC PERSONNEL MANAGEMENT,
     5, 2 (March-April 1976), 108-118.

Examines traditional OD theory and one
limited experience and knowledge of it in
public sector settings. Refers specifically to OD as increasing the ability of the
organization to do more effectively what
it is mandated to do--perform its work.
Spells out contextual factors which serve
as barriers to achieving planned change
in government. Relates these salient
differences to organizational variation,
long-range planning, the civil service
system, crisis atmosphere, and organization style and effectiveness. Contains a
number of middle-range theories which
deviate from the generally accepted OD theory and practice, but may, however, be more
applicable in severely ineffectual public
organizations.

513. Goldstein, Herman. "Police Response to Urban
     Crisis." PUBLIC ADMINISTRATION REVIEW,
     28, 6 (November-December 1968), 417-423.

Declares that the police now have to relate to more than just crime problems but
also to civil disorder and community conflict. Avers that this has created a crisis
in police response since traditional methods

are not always the best methods.

514. Golembiewski, Robert T.   "Infusing Organiza-
        tions with OD Values: Public   Sector
        Approaches to   Structural Change."
        SOUTHERN REVIEW OF PUBLIC ADMINISTRATION,
        4, 3 (December 1980), 269-302.

        Sketches the   senses   in   which common ap-
     proaches to structuring work   not   only can
     be mischievous but also   violate   OD values.
     Highlights bureaucratic principles which
     are the dominant public sector prescrip-
     tions for organizing work.   Reviews a
     variety of alternative structural forms
     more responsive to OD values that have been
     utilized in the public sector.   Argues that
     the bottom line is that existing experience
     suggests numerous ways in which, in incre-
     mental forms or comprehensively, individual
     freedom at work can be enhanced while OD
     values are approached and without jeopardizing
     usual notions of efficiency and effectiveness.

515. Golembiewski, Robert T.,   and David Sink.
        "OD Interventions in Urban Settings, I:
        Public Sector Constraints on Planned
        Change." INTERNATIONAL JOURNAL OF PUBLIC
        ADMINISTRATION, 1, 1 (1979), 1-30.

        Believes that common wisdom portrays a
     set of public sector characteristics as sig-
     nificant constraints on OD interventions.
     Points out that because of these obstacles,
     attempts to improve a public organization's
     problem solving and renewal processes
     through OD intervention have either
     failed, been modified considerably, or just
     not tried. Examines these bits of "conven-
     tional wisdom" by evaluating the impact of
     13 common constraints on reports of 44 OD
     applications. Admits that the constraints
     definitely operate and must be anticipated
     but they are not so binding as to negate all
     OD efforts. Contemplates a need for a sepa-
     rate body of theory, research and practice as

a result of difficulty in direct transfer of
OD technology from private to public sector.
Indicates that public   sector constraints
are confounding   though   not   immobilizing
impediments.

516. _____. "OD   Interventions   in   Urban   Set-
        tings, II: Public   Sector   Success   with
        Planned   Change." INTERNATIONAL JOURNAL OF
        PUBLIC ADMINISTRATION, 1, 2 (1979),
        115-141.

        Recognizes that   a   set   of   unique public
    sector constraints   work   against   OD   inter-
    ventions but they   need not   defeat   continued
    efforts   in   urban   governments   and   agencies.
    Refers to   the first indication that   these
    constraints   are   not all-powerful from the
    growing number and   range of OD applications
    in the   public   sector.   Determines that the
    success ratio takes on significance when the
    difficulty of task or   hard-to-achieve goals
    are considered.   Emphasizes that 90% of   the
    44 case reports studies   showed   at least a
    definite balance of   positive   effects.

        Cautions that despite this cause   for
    some optimism, OD   intervenors   must   anti-
    cipate real and numerous constraints, e.g.,
    the relatively short time frame and political
    nature   of   efforts   in the public sector.
    Denotes that these constraints often rede-
    fine   the   intervenor's   role   and measure
    of success.   Advises   against   direct   and
    unreflective adaptation of private sector
    intervention designs   to public agencies.

517. Golembiewski, Robert T., Carl W. Proehl, Jr.
        and David Sink. "Success of OD   Applica-
        tions in the Public Sector: Toting   Up
        the Score for a Decade, More or Less."
        PUBLIC   ADMINISTRATION REVIEW,   41, 6
        (November-December 1981),   679-682.

        Analyzes 270 OD applications out of a total
    574   OD   applications in   government agencies.

Considers the range of OD activities, modes and common emphases. Reveals the most common OD designs in order: skill-building (24%); team-building (19%); technostructural (16%); system-building or system-renewal (11%); coaching/counseling (7%); diagnostic (5%); and process-analysis (4%). Contains several perspectives on success rate.

518. Hollis, Joseph W., and Frank H. Krause. "Effective Development of Change." PUBLIC PERSONNEL MANAGEMENT, 2, 1 (January-February 1973), 60-70.

Investigates, with a theoretical model, why people fail to implement change. Enumerates reasons, such as: fear of failure, insecurity, unsureness of authority, momentum of consistency (of routinary work), lack of information, lack of decision making authority, and inexperience in implementing change.

519. Holzer, Marc. "Administrative Humour." PUBLIC ADMINISTRATION REVIEW, 34, 3 (May-June 1974), 280-282.

Reviews four books on "alternate" style management guides that are humourous. Believes that they are widely read and effect change more readily.

520. Hoos, Ida R. "Automation, Systems Engineering, and Public Administration: Observations and Reflections on the California Experience." PUBLIC ADMINISTRATION REVIEW, 26, 4 (December 1966), 311-319.

Deals with widespread use of electronic data processing that has brought great changes in organizational procedures and structure. Presents preliminary finding of research on California's experience in the application of systems analysis to five designated problem areas. Reports that it

is apparent that new patterns are developing
in intergovernmental relationships and that
new kinds of staff capability must be
developed.

521. Kemp, Thomas Harry. "The Administration of
     Equal Employment Opportunity in Utah
     State Government: A Study in Organiza-
     tional Change." Ph.D. Dissertation,
     University of Utah, 1976. 618 p.

     Uses participant observation approach in
     determining the status of compliance ef-
     forts with the State of Utah public
     service. Discovers resistance by key per-
     sonnel (administrators) and compliance to
     be simply a paper exercise. Reveals that
     attitudes of employees indicated ambivalence
     and misunderstanding about EEO, although
     females and minorities were underutilized
     and unemployed. Concludes that for public
     agencies to take meaningful strides toward
     change, strategies of EEO/AAP implementation
     have to be based on a mixture of in-
     voluntary compliance and a re-education of
     employees about their rights and respon-
     sibilities under EEO. Urges that this re-
     education will result in maintaining sup-
     port and facilitate lasting change based on
     an internalization of motives to accept EEO
     as an improvement.

522. Kim, Myoung Soo. "Improving Public Organiza-
     tions: The Means and Outcomes of Man-
     agerial Changes." D.P.A. Dissertation,
     State University of New York at Albany,
     1978. 180 p.

     Examines the relationship between the two
     elements in the process of managerial improve-
     ments efforts--the means and outcomes of
     change--through a survey of managers in pub-
     lic organizations. Finds, among others, that:
     (1) decentralization of the decision process
     and provision of positive incentives were po-
     sitively related to worker morale; (2) ins-

tallation of goal-setting process was more
highly related to the external image,
worker morale, and workload quantity of
outputs than other means of change;
(3) reduction of staff was more highly
related to economy savings than any other
means of change; (4) provision of training
was more highly related to the quality of
staff than any other means of change;
(5) managers who made goal setting-
evaluation-centered changes achieved significantly high improvement in the external
image and control-coordination; (6) managers who made structure-centered changes
were successful in improving the external
image, worker morale, and control coordination; (7) managers who made management information system-centered changes were able
to achieve significant improvement in the
external image, worker morale, control-
coordination, workload-quantity of outputs,
economy savings, and quality of staff; and
(8) all clusters of managers who made multiple changes were successful in achieving
improvement in control coordination.

523. Kline, Elliot H., and C. Gregory Buntz. "On
        Effective Use of Public Sector Expertise:
        or Why the Use of Outside Consultants
        often Leads to the Waste of In-House
        Skills." PUBLIC ADMINISTRATION REVIEW,
        39, 3 (May-June 1979), 226-229.

        Delivers an argument for expanded use of
in-house talent and expertise and for a re-
definition of the role of outside consultants.

524. Knowles, Malcolm. "Human Resources in OD."
        PUBLIC ADMINISTRATION REVIEW, 34,2
        (March-April 1974), 115-123.

        Expands the need for organizational de-
velopment to encompass human resources development purposes. Visualizes the evolving
meaning of human resources development as

something more crucial than any other role
in determining which organizations will be
alive 20 years from 1974 and which will be
extinct.

525. Lynn, Naomi B., and Richard E. Vaden. "Bu-
     reaucratic Response to Civil Service
     Reform." PUBLIC ADMINISTRATION REVIEW,
     39, 4 (July-August 1979), 333-343.

     Concerns the view of top level executives
     who constitute the target population of a
     significant portion of the reforms under the
     Civil Service Reform Act. Asks who will have
     the major responsibility for implementing
     these changes.

526. _____. "Federal Executives' Initial Reac-
     tion to Change: Views on Proposed Civil
     Service Reforms." ADMINISTRATION & SO-
     CIETY, 12, 1 (May 1980), 101-120.

     Studies the attitudes of 660 federal
     executives at the GS 15-18 levels toward
     proposed civil service reforms, before the
     passage of the 1978 Civil Service Reform
     Act. Identifies, through content analy-
     sis, areas of concern and potential bar-
     riers to meaningful transition, such as:
     fear of politicization of the civil service;
     affirmative action; bureaucratic image;
     bonuses, etc. Recommends that these issues
     must be identified and evaluated if the Of-
     fice of Personnel Management is to achieve a
     meaningful change.

527. Manley, T. Roger, and Charles W. McNichols.
     "OD at a Major Government Research
     Lab."   PUBLIC PERSONNEL MANAGEMENT, 6, 1
     (January-February 1977), 51-60.

     Compares the results of the 1973 and 1975
     analysis of one OD effort at a Midwestern
     government research laboratory. Evaluates
     the laboratory's present organizational

climate. Resolves that the program has
been a qualified success that could be a
viable model for other organizations.

528. Margulies, Newton. "Organization Development
     and Changes in Organizational Climate."
     PUBLIC PERSONNEL MANAGEMENT, 2, 2
     (March-April, 1973), 84-92.

     Reports on the monitoring results of
an organization development program conducted on three groups of a department.
Suggests that management's commitment to
the OD program and their behavior have an
impact on organizational climate and culture.

529. Morrison, Peggy, and Jack Sturges. "Evalua-
     tion of OD in a Large State Government
     Organization." GROUP AND ORGANIZATION
     STUDIES, 5, 2 (March 1980), 48-63.

     Measures the impact of a six-month OD ef-
fort by a top management group in a large
state government organization. Aims at
learning about the effects of OD on public
sector organizations. Uses six pre-post
measures to control for validity of the research. Appraises impact of OD by measuring change in collaboration, communication,
role clarity, and the manager's ability to
select and apply effective leadership
styles. Detects no change in management
style but demonstrates that OD in the public sector can result in mild to moderate
improvement in role clarity, collaboration,
and communication effectiveness among
participants.

530. Myrtle, Robert C. "Change, Changes, and
     Changing: The Views of Public Managers."
     INTERNATIONAL JOURNAL OF PUBLIC ADMIN-
     ISTRATION, 2, 1(1980), 103-115.

     Draws on responses of 40 public sector

managers who were asked three open-ended
questions relating to change: "What were the
beneficial effects of change? What are the
negative aspects of change? What are the
toughest problems faced when bringing about
change?" States that the ability of managers to bring about change was seen as being quite important. Feels that the change
has a very positive impact on the organization and on its people, even when conditions were less than ideal. Discusses
problems and costs of change: risks and uncertainties, temporary declines in productivity, unanticipated consequences, resistance to change, and management of change.

Provides a variety of insights into the
views of public managers regarding change.
Finds that the managers who participated
in the study welcomed change, desired to
become more successful in the management of
change and of the change processes, and were
quite concerned with the consequences associated with change.

531. Patten, Thomas H., and Lester E. Dorey.
"Long-Range Results of a New Team-Building
OD Effort." PUBLIC PERSONNEL MANAGEMENT,
6, 1 (January-February 1977), 31-50.

Follows up sample of 28 federal and military executives who were participants
in senior seminar/workshops on OD through
team building, contacted 6-21 months after
the initial OD effort was launched. Discovers that participants using MBO reported
noticeable changes in ability to resolve
interpersonal conflict, reward employees,
confront unacceptable performers, manage
time, motivate and communicate with subordinates, build trust, and set goals. Predicts that the design may have wide applicability in public employment. Suggests that
team building can be well adapted to complex
organizations employing thousands of managers and desiring a change of managerial style.

532. Rosenblum, Robert, and Daniel McGillis. "Ob-
     servations on the Role of Consultants in
     the Public Sector." PUBLIC ADMINISTRATION
     REVIEW, 39, 3 (May-June 1979), 219-226.

     Examines why consultants face tremen-
     dous challenges in attempting to work for
     the public sector. Attributes these dif-
     ficulties to the reason why consultants
     are hired and the manner they are used.
     Recommends that the public agency and the
     consultants must have a better understand-
     ing of each other's needs and constraints so
     that they can work together effectively.

533. Rouse, Andrew M. "Selecting Reorganizers."
     THE BUREAUCRAT, 1,1 (Spring 1972),
     11-23.

     Evaluates organization study mechanisms
     and levels of conflict on reorganization
     at the Federal level. Expresses bias in
     favor of agency head, as opposed to outside
     reorganization study group, in having
     substantial and real flexibility to reshape
     agency and meet new needs and policies.
     Sees more success for reorganization
     which reflects reorganizer's view of man-
     agement, agency objectives, and organiza-
     tional needs.

534. Sherwood, Frank P., and William Page, Jr.
     "MBO and Public Management." PUBLIC
     ADMINISTRATION REVIEW, 36, 1 (January-
     February 1976), 5-12.

     Analyzes MBO in terms of its use as a
     managerial tactic--not as a management system.
     Views the gaps between promise and perfor-
     mance, while specifying the assumptions of
     an "ideal world" that are preconditions to
     growth of MBO into a whole system. Antici-
     pates the direction that MBO takes to depend
     on the degree to which we are prepared to
     recognize organizational goal structures in
     their full complexity and to develop man-

agerial strategies reflecting such understanding and awareness.

535. Sipel, George A., J.C. Brown and M. Francis Kaufman. "The Management of Planned Change in Local Government: The Case of Palo Alto." SOUTHERN REVIEW OF PUBLIC ADMINISTRATION, 4, 2 (September 1980), 166-189.

Contributes to the limited supply of available literature on planned change in the public sector. Chronicles a very rich change experience accumulated over a ten-year period in the government of a medium sized California city. Tells this story, using a descriptive, exploratory and evaluative approach, from the perspective of the chief executive of the organization (the city manager) and two internal consultants.

536. Warrick, D.D. "Applying OD to the Public Sector." PUBLIC PERSONNEL MANAGEMENT, 5, 3 (May-June 1976), 186-190.

Raises the issues and special considerations that occur in each phase of the OD processes in the public sector. Adopts guideline for using OD in the public sector and makes some conclusions about the applicability of OD to the public sector. Urges that the need for OD is increasingly becoming apparent with the following: growing threat of unionization in public agencies, increased public concern over the efficiency and effectiveness of government programs, bankruptcy faced by cities, poor management, and depersonalizing effects of bureaucracy. Cites many of the obstacles, such as cumbersome civil service merit systems that result in overhauling or dropping change efforts altogether.

D. Management of Power

537. Alinsky, Saul D. "The War on Poverty-
     Political Pornography." JOURNAL OF SOCIAL
     ISSUES, 21, 1 (January 1965), 41-47.

     Evaluates Johnson's anti-poverty pro-
     gram. Yields findings about the program's
     emergence as a huge political pork barrel,
     as big business, and as a macabre mas-
     querade--with the mask growing to fit the
     face of political pornography.

538. Anagnoson, J. Theodore. "Bureaucratic Reac-
     tions to Political Pressures." ADMINIS-
     TRATION & SOCIETY, 15, 1 (May 1983),
     97-118.

     Addresses the question of how federal
     grant administrators handle the political
     pressures. Defines bureaucratic reactions
     to political pressures as requests or demands
     for an agency to approve measures it would
     otherwise decline. Declares that the key
     to handling project pressures in grant pro-
     grams lies in careful handling of project
     turndowns through pre-application procedures
     and quick decisions. Expresses policy
     tradeoffs in using pre-application proce-
     dures.

539. Bachrach, Peter. "A Power Analysis: The
     Shaping of Anti-Poverty Policy in Bal-
     timore." PUBLIC POLICY, 18, 2 (Winter
     1970), 155-186.

     Applies a two-dimensional approach to
     power--decisions and non-decisions--in ob-
     serving the manifold utilization of power.
     Relates utilization of power both to politi-
     cal ideology and to the political behavior of
     actors within and outside the system.

540. Ball, Howard. "To Curb Regulatory Sprawl."

THE BUREAUCRAT, 12, 2 (Summer 1983),
28-31.

Recognizes ongoing need for oversight
of agency policy making by the elected
representatives of the people. Places the
burden on the President in providing cen-
tralized coordination and balance when
directing actions of bureaucratic policy
makers who establish major regulatory
changes in our societal fabric.

541. Baum, Howell S. "Autonomy, Shame and Doubt:
     Power in the Bureaucratic Lives of Plan-
     ners." ADMINISTRATION & SOClETY, 15, 2
     (August 1973), 147-184.

     Questions why planners simultaneously
     say they should act more politically and
     powerfully and yet have ambivalence in
     doing so. Analyzes the peculiar nature
     of bureaucratic authority which tends to
     make power invisible and discourage organiza-
     tional members from learning to act power-
     fully. Illustrates ways in which organiza-
     tional experiences of shame and self-doubt
     discourage planners from acting powerfully.

   * Benze, James G. Jr. "Presidential Management
     and Presidential Power: The Bureaucratic
     Perspective." Cited as Item 436 above.

   * Bromage, Arthur W. "The Art of Management."
     Cited as Item 439 above.

542. Curtis, Donald A. "Management in the Public
     Sector: It Really is Harder." MANAGE-
     MENT REVIEW, 69, 10 (October 1980),
     70-74.

     Exposes the problem and starts a dialog
     on how to solve the paradox of an efficient
     yet democratic society. Believes that a cer-
     tain management inefficiency was deliberately

built into the American governmental system
because of an overriding need to preserve
individual freedom. Shows that the Founding
Fathers understood that to make the process
more efficient would be to make its leaders
more powerful. Stresses that in dealing with
the problem of making the present process
work better, all dialog must take as its
starting point our nation's basic constitutional framework. Asserts that to achieve
management efficiency at the expense of individual freedom would be without conscience.

543. Daley, Dennis. "Controlling the Bureaucracy
     Among the States." ADMINISTRATION &
     SOCIETY, 15, 4 (February 1984), 475-488.

     Appraises attitudes of state administra-
     tors, executives, and legislators toward
     proposals for controlling the bureaucracy:
     executive control, pluralism, and represen-
     tative bureaucracy.

544. Gilbert, Neil, and Harry Specht. "Picking
     Winners: Federal Discretion and Local
     Experience as Bases for Planning Grant
     Allocation." PUBLIC ADMINISTRATION RE-
     VIEW, 34, 6 (November-December 1974),
     565-574.

     Describes how funding agencies, both pub-
     lic and private, are continually engaged in
     selection processes that attempt to dis-
     tinguish those applicants most likely to
     succeed. Concludes that these processes
     usually rely on some form of expert judg-
     ment. Evaluates the Department of Housing
     and Urban Development's procedures for
     selecting 75 cities from among 193
     participants.

545. Harrell, C.A. "The City Manager as a Com-
     munity Leader." PUBLIC MANAGEMENT,
     30, 10 (October 1948), 290-294.

Notes the distinctions in the roles of a
city manager vis-a-vis an elected mayor.
Heightens the fundamental differences between community and political leadership.
Emphasizes the fact that a city manager
acts as an administrator and adviser to the
community while an elected mayor partici-
pates in political campaigns to promote
factional interests.

546. Hughes, G. Philip. "Congressional Influence
     in Weapons Procurement: The Case of
     Lightweight Fighter Commonality." PUBLIC
     POLICY, 28, 4 (Fall 1980), 415-449.

     Explores the reasons for limited Congres-
     sional influence in weapons procurement de-
     cisions. Cites the reasons as: fragmen-
     tation of power among Congressional commit-
     tees, power and professional rivalry of
     Congressional staff, weak commitment of
     members of Congress on technical weapons
     issues, and dominance of regional economic
     interests in Congress.

547. Hunter, Floyd. COMMUNITY POWER STRUCTURE:
     A STUDY OF DECISION MAKERS. Chapel
     Hill: The University of North Carolina
     Press, 1953. 297 p.

     Studies power relations using concept of
     community as a frame of reference. Demons-
     trates the nature of exercise on program
     in a selected community (called Regional
     City) as this relates to the larger society.

548. International City Management Association.
     "How the Manager Controls Activities."
     PUBLIC MANAGEMENT, 27, 4 (April 1945),
     105-107.

     Synthesizes a panel discussion on some
     techniques used by city managers: moni-
     toring of records and statistical data on
     department's work program, personnel ins-

pections, conferences with department heads,
independent surveys, appraisals by outside
agencies, and citizen complaints. Recommends balance in the delegation of authority
to department head and his own final responsibility to do a good job.

549. _____. "The City Manager's Relations with
the Council." PUBLIC MANAGEMENT, 24, 2
(February 1942), 39-45.

Brings to light principles underlying a
sound working relationship between council
and manager. Places on city manager the
primary responsibility to the Council,
avoiding participation in factional disputes, and lessening effect of partisan
politics on government through intelligent
leadership.

550. _____. "The Manager's Role in Public Relations." PUBLIC MANAGEMENT, 24,4 (April
1942), 103-107.

Supports the city manager's role as
chief public relations officer of the
City government by his own contacts with
the public and control of his subordinates'
contacts.

551. Johannes, John. "Congress, The Bureaucracy,
and Casework." ADMINISTRATION & SOCIETY,
16, 1 (May 1984), 41-49.

Provides data on attitudes and behavior
of executive branch administrators, members
of Congress, and congressional staffs involved in the casework process. Examines
effect of Congressional casework efforts
on the executive. Addresses two theoretical questions: agreement or disagreement
between congressional and executive participants in the casework process; and effects of individual's position or duties on
his/her judgments about casework.

218   Managerial Behavior

* Johnson, Richard T. MANAGING THE WHITE
       HOUSE. Cited as Item 457 above.

552. Kaufman, Herbert. "Administrative Decentral-
       ization and Political Power." PUBLIC AD-
       MINISTRATION REVIEW, 29, 1 (January-
       February 1969), 3-15.

       Discusses the quest for representativeness
     centered primarily on administrative agencies.
     Forecasts that demands for administrative
     reorganization and decentralization propo-
     sals are but part of cyclical new waves
     that will be superseded by other waves
     brought about by changing values.

553. Kneier, Charles M. "The City Manager and
       the Courts." PUBLIC MANAGEMENT, 33, 7
       (July 1951), 148-154.

       Surveys court decisions from 1931 invol-
     ving the powers, duties, rights, and lia-
     bilities of the city manager. Declares that
     the judiciary has not become an obstacle to
     the use of the council-manager plan since the
     courts recognize the intent of the plan to
     vest administrative powers in the city
     manager. Points out the importance of the
     enabling act, home rule charter, or city
     ordinance in defining clearly the powers of
     the city manager.

554. Maas, Arthur. "Public Investment Planning
       in the United States: Analysis and Cri-
       tique." PUBLIC POLICY, 18, 2 (Winter
       1970), 211-243.

       Analyzes public investments in water re-
     sources development planning through the
     use of multi-purpose planning and benefit-
     cost analysis. Relates the reasons for
     uneven accomplishments of these two ana-
     lytical techniques to bureaucratic conduct
     and to executive-legislative relations.

555. Meier, Kenneth J. "Measuring Organizational
     Power Resources and Autonomy of Govern-
     ment Agencies." ADMINISTRATION & SO-
     CIETY, 12, 3 (November 1980), 357-375.

        Delineates power as a major concern of
     organization theory although little research
     has focused on the horizontal dimension of
     power between organizations at relatively
     equal hierarchical levels. Attempts to fill
     that void by operationalizing power for 127
     federal government agencies. Subjects the de-
     rived measure to tests for internal and ex-
     ternal validity by empirically testing one
     promising theory of agency power.

556. Pfiffner, John M. "Management Must Manage."
     PUBLIC MANAGEMENT, 35, 11 (November
     1953), 242-245.

        Advises a manager to organize his office on
     the basis of delegation so that he can
     have time for planning, policy, and public
     relations. Indicates that a manager can
     be effective by encouraging participation,
     communication and consultation among his
     people. Recommends the implementation of
     internal checks plan to take corrective ac-
     tions if necessary without unduly burdening
     himself.

557. Presthus, Robert. MEN AT THE TOP: A STUDY
     IN COMMUNITY POWER. New York: Oxford
     University Press, 1964. 485 p.

        Provides a comprehensive explanation of
     power at the community levels. Determines
     the extent to which the political process
     in two small communities (Edgewood and
     Riverview) may be called pluralistic.

558. Schuck, Victoria. "A Mini-Symposium, The
     Strong Governorship: Status and Problems."
     PUBLIC ADMINISTRATION REVIEW, 36, 1
     (January-February 1976), 91-92.

Traces historical development of the role
of governor in the state of Massachusetts.
Evaluates position of governor regarding
status and authority in the state legislative process and control of the state
bureaucracy.

559. Smith, J. Clay Jr. "Management by Delega-
     tion." THE BUREAUCRAT, 13, 2 (Summer
     1984), 29-31.

Focuses on the delegation of authority from
the legislative arm of the government to
public administrators. Expresses the view
that federal and state legislatures cannot
manage the republic without delegating some
of their functions to public administrators.
Enjoins continued scrutiny of management by
delegation to assure non-abdication by
elected representatives of their constitutional responsibilities.

560. Sorensen, Theodore C. WATCHMEN IN THE
     NIGHT: PRESIDENTIAL ACCOUNTABILITY AFTER
     WATERGATE. Cambridge, Mass.: The MIT
     Press, 1975. 178 p.

Examines, from a lawyer's viewpoint, the
effect of Watergate on the future of the
American Presidency. Discusses the basic
thesis that in making certain changes, Watergate and other recent events must not
distort the long-range perspective--that
the nation will continue to need great
power in the Presidency, but must make
it more accountable to Congress, to the
courts, and to the American people.

561. Stillman, Richard. "The City Manager: Pro-
     fessional Helping Hand, or Political
     Hired Hand?" PUBLIC ADMINISTRATION RE-
     VIEW, 37, 6 (November-December 1977),
     659-670.

Differentiates the views of "professional

helping hands" versus "political hired
hands." Avers that managers cannot to-
tally embrace either role of professional
or politician--instead they have tried a
middle ground between the two poles of politics and expertise. Warns of an ever increasing role of the national government as
a result of grants and other revenue sources.

562. Swingle, Paul G. THE MANAGEMENT OF POWER.
     Hillsdale, N.J. : Lawrence Erlbaum As-
     sociation, 1978. 178 p.

     Reviews some of the concepts from both
polemology (the science of contention) and
organizational behavior. Directs the book
at providing managers with a workable
understanding of the situations that give
rise to stress and the workings of organizations that render them stupid and un-
changeable, except by major confrontation.
Writes the book specifically for managers
or bureaucrats because what is needed is
good administrators who have to generate
changes from the inside to carry out important changes in society. Focuses on the
structural features of organizations which
generate conflict, affect decision making
processes, and affect the veracity of the
information. Presents the basic premise that
good managers are intelligent people who
understand organizations and the dynamics of
group decision making. Examines conflict
models and problem of regulation of societal
units. Proposes a regulatory principle of
power distribution and advocates a simple
organizational structure that can be used
for small departments within organizations.

563. Van Wagner, Karen, and Cheryl Swanson. "From
     Machiavelli to Ms: Differences in Male-
     Female Styles." PUBLIC ADMINISTRATION
     REVIEW, 39, 1 (January-February 1979),
     66-72.

     Develops a conceptual framework for

analyzing power-related behavior in an organizational setting. Applies this framework to the problem area of whether or
not women managers can be expected to
behave differently than male counterparts
due to possible differences in their
orientations toward power. Declares that
differences in power needs will not im-
pede the effectiveness of female managers.
Notes, however, that in the work environment, women may be at a disadvantage because
of the various ways these needs are
expressed.

E.   Management of Conflict

564. Auerbach, Arnold. "Confrontation and Adminis-
      trative Response." PUBLIC ADMINISTRATION
      REVIEW, 29, 6 (November-December 1969),
      639-646.

      Delves into some of the sociological
and psychological effects of organizational
principles to guide administrators of public institutions in meeting the confronta-
tional tactics of activist-groups.

565. Borrego, Vicky K. "A Study of Organizational
      Stress." Ph.D. Dissertation, University
      of Southern California, 1981. 135 p.

      Proposes a conceptual scheme to better
understand stress within organizations. Explores eight general models of stress
which could explain some relationships found
in the organizational setting. Examines
findings in empirical studies and finds
that psychosocial and psychosomatic models
tended to explain relationships. Indicates
that psychosocial model explains relationships by showing cause of strain as
originating in the social environment,
with the stress effect resulting in a

psychological response. Reveals that the
psychosomatic model shows the cause of the
stress as originating in psychological
area and eliciting a physiological response.
Finds two factors that positively and ne-
gatively affect organizational members--
amount of control and support relate to
increasing or moderating stress events.
Asserts that the organizational groups with
least amount of control in the work place
showed highest levels of stress problems--
women, minorities, younger and older groups,
and organizational members with low-status
roles. Demonstrates that support of a
generic nature moderates stress event for
organizational members.

566. Cornelius, Loretta. "A Possible Resolution."
     THE BUREAUCRAT, 13, 6 (Fall 1984),
     22-24.

     Claims that present political/career in-
terface is especially turbulent because
of effective innovations. Raises several
issues that can be considered as causes
for the current tension between these groups:
size, time factor, stability versus change,
merit versus political selection, and spheres
of responsibility. Suggests, among others,
that team building and partnership can develop healthy working relationships and
effective communication.

567. Cowley, Geoffrey. "Another Terrible Idea."
     THE BUREAUCRAT, 13, 1 (Spring 1984),
     16-19.

     Argues that comparable worth is a prin-
ciple that will ultimately prove not merely
inadequate, but destructive when it comes to
larger problems of inequality faced by
both women and society at large. Brings up
better ways of fighting sexual discrimination
in the workplace, such as: anti-
discrimination lawsuit, combatting deep-
seated cultural prejudices that funnel

women into jobs like that of nurse and
secretary, and fighting rigid rules that
keep women--and men--who occupy lower status
rungs in their place.

568. Cummings, L.L., and T.A. Decotiis. "Organi-
     zational Correlates of Perceived Stress
     in a Professional Organization." PUBLIC
     PERSONNEL MANAGEMENT, 2, 4 (July-August
     1973), 275-283.

     Contains the results of a study of per-
     ceived stress in a large professional or-
     ganization. Claims that stress is an
     attribute of organizational climate--"per-
     ceptions of the way the organization deals
     with its members."

569. Hunt, Deryle G. "The Black Perspective in
     Public Management." PUBLIC ADMINISTRA-
     TION REVIEW, 34, 6 (November-December
     1974), 520-525.

     Considers the conflict between the in-
     dividual perspective in public administra-
     tion versus the group activity of the
     black perspective. Gives specific sugges-
     tions to help realize the group perspec-
     tive in public administration.

570. Irland, Lloyd C. "Citizen Participation: A
     Tool for Conflict Management in the Public
     Lands." PUBLIC ADMINISTRATION REVIEW,
     35, 3 (May-June 1975), 263-269.

     Develops citizen participation systems to
     improve the responsiveness of decisions by
     public land agencies. Pays attention to
     the conflict on public lands and the use
     of citizen groups as a tool for conflict
     management. Proposes some alternative
     structures for implementing citizen in-
     volvement in decision making.

571. Johansen, Elaine. "Surveying the Contro-
     versy." THE BUREAUCRAT, 13, 1 (Spring
     1984), 8-11.

     Concerns comparable worth's various
     aspects: ideology and methodology, social
     and political background, problems, reme-
     dies sought, and implications for public
     managers. Specifies other factors of beh-
     avior related to sex roles that affect econ-
     omic mobility of women workers: discon-
     tinuities in employment related to home-
     making, pay differentials because of
     unionization, multiplicity of unions,
     specialized skill markets, and supply fac-
     tors. Predicts that much of the approach
     to change in upgrading work classifications
     will be by managers who design and implement
     appropriate remedies.

572. Kochan, Thomas A, G.P. Huber, and L.L.
     Cummings. "Determinants of Intra-
     Organizational Conflict in Collective
     Bargaining in the Public Sector." ADMIN-
     ISTRATIVE SCIENCE QUARTERLY, 20, 1
     (March 1975), 10-23.

     Presents initial test of a model of
     intraorganizational conflict by examining
     conflicts among city management officials
     engaged in collective bargaining with unions
     in 228 cities. Hypothesizes that: (1) goal
     incompatibility among interdependent parties
     provides the motivation to engage in con-
     flict; and (2) for overt conflict to occur
     among parties with incompatible goals, the
     parties must have the ability to interfere
     with the goal attainment of one another.
     Shows that goal incompatibility and fac-
     tors regarding the ability to interfere
     with goal attainment of others are sig-
     nificantly correlated with conflict. Identi-
     fies several possible modifications of the
     original theory and measurement of its
     concepts. Discusses briefly the relation-
     ship between the internal organizational
     conflicts and the union-management bargain-

ing process and the strategies for internal
conflict resolution.

573. LaBier, Douglas. "Emotional Disturbances in
the Federal Government." ADMINISTRATION &
SOCIETY, 14, 4 (February 1983), 403-448.

Undertakes exploratory sociopsychoanalytic
research between psychopathology and bureaucratic work within the U.S. government.
Studies individuals, work roles, and organizational culture. Indicates that career
within bureaucracy plays a significant role
in stimulating either healthy or pathological development.

Hypothesizes that in government, presence
or absence of psychiatric symptoms per se
does not necessarily indicate presence
or absence of psychopathology. Alleges
that some types of work and management support pathological attitudes that result in no
overt symptoms since the pathology is
adaptive to the situation. Finds that other
pathological attitudes are not adaptive and
do result in overt symptoms. Contends
that some people, within the normal range
of character, develop some symptoms because
of stress reaction to an unhealthy situation; others develop more positively under
certain conditions of work and management.

574. Manet, Alfred, and Mark Burns. "Administrative Freedom for Interorganizational
Action: A Life Cycle Interpretation."
ADMINISTRATION & SOCIETY, 16, 3 (November
1984), 289-305.

Speculates that the applicability of
specific models of interorganizational relations for public agencies may be linked
to the stage of the organizational life cycle
in which a particular agency is located.
Examines five classes of models, each of
which implies different types of interorganizational problems and different amounts

of freedom for public administrators to
handle these problems. Recommends that administrative freedom of action in interorganizational relations is at the maximum
near the "midlife" of public organizations,
and at the minimum near their "birth"
and "death."

575. Mars, David. "Governing Megacentropolis:
     The Problem." PUBLIC ADMINISTRATION RE-
     VIEW, 30, 5 (September-October 1970),
     474-480.

     Outlines the difficulties and problems
concerning large cities and their governments: large populations, national significance and newsworthiness, homes of cultural
complexes and unique facilities, centers of
considerable political weight and influence,
and sociological phenomenon of isolation,
rootlessness or anomie. Contemplates
changes at all levels--substantive, process,
and design changes.

576. Mulrooney, Keith R. "Prologue: Can City Man-
     agers Deal with Major Social Problems?"
     PUBLIC ADMINISTRATION REVIEW, 31, 1
     (January-February 1971), 6-14.

     Deals with the challenges that city man-
agers confront in the 1970's. Feels that
managers should be capable of responding
to the major social problems of the future, given the strong desire and the
necessary training to do so.

577. Nachmias, David. "Organizational Conflict
     in Public Bureaus: A Model." ADMINIS-
     TRATION & SOCIETY, 14, 3 (November
     1982), 283-298.

     Evaluates the direct, indirect, and
common causes and effects of three organizational attributes of public bureaus--size,
specialization, and centralization of

authority--on lateral and vertical conflict.
Tests developed model separately for eth-
nically homogeneous and heterogeneous bureaus. Examines differentials in individual's adaptations to general organizational
arrangements. Discovers that variations in
the two types of conflict result from the
interaction of organizational variables
with the ethnic composition of the bureaus.

578. Rourke, John T. "The GAO: An Evolving Role."
     THE BUREAUCRAT, 38,5 (September-October
     1978), 453-457.

     States that the role of the General Ac-
counting Office has changed considerably
since its creation in 1921. Describes the
reorientation of the GAO efforts during the
past decade toward "program" auditing.
Finds much resistance to this change with-
inthe GAO. Urges that Congress should attempt to clearly establish the role it wishes
the GAO to play.

579. Saltztein, Alan, and Virginia Bott. "Per-
     sonnel Policy Making in Times of Cri-
     sis: California Personnel Directors Face
     the Aftermath of Proposition 13."
     AMERICAN REVIEW OF PUBLIC ADMINISTRATION,
     16, 2/3 (Summer/Fall 1983), 195-207.

     Looks closely at problems experienced by
city personnel directors in 37 of the 40
largest cities in California in the after-
math of Proposition 13. Evaluates the effect
of changes on the personnel director's job,
his perception of his role, and the sources
of his frustrations. Makes conclusion that
some cities resolved problems of personnel
management rather peacefully, uneventfully,
and perhaps creatively in dealing with severe changes in public perceptions, resources, and rights of workers.

580. Schweitzer, Glenn E. "The Rights of Federal

Employees Named as Alleged Discriminatory Officials." PUBLIC ADMINISTRATION
REVIEW, 37, 1 (January-February 1977)
58-63.

Alleges that a number of complaints of
discrimination filed by federal employees
under the EEO complaint process has increased significantly. Discusses the weaknesses in the system, specifically focusing
on unsustained allegations toward alleged
discriminatory officials (ADO) which have
serious personal and professional implications. Enjoins congressional committees
to conduct hearings into the matter and
urges the Civil Service Commission to amend
regulations that would guarantee a greater
degree of fairness to the complaint process.

581. Seashore, Charles. "The Interpersonal Dynamics of the Manager's Role." PUBLIC MAN-
AGEMENT, 55, 4 (April 1973), 6-9.

Investigates the relationship between
the city manager and the police chief.
Identifies five areas of conflict:
(1) power, competition and testing of limits
of authority; (2) isolation and withdrawal
of both individuals resulting in a communication gap; (3) techniques of modern
management which the manager has at his
disposal and which the chief finds
difficulty in adaptation; (4) defensive
stands towards intrusion from outside
forces; and (5) special treatment for the
police department.

Studies key dimensions in interpersonal
relationships, which include: initiative,
conflict style, status preference, degree
of connection or relationship, time spent
with each other, self-disclosure to the
other persons, expectations, depending on
each other, and resource allocation for
operating programs. Calls for the implementation of an interpersonal contract
that will encourage both parties to meet

in more serious ground   on a regular   basis.

582. Sherif, Carolyn W.,   and   Norman R. Jackman.
     "Judgments of Truth   by   Participants in
     Collective Controversy." PUBLIC OPINION
     QUARTERLY,   30, 2(Summer 1966),   173-186.

     Reviews the   Oklahoma   battle over pro-
     hibition repeal in 1959   by   investigating
     the ways in which participants assessed the
     truth of conflicting statements of fact.
     Finds that participants on   both   sides   fol-
     lowed   common   psychological   principles. Ad-
     dresses the interdependence of   psychological
     functioning and social process, i.e.,
     common psychological principles operated
     to enhance   solidarity   by affirming   the
     correctness of   one's own side   and the error
     of the opposition.

583. Stahl, Glenn.   "Neo-Job-Evaluation   and   Old
     Obstacles (A Commentary   on the Compara-
     ble Worth Controversy.)"   THE BUREAUCRAT,
     13, 1 (Spring 1984),   12-14.

     Claims that argument on comparable worth
     occurs when   the   means to   attain   the   ob-
     jective are brought up. Declares that   the
     real   question   is how well, how thoroughly
     we are   giving   effect   to a long-hallowed
     principle,   not whether we need a new one.
     Notes that   concepts of comparable   worth,
     as well   as principles and   techniques   of
     job   analysis, job evaluation, and job
     classification originated in the public
     service.   Questions the ignoring of gross
     inequities existing in   many other pay compa-
     risons, e. g., executive   salaries and
     overpayment.

584. Weckler, J.E., and Theo E. Hall.   "Organizing
     the Police to Prevent Riots." PUBLIC
     MANAGEMENT,   26, 7 (July 1944),   194-199.

     Stresses   the   importance   of   the   police

force in preventing race riots. Suggests
that the deployment of special tactics and
the possession of adequate information on
group attitudes and racial behavior can help
in the development of a more effective police
program to combat these problems.

F.   Management of Managers

585. Allan, Peter, and Stephen Rosenberg. "Getting
a Managerial Performance Appraisal System Underway: New York City's Experience." PUBLIC ADMINISTRATION REVIEW,
40,4 (July-August 1980), 372-379.

Uses New York City as a case study to
put together guidelines for installing a
performance evaluation system to: (1) ob-
tain top level support; (2) ascertain the
goals of top level leaders; (3) provide
systematic monitoring and follow-up;
(4) keep the program simple; (5) build
concrete reward incentives into the program; (6) utilize existing preferences and
practices as much as possible; (7) allow
sufficient time; and (8) minimize interference or disruption of management practices and styles.

586. Anderson, W., C. Newland, and R. Stillman II.
THE EFFECTIVE LOCAL MANAGER. International City Management Association, May
1983. (Chapter 3: "Helping the Governing
Body Work Effectively.")

Points out that confidence is the foundation of a successful manager-council relationship. Offers following techniques for
maintaining confidence of council: (1) preparing good agendas; (2) identifying all
tenable alternatives; (3) developing
special review techniques; (4) avoiding
peaks and valleys in meetings; (5) with-

drawing from the final decision; (6) respecting council decisions; (7) losing gracefully; (8) being generous with credit; (9) taking the heat; and (10) paying attention to timing. Cites keys to conflict resolution as: self-understanding, awareness of relationships, cultivation of allies and support systems, and willingness to be open and candid in confronting conflict solutions.

587. Ascher, Charles S. "Manager Plan Under the Microscope." PUBLIC MANAGEMENT, 22, 6 (June 1940), 166-169.

Presents appraisal of the operation of the manager plan in a large group of cities. Finds that the strongest points of many managers are community leadership and skillful use of administrative tools. Lists managers' weaknesses as lack of imagination, failure to delegate, lack of systematic information system, and failure to coordinate.

588. Barkley, Bruce. "The Program Management Officer in the Public Service: His Role in Policy Formulation and Administration." PUBLIC ADMINISTRATION REVIEW, 27, 1 (March 1967), 25-30.

Designs the position to bring to the administration of health research a high level of management competence. Combines line and staff functions in the position. Describes experiences in the position and offers suggestions to make it effective.

589. Barton, Allen H. "Consensus and Conflict Among American Leaders." PUBLIC OPINION QUARTERLY, 38, 4 (Winter 1974), 507-530.

Determines that sharp divisions and practical alignments exist among 500 American leaders of powerful organized

groups (private and public sectors) on
economic, foreign policy, and social issues.
Includes respondents from Administration
officials (assistant secretary level), career civil servants (GS-17 and 18), Repub-
lican and Democratic congressional leaders
from both houses.

590. Belk, John M. "A Mayor-Administrator Partnership." PUBLIC MANAGEMENT, 55,6 (June
1973), 10.

Shows that a mayor and an administrator
can work in harmony with each other
through exchange of views and opinions,
support from administrative staff, and
participation in special training programs.
Views both mayor and manager as "symbols of
the city."

591. Bocher, Rita Bonaccorsi. "A Study Into the
Representation of Women in the Middle
Management Levels of the Pennsylvania
State Government." Ph.D. Dissertation,
Temple University, 1980. 383 p.

Concentrates on the representation of
women in the middle management levels of
the Pennsylvania state civil service. Emphasizes that the overall percentage of
women rose from 47.5% to 50.0% from the
initiation of the affirmative action network of the state civil service in 1972 to
1980. Shows that the position of women
changed from 11.9% to 15.1% within the
middle management positions ($17,000-
$30,000). Indicates that managerial women
in the new positions tended to have a strong
image of self as expressed by a high absence
of feelings of discrimination, and also
tended to be equal to men in education and
experience.

592. Dubin, Samuels, E. Alderman, and L. Marlow.
"Keeping Managers and Supervisors in Local

Government Up-to-Date." PUBLIC ADMINIS-
TRATION REVIEW, 29, 3 (May-June 1969),
294-298.

Reports on results of study using
questionnaires distributed to managers and
supervisors. Compiles profile of their
educational background, methods of updating, and their perception of municipali-
ties' attitudes toward education.

593. Elliot, Clarence H. "Training Supervisors
    in Human Relations." PUBLIC MANAGEMENT,
    31, 7 (July 1949), 194-196.

Recognizes the relevance of supervisor
development programs to improved employee
relationships and better job performance.
Uses participative conferences and audio-
visual aids to improve supervisory skills
and abilities, and to make supervisors aware
of the human factor in relationships.

594. Fenn, Dan H. "A View of the Practical
    Problems." PUBLIC ADMINISTRATION REVIEW,
    27, 4 (November 1967), 373-382.

Expresses concern with the means for
finding, attracting, developing and keeping top leadership for government at all
levels. Promotes the finding of the best
man for the job and not simply promoting
mobility. Recommends that managers must use
system to do this.

595. Fletcher, Thomas. "Team Building for Mayors
    and Administrators." PUBLIC MANAGEMENT,
    55, 6 (June 1973), 26-27.

Emphasizes the importance of team building
for a better job for their community.
Suggests some techniques to maintain involvement and contact between mayors and
administrators to achieve better administrative understanding.

596. Gish, Lawrence. "The Storms of our Lives."
       PUBLIC MANAGEMENT, 65,5 & 6 (May-June
       1983), 7-8.

       Reveals a strategy for a transition
    process of coping with forced resignation
    after sixteen years as city manager of
    Stillwater, Oklahoma. Advises development
    of multiple support systems--spiritual, phy-
    sical, professional and personal natures.

597. Haider, Donald. "Presidential Management
       Initiatives: A Ford Legacy to Executive
       Management Improvement." PUBLIC ADMIN-
       ISTRATION REVIEW, 39, 3 (May-June 1979),
       248-259.

       Appraises the seven month old attempt by
    President Ford to combine management and
    budget by incorporating PMI into the Office
    of Management and Budget. Finds that PMI
    added no new staffs or divisions and
    avoided jurisdictional battles with OMB.
    Attributes PMI's demise to the attempt to
    impose an entirely new process on top of an
    existing process set against inelastici-
    ties of the clock and the already her-
    culean work demands placed upon OMB's
    budget examiners. Records PMI, however, as
    a major attempt to respond to very real
    problems of presidential involvement in
    executive branch management.

598. Harman, Douglas, and Steven C. Carter.
       "Currents of Change." PUBLIC MANAGE-
       MENT, 55, 6 (June 1973), 7-9.

       Capitalizes on the ability of both the
    mayor and the manager to work jointly and
    to establish mutually supportive roles to
    meet the demands of local government.

599. Henry, Nicholas. "Are Internships Worth-
       while?" PUBLIC ADMINISTRATION REVIEW,
       39, 3 (May-June 1979), 245-247.

Presents the results of a questionnaire
survey of graduates of MPA and MPP programs across the nation. Shows that non-
interns as a group appear to have higher
levels of supervisor responsibilities and
a greater commitment to the public service than do former interns.

600. Herbert, Adam W. "The Minority Administra-
        tor: Problems, Prospects and Challenges."
        PUBLIC ADMINISTRATION REVIEW, 34, 6
        (November-December 1974), 556-563.

        Outlines problems facing black adminis-
        trators since there is an increase in the
        employment of minority administrators. Dis-
        cusses how minority communities expect too
        much from minority administrators.

601. Hooyman, Nancy R. , and Judith S. Kaplan.
        "New Roles for Professional Women:
        Skills for Change." PUBLIC ADMINISTRA-
        TION REVIEW, 36, 4 (July-August 1976),
        374-378.

        Describes the concentration of women in
        lower-level positions. Suggests changes
        necessary to enable women to assume higher
        level administration on planning jobs. De-
        monstrates, from experience, the implemen-
        tation of a training program as one means
        to remove barriers to women's participation
        in decision making processes.

602. International City Management Association,
        "Relations with Other Local Governments."
        PUBLIC MANAGEMENT, 24, 3 (March 1942),
        73-79.

        Identifies some important opportunities
        for cooperative action among city man-
        agers: membership in independent boards
        and offices, joint service delivery with
        other local governments, exchange of general
        services, performance of a service by one

governmental unit for another, temporary
loans and joint use of equipment and personnel, conferences, and cooperative administration through State Leagues.

603. Imundo, Louis B. "Ineffectiveness and Inef-
     ficiency in Government Management."
     PUBLIC PERSONNEL MANAGEMENT, 4, 2
     (March-April 1975), 90-95.

     Makes strong charges against public
     executives that inefficiencies in public
     agencies could be traced to four major
     reasons: (1) political appointees lacked
     executive skills for their positions;
     (2) no progress had been made in govern-
     ment to define measures of productivity;
     (3) budgeting systems were outdated; and
     (4) decision making is centralized.

*   Johnson, Richard T. MANAGING THE WHITE
    HOUSE. Cited as Item 457 above.

604. Kahn, Bernard. "Improving Managerial Use
     of Statistics." PUBLIC ADMINISTRATION
     REVIEW, 19, 4(Autumn 1959), 233-237.

     Emphasizes the need for statistics
     knowledge by managers so that they can
     maintain control of large, complex, decen-
     tralized programs. Gives examples of man-
     agement weaknesses caused by poor grasp of
     statistics among business and government
     administrators. Describes a course in
     teaching managers just enough statistics
     to improve their work.

605. King, Albert S., and Richard E. Vaden. "Re-
     visiting the Military Organization."
     MILITARY REFIEW, 53, 3 (March 1973),
     60-71.

     Poses the critical challenge for mili-
     tary decisions as the more effective utili-

zation of people: (1) utilization of younger
and more educated members; (2) more effective use of junior officers' skills and ap-
titudes; (3) utilization of leadership; and
(4) development of military philosophy of
organization conducive to social changes influencing the individual's behavior.

606. Levin, Lesley J. "Managing the Two-Career
     Marriage." PUBLIC MANAGEMENT, 65, 5 & 6
     (May-June 1983), 9-10.

     Discusses ways of overcoming difficul-
     ties of husband and wife having manag-
     erial careers. Concludes that a strong
     marriage and family can be built based
     on open communication, mutual respect,
     romance, and role sharing.

607. Likert, Rensis. "System 4: A Resource for
     Improving Public Managers." PUBLIC AD-
     MINISTRATION REVIEW, 41, 6 (November-
     December 1981), 674-678.

     Clarifies characteristics of a system 4
     leader: (1) is supportive, approachable,
     easy to talk to, interested in well-being
     of subordinates; (2) builds subordinates
     into cohesive, highly effective, coopera-
     tive problem-solving teams linked together
     by persons who hold overlapping memberships;
     (3) helps subordinates with their work by
     providing all necessary resources and keep-
     ing open commmunication lines;and (4) has
     high performance, no nonsense goals, and
     (5) expects high quality performance
     from himself and others. Discusses req-
     uirements for the shift to system 4:
     (1) clear understanding of system and its
     leadership and interactional processes and
     structure; (2) gradual shift to system 4;
     and (3) periodic measurement by managers
     of their subordinates' views.

 *   Lorentzen, Paul. "A Time for Action." Cited

as Item 427 above.

608. Mathiasen, David G. "Rethinking Public
     Management." THE BUREAUCRAT, 3, 2
     (Summer 1984), 9-13.

     Contends that the basic conceptual and
empirical analysis for what might be called
modern governmental management is largely
non-existent. Summarizes three goals for
public management: (1)define what consti-
tutes a shared body of information on how
to manage public sector activities; (2) establish criteria by which good management
can be defined in the public sector;
(3) analyze kinds of resources bought to
carry out goals of public programs; and
(4) develop some set of criteria for efficient and effective use of these resources.
Hopes that goals would change what most
Americans now think--almost seem to assume--
that their government is grossly ineffi-
cient.

609. McGill, Michael E. "Learning from Administra-
     tive Experience." PUBLIC ADMINISTRATION
     REVIEW, 33, 6 (November-December 1973),
     498- 503.

     Argues in favor of helping administrators
learn from their experience rather than
from continuing education alone. Presents
a pattern to use in accomplishing this.

610. McGowan, Robert P. "The Professionalization
     of Public Organizations: Lessons from
     the Private Sector?" AMERICAN REVIEW
     OF PUBLIC ADMINISTRATION, 16, 4 (Winter
     1984), 337-349.

     Distinguishes between the "professional"
and the "executive/administrator/manager"
in public organizations. Raises issue of
professionalism in the public sector. Contends that it is not possible to pattern

development of public management along
lines of business administration due to
three major factors: distribution of resources across organizations and levels
of government, broad policy impacts, and
equity considerations.

611. Neustadt, Richard E. PRESIDENTIAL POWER:
     THE POLITICS OF LEADERSHIP. New York:
     John Wiley & Sons, 1960. 244 p.

     Explores the power problem of the man
in the White House: how to be on top in
fact as well as in name. Looks closely at
the American presidency. Analyzes presidential leadership by defining his role as
either leader or clerk, his power to per-
suade, professional reputation, and public
prestige. Concludes that the President
remains the Great Initiator, becomes the
Final Arbiter when he makes judgment which
then becomes the mark of leadership.
Declares that regardless of the dangers,
presidential power has to be sought and
used, and cannot be escaped.

612. Paget, Richard M. "Strengthening the Federal
     Career Executive." PUBLIC ADMINISTRATION
     REVIEW, 17, 2 (Spring 1957), 91-96.

     Outlines a program which would yield
a high caliber administration in the
Federal government, such as improved selection process and realistic compensation
scales.

613. Pak, Chong M. "Public Executives Can't."
     THE BUREAUCRAT, 13, 2 (Summer 1984),
     19-22.

     Analyzes why government is not run
like business. Claims that public executives **can't** run government like a
business because of the intended and un-
intended consequences of the American

political system. Argues that public executives are productive only if the political
system permits them to function at their
highest levels of competence.

614. Preston, Edward. "Orienting Political Ap-
     pointees." THE BUREAUCRAT, 13, 3 (Fall
     1984), 40-43.

     Raises the question of why some top
level officials succeed and enjoy their
experiences while others fail and go away
frustrated. States that the answer lies
in acquiring skills to manage a big or controversial federal agency. Describes the
Reagan approach in providing political appointees the necessary management skills
through: (1) Seminar series with Harvard
faculty; (2) Conference Series--in-house
sessions for non-career SES appointees; and
(3) "briefing" series of short current
issue sessions for top level appointees.

615. Ray, Joseph M. "Reflections of a Professor
     Turned Bureaucrat." PUBLIC ADMINISTRA-
     TION REVIEW, 19, 4 (Autumn 1959),
     238-242.

     Gives examples showing the differences
between public administration textbooks
and experience. Pays particular attention
to delegation, coordination, and control
based on United States Air Force experience.

616. Scott, K. Dow, and Michael Moore. "Instal-
     ling MBO in a Public Agency: A Compari-
     son of Black and White Managers, Super-
     visors and Professionals." PUBLIC AD-
     MINISTRATION REVIEW, 43,2 (March-April
     1983), 121-126.

     Appraises MBO implementation at the
City of Detroit Department of Transportation with four groups: blacks supervising
blacks, blacks supervising whites, whites

supervising whites, and whites supervising
blacks. Discovers significant cultural
differences between the races in MBO assessment. Reveals existence of behavioral
differences with blacks giving more favorable perception of MBO. Attributes this
perception to several reasons: (1) better
performance in participative goal-setting
conditions; (2) more objective performance
review; (3) enhanced feeling of security
through more explicit job requirements;
and (4) initiation of program by black
director.

617. Sickels, Robert J. PRESIDENTIAL TRANSAC-
      TIONS. Englewood Cliffs, N.J: Prentice-
      Hall, 1974. 184 p.

      Applies the insights of exchange theory
in revealing primary patterns of presidential behavior and dispelling some of
its mystery. Views the President, one of
the participants in the political system,
as calculating probable costs and benefits in transactions with party leaders,
congressmen, judges, his advisors, bureaucracy, and the public. Distinguishes normal patterns of exchanges from the more
intense to the less intense. Notes the
special features in each relationship as
well as the behavior that cannot be ex-
plained as self-interest, i.e., acting on
principle alone, or by impulse.

618. Sisneros, Antonio. "Hispanic Executive Per-
      sonnel in the Federal Service." AMERI-
      CAN REVIEW OF PUBLIC ADMINISTRATION,
      16, 1 (Spring 1981), 23-35.

      Provides initial, exploratory step in
compiling comprehensive data on the
background of Hispanic federal executives. Includes discussion on executive
mobility and management training, causes
for entry, and career intentions and dissatisfactions in federal civil service.

Observes concern for stereotyping of Hispanic federal executives and lack of concern for minorities.

619. Steene, Edwin O. "Historical Commentary-- Mayors and Administrators." PUBLIC MANAGEMENT, 55, 6 (June 1973), 4-6.

Reviews the roles and responsibilities of mayors and administrators. Suggests that conflicts may occur between these two in- dividuals because of differences in per- sonalities, interests, and community needs. Encourages the manager to act with initiative and foresight to attain the goals and objectives he seeks and that will also conform to societal goals.

620. Stewart, Debra W. "Women in Top Jobs: An Opportunity for Federal Leadership." PUBLIC ADMINISTRATION REVIEW, 36, 4 (July-August 1976), 357-364.

States that expansion of employment opportunity for women in American society calls for a focus on job stratification. Reviews three broad explanations for the blockage of female entry into high-level decision making positions: political, biological, and sociological. Asserts that of the three, the sociological ex- planation casts the most revealing light. Sees the structure of contemporary career systems as the principal impediment for the expansion of women in top level federal jobs. Suggests some recommendations for improvement in the federal government's personnel system.

DIRECTORY OF PROFESSIONAL ASSOCIATIONS

American Legislative Exchange Council
418 C Street, N.E., Suite 200
Washington, D.C. 20002

American Management Association
135 West 50th Street
New York, N.Y. 10020

American Society for Public Administration
1120 G Street, N.W., Suite 500
Washington, D.C. 20005

American Society for Training and Development
600 Maryland Ave., S.W., Suite 305
Washington, D.C. 20024

American Sociological Society
1772 17th Street, N.W.
Washington, D.C. 20036

Foundation for Public Affairs
1220 16th Street, N.W.
Washington, D.C. 20036

Governmental Research Association
P.O. Box 387
Ocean Gate, N.J. 08740

International Association of Professional
  Bureaucrats
National Press Building
Washington, D.C. 20045

International City Management Association
1120 G Street, N.W.
Washington, D.C. 20005

International Personnel Management Association
1850 K Street, N.W. Suite 870
Washington, D.C. 20006

National Association of Government Employees
3300 W. Olive Ave.
Burbank, CA 91505

National Urban League
500 E. 62nd Street
New York, N.Y. 10021

Policy Studies Organization
361 Lincoln Hall
University of Illinois
Urbana, Il. 61801

Public Affairs Program
1822 R Street, N.W.
Washington, D.C. 20009

Public Service Research Council
8320 Old Courthouse Rd.
Suite 430
Vienna, VA 22180

Robert A. Taft Institute of Government
420 Lexington Ave.
New York, N.Y. 10017

Western Governmental Research Association
109 Moses Hall
University of California
Berkeley, CA 94720

AUTHOR INDEX

Abney, G., 89
Adams, B.   369
Alderman, E.   592
Aleshire, R.A.   506
Alexander, E.R.   90
Alexander, J.B.   170
Alinsky, S.D.   537
Allan, P.   585
Allen, E.R.   431
Alpern, A.F.   422
Altemose, J.   169
Altman, I.   370
Altshuler. A.   476
Ammons, D.N.   280, 281
Anagnoson, J.T.   538
Andersen, R.   17
Andersen, W.   586
Anderson, J.   1, 219
Aplin, J.C.   507
Arellano, E.   30
Argyle, N.J.   396
Ascher, C.S.   587
Ash, P.   18
Auerbach, A.   564
Austin, D.M.   91
Baber, W.F.   256
Bachrach, P.   539
Bailey, J.J.   134
Bailey, S.   282
Balk, W.E.   284
Ball, H.   540
Balloun, J.   135
Balzer, A.J.   477
Barbour, G.P.   285
Barkdoll, G.L.   371
Barkley, B.   588
Barlotta, S.J.   51
Barton, A.H.   188, 589

Bass, W.R.   508
Bathory, P.D.   432
Baum, H.S.   541
Beaumont, R.A.   52
Becker, T.L.   286, 356
Beckman, N.   189
Belk, J.M.   590
Bell, W.   433
Bennet, D.H.   434
Bennis, W.G.   435
Benson, G.C.S.   190
Benze, J.G. Jr.   436
Bercal, T.E.   92
Berg, B.   136
Berkeley, C.S.   19
Berkes, L.J.   455, 456
Bernick, E.L.   125
Bernstein, M.H.   452
Bernstein, S.J.   287
Berrodin, E.F.   397
Best, F.   288
Beutel, A.E.   289
Bingman, C.F.   233
Bishop, G.T.   93
Bissel, D.M.   354
Blachly, F.F.   257
Blake, R.R.   437
Blau, P.   372
Bledsoe, R.C.   171, 438
Blum, J.   140
Bocher, R.B.   591
Bollens, J.C.   2, 20, 53
Bomer, J.   94
Boone, R.W.   95
Borrego, E.A.   137
Borrego, V.K.   565
Borut, E.   388

Botner, S.B.   138, 139
Bott, V.   579
Bouchard, G.R.   290
Bowman, A.O.   478
Brady, F.N.   191
Branch, T.   220
Brenneman, D.S.   234
Brianas, J.G.   235
Brockman, P.R.   54
Bromage, A.
Brouillete, J.R. 96
Brown, D.   192, 373
Brown, J.C.   535
Brown, K.   291
Brudney, J.   97
Bruno, C.J.   21
Bryant, S.   292
Buchanan, B.   193
Buck, J.H.   440
Bulgaro, P.   441
Bullock, C.S. III   509
Buntz, C.G.   523
Burkhead, J.   293, 341
Burns, M.   574
Bush, M.   194
Bushnell, D.S.   434
Bussey, C.D.   442
Cadoo, J.C.W.   317
Cafanga, D.   331
Caiden, N.   141, 195
Calbos, D.P.   172
Caldwell, L.K.   374
Campbell, J.T.   22
Carey, S.W.   142
Carroll, M.A.   143
Carter, S.C.   598
Cates, C.   479
Cave, C.A.   480
Chadwin, M.L.   391
Chaison, G.N.   399
Chambliss, W.J.   98
Chaney, B.W.   443
Chase, P.   444
Chatman, L.   99
Chisholm, R.   258
Chitwood, S.   445
Christofferson, C.   189
Clary, T.C.   294

Cleveland, H.   236, 446
Cohen, R.   196
Colby, W.   375
Cole, J.D.R.   382
Coleman, C.   259
Collinge, F.B.   100
Congressional Quar-
    terly   3
Connely, M.D.   144
Copeland, R.   237
Coplinger, J.L.   295
Cornelius, L.   424, 566
Cornia, G.C.   167
Costello, J.M.   296
Coulter, P.   291
Covello, V.   426
Cowley, G.   567
Cox, R.A.   107
Crane, E.G.   297
Crompton, J.L.   348
Crow, M.M.   174
Cummings, L.L.   568,
    572
Curtis, D.A.   542
Dahl, R.A.   238
Dale, B.E.   437
Daley, D.   543
Danet, B.   10
Danziger, J.N.   173
Davis, R.V.   4
Davison, W.P.   376
Davy, T.J.   23
Decotiis, A.R.   298,
Decotiis, T.A.   568
Dempsey, C.L.   197
Denhardt, R.B.   260
Desai, U.   174
Diegelman, R.F.   266
Dixon, J.   101
Dodson, C.   55
Dolbeare, K.   102
Dorey, L.E.   531
Douglas, P.H.   198
Douglas, S.R.   148
Downey, E.H.   510
Dubin, S.   592
Duffee, D.   495
Dumler, M.   251

Dworak, R.J.   103
Eaton, J.W.   299
Eddy, W.B.   5, 8, 511
Elkins, R.E.   400
Elliot, C.H.   104, 593
Engel, H.M.   401
England, R.   97
Ewell, J.J.   300
Exley, C.M.   145
Fagin, R.F.   262
Feller, I.   349
Fenn, D.H.   594
Ferguson, K.E.   263
Fessler, D.R.   105
Feuille, P.   403
Fitton, R.A.   447
Flanders, L.R.   56
Fletcher, T.   595
Flink, J.   487
Floyd, P.B.   57
Flynn, J.M.   199
Forbath, P.   375
Fosler, R.S.   301
Foster, G.D.   200
Foster, J.L.   261
Fox, W.H.   481
Frendreis, J.P.   377
Fried, R.C.   6
Friedman, R.S.   201
Friedrich, C.J.   106
Fritscher, L.   482
Fry, L.   456
Gabriel, R.A.   468
Gabris, G.   302
Gain, C.R.   448
Galnoor, I.   239
Galonis, P.E.   175
Galvin, R.T.   448
Garcia, R.L.   303
Gardiner, J.A.   202, 203
Gardner, B.B.   449
Gardner, N.   264
Gawthrop, L.   265, 304
Gerhardt, I.D.   483
Giblin, E.J.   512
Giles, K.W.   28
Giles, W.   302

Gill, M.R.   350
Ginsbury, M.C.   27
Gish, L.   596
Goetze, D.B.   7
Goldberg, J.A.   305
Goldich, R.L.   24
Goldstein, H.   484, 512
Goldy, F.B.   378
Golembiewski, R.T.   8, 240, 351, 514, 515, 516, 517
Goode, L.F. Jr.   306
Gordon, F.C.   194
Goriller, E.   63
Gosling, J.G.   146
Gotbaum, V.   307
Granger, C.E.   241
Gregg, J.M.H.   266
Greiner, J.M.   308
Grode, G.   25
Grossman, H.   107
Grykski, G.B.   298
Gulick, L.   58
Gunter, E.   393
Guttman, D.   108
Haefele, E.T.   204
Hagebak, B.R.   267
Hagstrom, J.   416
Haider, D.   597
Hale, G.E.   147, 148
Hale, T.M.   309
Hall, L.   18
Hall, T.E.   89, 584
Halliday, M.S.   317
Halperin, M.H.   485
Hammond, P.   102
Handman, E.   307
Hanks, D.E.   268
Hansell, W.H. Jr.   399
Hanson, J.A.   402
Harman, D.B.   109, 598
Harmon, M.M.   242
Harrel, C.A.   545
Harris, B.M.   450
Harrison, E.   59
Hart, D.K.   205
Hartwig, R.   206

Haskew, B. 55
Hassler, J.F. 269
Hatry, H.P. 310, 311
Hauptman, J. 26
Havelick, F.J. 392
Hayes, F.O. 312
Hayward, N.S. 313, 314
Heclo, H. 425
Helfand, G. 270
Henderson, K.M. 379
Hennigan, P.J. 293
Henning, D.H. 207
Henry, C.T. 451
Henry, N. 599
Herbert, A.W. 600
Herrick, J.S. 315
Highsaw, R.B. 208
Hildreth, W.B. 209
Hill, D.B. 316
Hill, R.A. 317, 433
Hollis, J.W. 518
Holzer, M. 25, 318, 519
Hooper, M. 319
Hoos, I.R. 320
Hooyman, N. 601
House, P. 426
Howe, H. II 352
Howell, M.A. 27
Hoy, J.C. 452
Huber, G.P. 572
Hughes, A. 176
Hughes, G.P. 546
Hulpke, J.F. 149
Hummel. R.P. 9
Hunt, D.G. 569
Hunter, F. 547
ICMA 110, 210, 320,
   321, 353, 548, 549,
   550, 602
Imundo, L.V. Jr. 404,
   405, 406, 603
Ingraham, L.H. 60
Irland, L.C. 570
Jackman, N.R. 582
Jackson, D.M. 99
Jackson, H.M. 486
Jacob, P.E. 467
James, R.W. 401

Jawad, A. 119
Jehring, J.J. 322
Jennings, E.E. 453
Jennings, M.K. 454
Johannes, J. 551
Johansen, E. 571
Johnson, B.W. 111
Johnson, G.R. 211
Johnson, R.T. 457
Jones, J.H. 261
Jones, R.W. 61
Joyce, R. 292
Kahn, B. 604
Kaplan, I. 380
Kaplan, J.S. 601
Katz, E. 10
Katz, R. 323
Katzell, R.A. 62
Kauffman, K. 112
Kaufman, H. 552
Kaufman, M.F. 535
Keating, W.T. 243
Keevey, R.F. 324
Kemp, T.H. 521
Kenned, G.W. 28
Kerr, S. 456
Kim, M.S. 522
King, A.S. 605
King, J. 281
King, J.L. 177, 325
Kittredge, L.D. 234
Klein, B. 201
Klein, R. 354
Kline, E.H. 523
Kneier, C.M. 553
Knight, F. 178
Knowles, M. 524
Kochan, T.A. 572
Koontz, R.D. 380
Korb, L.J. 440
Kraemer, K.L. 177, 360
Kramer, F.A. 244
Kranz, H. 29
Krause, F.H. 518
Kuespert, E.F. 150
Kuper, G. 314
Kusserow, R.P. 212
LaBier, D. 573

LaCapra, L.V.   355
Lamare, J.   326
LaPorte, T.A.   179
Lasky, V.   213
Lauth, T.P.   89
Layden, D.R.   327
Lee, R.   407
Lee, S.M.   296
Levin, L.J.   606
Levine, C.   151, 152
Levine, E.   30, 248
Levine, J.P.   356
Levy, S.J.   113
Lieske, J.A.   114
Likert, R.   328, 607
Lindblom, C.E.   488, 489
Littlejohn, R.F.   438
Loehr, V.M.   30
Loevi, F.J. Jr.   408
Long, G.   403
Lorentzen, P.   427
Lovell, C.   329
Lucy, W.   115, 153
Lundsted, S.   458
Lyden, F.J.   63
Lyman, T.R.   203
Lynn, N.   525, 526
Maas, A.   554
Macy, J.W. Jr.   180, 459
Mailick, S.   490
Makieliski, S.J. Jr.
  460
Malek, F.V.   31
Malone, J.E.   32
Maloney, J.F.   135
Mandell, M.M.   33
Manet, A.   574
Manley, T.R.   527
Manning, B.   214
Manning, F.J.   60
Marcus, P.M.   330
Margolis, L.S.   561
Margulies, N.   528
Mark, J.A.   331
Markoff, H.S.   462
Marlow, L.   592
Mars, D.   357, 575
Marsh, B.W.   116

Marsh, J.T.   64
Martin. D.L.   409
Martin, D.W.   491
Martin, J.E.   410
Martin, J.W.   215
Marton, T.   501
Marver, J.   117
Marx, F.M.   216
Mathewson, K.   463
Mathiasen, D.G.   608
Maxwell, T.F.   118
May, G.   34
Mazmanian, D.A.   271
McCabe, W.R.   75
McCaffery, J.L.   35,
  154
McClung, G.G.   36
McClure, R.E.   393
McDonald, R.J.   163
McEachern, A.W.   119
McGehee, R.W.   492
McGill, M.E.   272, 609
McGillis, D.   532
McGowan, R.P.   610
McKenzie, R.H.   469
McKinley, T.M.   37
McKinney, J.B.   358
McNichols, C.W.   527
McTighe, J.J.   155
Mead, L.   493
Meade, M.   411
Medina, W.   11
Meier, D.H.   306
Meier, K.J.   66, 555
Menges, E.D. Jr.   332
Menzel, D.C.   156, 181
Mercer, G.E.   464
Merriam, C.E.   65
Methe, D.T.   412
Meyer, E.C.   465
Meyers, P.R.   286
Michael, D.N.   182
Mikesell, J.L.   120
Miles, R.E. Jr.   217,
  218, 333
Miller, D.R.   273
Miller, G.W.   359
Mills, C.   38

Milward, H.B.   251
Moore, M.   616
Mordecai, L.   271
Morgan, D.   494
Morris, R.B.   39
Morrison, P.   529
Mouton, J.   437
Muchmore, L.   40
Mulrooney, K.R.   576
Murray, M.A.   41, 381
Myrtle, R.C.   530
Nachmias, D.   577
Nalbandian, J.   428
Neugarten, D.A.   334
Neuse, S.   12
Neustadt, R.E.   611
Newhouse, M.L.   121
Newland, C.   245, 586
Nigro, F.A.   413
Nigro, L.G.   66
Oatman, M.E.   257
O'Connor, R.J.   134
Odom, T.   67
Ogden, D.M. Jr.   157
O'Harrow, D.   42
O'Leary, V.   495
Olsen, A.S.   68
Olsen, D.J.   202
Olsen, J.B.   122
Overton, C.E.   421
Owen, S. Jr.   183
Owstrowski, J.   382
Page, W. Jr.   534
Paget, R.M.   612
Pajir, R.G.   383
Pak, C.M.   613
Paine, T.O.   274
Pati, G.C.   43
Patten, T.H.   531
Patton, C.V.   158
Paulionis, A.N.   69
Peabody, R.L.   335
Pearson, D.   219
Peirce, N.R.   416
Peitzsch, F.C.   336
Perkins, J.   260
Perkins, J.A.   44
Perkins, L.   160

Pernick, R.   70
Perry, J.L.   74, 360   412
Peters, C.   220
Pfiffner, J.M.   71, 556
Pickering, T.J.   72
Pitsvada, B.T.   159
Platt, C.S.   246
Plyman, J.   160
Pope, H.G.   275
Porter, W.   30
Posegate, J.   30
Posey, R.B.   414, 415
Preble, J.F.   123
Presley, R.W.   359
Press, F.   184
Presthus, R.   161, 557
Preston, E.   614
Price, D.K.   466
Proehl, C.W. Jr.   517
Prottas, J.   361
Pruefer, C.H.   496
Quinn, T.A.   221
Rabin, J.   50
Rafferty, R.R.   185
Ragoff, M.   400
Rainey, G.   362
Rainey, H.G.   337
Ray, J.M.   615
Raymond, J.   501
Ready, R.R.   395
Reaume, P.A.   45
Reeves, E.J.   384
Rehfuss, J.   500
Relyea, H.C.   385
Reinharth, L.   287
Rennagel, W.C.   497
Richards, F.M.   13
Richter, A.   247
Ridgley, E.E.   14
Ridley, C.E.   73
Riethmayer, L.C.   124
Rigos, P.N.   165
Rinehart, J.C.   125
Ring, P.S.   74
Roberts, N.C.   46
Roberts, S.L.   75
Robertson, G.W.   165

Roderick, S.S.   126
Roessner, J.D.   363
Rogers, G.L.   467
Rogers, W.G.   338
Rohr, J.A.   222, 223
Roll, D.   276
Roll, J.   276
Romani, J.H.   201
Rommel, R.B.   76
Rosen, B.   77
Rosener, J.B.   127
Rosenbaum, A.   339
Rosenberg, S.   585
Rosenbloom, D.   47
Rosenblum, R.   532
Rosenthal, A.   386
Rosenthal, A.H.   128, 162
Rosenthal, S.   248
Ross, J.P.   341
Rosow, J.M.   340
Rourke, J.T.   578
Rouse, A.M.   533
Rowat, D.C.   129
Rubin, I.S.   152
Rubin, R.S.   364
Rushin, E.R.   249, 417
Ryan, R.   342
Saltztein, A.   579
Saroff, J.R.   277
Saunders, R.J.   511
Savage, P.L.   468
Savitz, L.   387
Sayre, W.S.   250
Schmandt, H.   2
Schneider, M.   498
Schroeder, P.   343, 471
Schubert, G.   499
Schuchman, J.   487
Schuck, P.H.   130
Schuck, V.   558
Schweitzer, G.E.   580
Scioli, F.P. Jr.   344
Scott, K.D.   616
Scott, P.   163
Seashore, C.   581
Shapek, R.   48
Shelby, L.W.   469

Shepard, J.M.   251
Sherif, C.W.   582
Sherman, B.   369
Sherwood, F.P.   164
Sherwood, F.P.   164, 224, 470, 534
Shorett, A.   112
Sickels, R.J.   617
Sigelman, L.   251
Sikula, A.F.   225
Simon, H.A.   388
Simon, M.E.   394
Sink, D.   514, 515, 516, 517
Sipel, G.A.   535
Sisneros, A.   618
Smith, J.C. Jr.   559
Smith, M.P.   252
Sniderman, M.S.   359
Sommers, W.A.   49
Sorensen, T.C.   560
Specht, H.   544
Sproule, C.F.   19
Staats, E.B.   226
Stahl, G.   583
Stanley, D.   78
Staudohar, P.D.   418
Staufenberger, R.A.   79
Steene, E.O.   619
Steinhauer, M.B.   365
Stewart, D.W.   620
Stewart, J. Jr.   509
Stillman, R.   561, 586
Stipak, B.   131
Stockard, J.G.   80
Stone, D.   366
Stone, D. B.   81
Stowe, E.   500
Sturgess, J.   529
Swanson, C.   563
Swierczek. F.W.   165
Swingle, P.G.   562
Swiss, J.E.   227, 345
Taylor, N.   18
Taylor, W.J. Jr.   82
Teasley, C. III   395
Tedesco, T.   253
Theony, A.R.   83

Thomas, D.   17
Thompson, D.E.   507
Thompson, D.F.   228
Thompson, H.   472
Thompson, K.   368
Thurow, L.   166
Todd, R.J.   501
Tomkin, S.L.   502
Torrence, W.D.   419
Totten, M.W.   229
Townsend, J.R.   84
Tretten, R.W.   230
Uhlman, F.W.   85
Ukeles, J.B.   503
Urwick, L.F.   473
Usher, C.   167
Vaden, R.E.   525, 526, 605
Vanderbilt, D.H.   168
Van Ness, E.H.   490
Van Straten, J.G.   389
Van Wagner, K.   563
Vaughn, T.B.   474
Villanueva, A.B.   16
Vocino, T.   50
Waldron, R.   169
Walfron, S.M.   215
Walker, A.G. III   28
Walker, D.C.   254
Warrick, D.D.   16, 536
Watne, D.A.   149
Waugh, W.   464
Weckler, J.E.   87, 584

Weddle, P.D.   186
Wedin, W.D.   255
Weimer, D.L.   367
Weir, M.   346
Weiss, C.H.   15
Welch, S.   368
Werling, R.P.   429
White, L.G.   382, 504
Wikstrom, N.   475
William, G.L.   187
Willner, B.   108
Wilson, J.   278
Wise, D.   231
Witcover, J.   196
Wolf, L.   362
Wolohojean, G.G.   152
Woodard, J.D.   232
Woolpert, E.D.   132, 390
Wooten, L.M.   272
Word, W.R.   420
Wortman, M.S.   421
Wright, C.R.   433
Wurf, J.   422
Yeager, S.   50
Young, A.R.   187
Young, J.D.   279
Zagoria, S.   347
Zawacki, R.A.   16
Zeina, Y.   88
Zinke, R.C.   505
Zuck, A.M.   430
Zukin, C.   133

Administrative humour, 519
Affirmative action,
  elephant burial grounds, 251

Benefit-cost analysis, 166, 554
  action-forcing, 138
  and policy analysis, 138
  and social planning, 153
  and technology, 172, 173
  and urban planning, 143
  and wellness program, 160
  appropriations, 138, 142
  beyond ZBB, 157
  budget execution, 148, 159
  budget innovation, 165
  budget process, 140, 146, 158
  budgetary behavior, 147, 149
    156
  cost improvement, 135
  decremental approach, 154
  executive control, 164
  fiscal decisions, 161
  for recreation services, 145
  grant-in-aid programs, 156,
    162, 163, 544
  information system, 172
  performance assessment, 167
  PPBS, 172
  program budget-oriented
    system, 165, 244
  published versus working
    documents, 137
  reforms, 141
  revenue budgeting, 154
  revenue sharing, 140, 143
  scarcity, 136, 139, 150,
    151, 152, 155
  target budgeting, 168

ZBB, 157, 168, 169
Bureaucracy,
  and democracy, 482
  and post-modern society,
    374
  and public life, 263
  bureaucratic reform, 261
  changing bureaucracies, 11
  controlling, 543
  contract-consulting, 108
  countervailing force, 436
  dynamics of, 372
  good bureaucracy, 34
  irresponsible criticism, 77
  maladies and remedies, 15
  official-client relations,
    10
  performance, 6
  reforming upper levels, 74
Bureaucrats,
  guide to survival, 431
  policy makers, 540
  political pressures, 538
  reluctant, 286

Citizen Participation,
  and administrative
    innovation, 348
  and coordination, 107
  and Economic Opportunity
    Act, 95
  and minority groups, 99
  and public lands conflict,
    570
  citizen interest, 111
  citizen satisfaction, 131,
    291
  community action, 91

consumer demands and police
  executive, 92
co-production, 97
group process, 105
in municipal affairs, 118
measurement of participa-
  tion, 127
parking problems, 116
public employee view of
  public management, 115
public interest groups, 130
public involvement in water
  management, 112
public relations program,
  110, 118
sunset implementation, 369
techniques of involvement,
  111, 112
City manager,
and courts, 553
and ethics, 232
and public relations, 110,
  550
and social problems, 576
art of management, 439
control of activities, 548
cooperative action, 602
labor relations, 398
relations with council,
  549, 586
teleconferencing, 253
Communication,
accessible information, 385
and leadership styles, 380
federal agencies and minorities, 384
hot questions, 379
intelligence secrecy, 375
municipal publicity, 390
oral and written, 381
peer communication, 377
research information, 383
sharing of knowledge, 374
third-person effect, 376
Conflict, Management of
black perspective, 569
city manager-council, 549
collective controversy, 582

comparable worth, 567,
  571, 583
confrontation, 564
determinants, 572
discriminatory officials,
  580
emotional disturbances, 573
GAO, resistance to, 578
interorganizational rela-
  tions, 574
interpersonal dynamics, 581
megacentropolis, 575
on public lands, 570
personnel directors, 579
professional organization,
  568
public bureaus, 577
race riots, 584
reorganizers, 533
social problems, 576
team building, 566
Corruption,
from petty crooks to pre-
  sidents, 98
in highway construction,
  215
in land use, 203
  political, 2, 107, 190,
  195, 203, 213
Congress,
casework process, 551
congressional influence,
  546, 561
presidential accountabi-
  lity to, 560
Cost-benefit analysis,
and administrative deci-
  sion making, 505
Creativity
creative behavior, 357
creative of intergovern-
  mental relations, 358

Decision making
ad hoc, 486
administrative duality, 497
administrative rationality,
  497

and community change, 105
and correction policy, 495
and cost-benefit analysis,
    505
and creativity, 479
and discretionary authority,
    481, 484
and social indicators, 498
and values, 487
barriers to problem solving,
    494
CIA and presidential policy,
    492
fiscal decisions, 161
foreign policy, 485
formal and informal con-
    trols, 482
impact of personnel deci-
    sions, 480
institutional analysis, 493
military, 483, 497
muddling through, 477, 488,
    489, 500
OMB examiners, impact, 502
national, 485, 486
policy analysis, 503
policy innovation, 478
problem solving, 494
process, 386, 490
psychometric model, 499
risk in making decision,
    483
technical advice for, 491
Delegation, 556, 559, 615
Disaster preparedness,
    and Department of Public
    Works, 96

Environment
    environmental education, 207
    environmental quality man-
        agement, 350
    State Air Pollution Control
        Agencies, 7
Ethics,
    and city manager, 232
    and education, 207
    and financial analysis, 209

and job performance, 211
and local administration,
    216
and organization struc-
    ture, 206
bureaucratic accountabi-
    lity, 194, 227
bureaucratic maladies,
    15, 188
challenge of public serv-
    ice, 226
code of ethics, 209, 210,
    223, 232
competing interest, 191,
    208, 214, 221
congressional ethics, 3,
    219
for SES, 222
managerial accountability,
    192
moral philosophy, 205
professional standards,
    229
service ethics, 337
to particular groups, 201
value systems, 225
External relations,
    with political actors, 89

Flexitime, 351, 362, 364

GAO, 579
Goal-setting,
    and performance assess-
        ment, 167
    and planning, 90
    goal-setting process, 504
Government,
    and citizen orientations,
        121
    and public affairs, 93
    and technology, 171, 177,
        178, 179, 180, 181
    deception, 231
    federal, 1, 105, 107, 245,
        282, 283, 304, 383, 384,
        385, 386, 454, 612

local, 30, 32, 104, 107,
  118, 121, 122, 132, 281
  283, 303, 325, 326, 341
  377, 382
reorganization, 256
secrecy, 239
shadow government, 108
state, 12, 301, 324, 342,
  344
Group conflicts,
  in bureaucratic change, 426
  political-career executive
    interface, 423, 424, 425,
    426, 427, 430, 614
Group dynamics,
  administrator-teacher re-
    lations, 386
  CIA, 375
  group process techniques,
    382
  lower officialdom, 372
  medical support, airland
    battle, 389
  organizational interaction,
    378
  personal interaction, 377
  police, code of mutual aid,
    387
  positive partnership, 369
  program evaluations, 371
  social sharing, 374
  staff men, 373

Incrementalism, 134, 345
Internship, 599
  satisfaction-dissatisfac-
    tion, 35
  trainee program, 39, 50
Intergovernmental finance,
  and process accountability,
    358
  and productivity, 326
Innovation
  administrative, 348, 350
  budget, 165
  chief executive support,
    360

federal intervention, 367,
  368
flexitime, 351, 362, 364
five-day week, 353
four-day week, 355
futuristic methods, 123
impacts of, 361
incentives, 363
innovative managers, 366
Japanese management, 270
medical audit, 356
multijobholding, 359
new approaches and proce-
  dures for Supreme Court,
    356
organization for, 352
policy, 479
technological, 349
technological change, 361
technology transfer, 365

Job satisfaction,
  job longevity, 323
  role expectation, 299
  role orientations, 298

Leadership,
  actualization and con-
    flict, 464
  anatomy of, 453
  and communication, 380
  and sleep research, 472
  and social power, 458
  approaches to, 433
  art of management, 439
  city manager as commu-
    nity leader, 545
  county, 444
  effectivemanager, 434
  executive administration,
    445
  federal executives, 435
  female executives, 315
  institutional, 431
  mayor as policy leader, 475
  megacentropolis leader,
    463

military, 437, 440, 442,
    447, 450,   465, 467,
    468, 474
personal attributes,
    473
police management, 448, 456
political, 432
preconditions to effective
    administration, 460
presidential management,
    436, 443, 452, 457, 461,
    471, 611, 617
public leaders, 432, 464
styles of, 458
to decentralize, 459
traits, successful and un-
    successful, 449
trusted leaders, 454
types, 453
urban manager, 451, 466
Women's Program, 462
versus management, 469
Loyalty, 65
administrative, 217, 269
civil servants, 218
constructive program, 65
police, 387
to American regime values,
    205

Management of change
civil service reforms, 525,
    526
consultants, 117, 523, 532,
    535
feedback process, 507
human resources develop-
    ment, 524
managerial changes, 522
mandated change, 14
MBO, 234, 438, 534
organizational climate,
    527, 528
OD, 4, 8, 16, 508, 511,
    512, 514, 515, 516, 517,
    527, 528, 529, 531, 536
police, 513
program teamwork, 506, 531

reasons for failure, 518
reorganization, 256, 533
suggestion systems, 510
Managers, management of
administrative experience,
    609
American leaders, 589
and political system, 613
cooperative action, 602
delegation, 615
executive corps, 27
executive management im-
    provement, 597
federal career executive,
    612
forced resignation, 596
goals, public management,
    608
Hispanic federal execu-
    tives, 618
inefficiency in govern-
    ment management, 603
internships, 599
local manager, 586
manager plan, 587
managerial careers, 606
managerial performance,
    585
mayor-administrator, 590
mayor-manager relations,
    595, 598, 619
MBO, 616
military, 605
minority administrator, 600
presidential leadership,
    611, 617
political appointees, 614
professionalism, 12, 79,
    601, 610
profile, managers, 592
program management officer,
    588
statistics, managerial use,
    604
supervisors' training, 593
system 4, 607
top leadership development,
    594

women managers, 591, 620
Management philosophy
  case management, 248
  changes in communication
    field, 255
  democratic administration,
    250
  elephant burial grounds, 251
  employer-management parti-
    cipation, 249
  existentialism, 247
  government secrecy, 239
  humanization, 235, 244, 246
  ignorance, management of,
    243
  management systems and or-
    ganizational reality, 234
  muscle administration, 254
  negotiation and realignment,
    233
  openness and participation,
    236
  organizational democracy,
    252
  professionally-oriented,
    244
  projections of the future,
    241
  science of public adminis-
    tration, 238
  work democratization, 252
Manpower planning, 61, 187
  human resources management,
    70
  key people, replacement, 84
  manpower programs, 114
  psychiatric battle casual-
    ties, 60
Matrix organization
  dual responsibility, 497
  employees council, 393
  headquarters units, 391
  human service matrix, 395
  joint union-management
    committees, 410
  managerial matrix, 235
  matrix management, 394
  third party mechanism, 392

MBO, 438, 532, 533, 617
Merit system
  administrative selection,
    33
  and representative bureau-
    cracy, 29
  competitive merit selec-
    tion, 36
  employment tests, 18
  test-anxiety, 19
Metropolitan desk, 506
Motivation
  authority relations, 335
  control, 330
  difficulties, 300
  employee recognition, 321
  fringe benefits, 290, 295,
    402, 422
  job longevity, 323
  job satisfaction, 298, 299
  leisure tradeoffs, 288
  motivational bases, 319
  needs-fulfillment, 296
  non-economic incentives,
    302
  organizational incentives,
    367
  participation bonuses, 322
  positive stroking, 294
  public sector benefits, 340
  retirement pay, military,
    309
  reward preferences, 337
  salary increases, 321
  self-actualization, 315
  shifts in assignment, 333
  sick-time usage, 303
  supportive tactics, 286
  trends, 336

Office politics
  political career-executive
    interface, 423, 424, 425,
    426, 427, 430, 614
Ombudsman, 128, 129
Organization behavior, 407
  administrative systems, 6
  and social behavior, 407

budgetary behavior, 147
bureaucratic behavior, 136
economizing behavior, 103
federal civil servants, 125
macro-organizational beh-
  avior, 103
socio-technical experience,
  13
with management-employee
  conflict, 407
Organizational change
  all volunteer force, 38
  and technological changes,
    180
  automation, 520
  contracting, 233
  EEO implementation, 521
  external management train-
    ing, 88
  futuristic methods, 123
  managerial matrix, 235
  mandated change, 14
  Office of Civil Rights, 509
Organization design
  changing personnel func-
    tions, 259
  death of administrative
    man, 260
  femininization, 263
  integration, 275
  public inspector general,
    262
  quality circles, 270, 275
  quality of working life, 258
  rule orientation, 262
  temporary society, 277
Organization development, 511
  512, 536
  and applied behavioral
    sciences, 511
  human resources develop-
    ment, 524
  impact, CEO, 508
  interventions, 514, 515,
    516, 517
  public sector, 4, 8, 16
  state welfare system, 4
Organizational reality

PL-89-306, 429
to management systems, 234
Organization structure
  for innovation, 352
  non-hierarchical, 264
  organismic structure, 264
  third sector, 272
  transportation depart-
    ments, 273

Performance Appraisal
  determinants, 289
  evaluation of government,
    316
  management systems review,
    317
  managerial performance ap-
    praisal, 585
  measurements, 291, 338
  peer evaluation, 280, 378
Planning
  and power, 541
  and revenue sharing, 143
  army readiness, 278
  force-field analysis, 501
  to maintain peace, 241
  transportation, 273
Policy Evaluation, 344
  politics, 343
  problems, 344
  program evaluations, 371,
    378
Political Behavior
  and planners, 109
  and psychological theory,
    100
  and shadow government, 108
  motivational bases, 319
  of Federal civil servants,
    125
  political party and Sup-
    reme Court, 102
  political pornography, 537
  political pressures, 538
  political programming, 133
  politics of productivity,
    343
  professional manager, 428

Power, management of, 562
  and planners, 541
  art of management, 439
  by delegation, 559
  city manager, 548, 561
    and courts, 553
    and public relations, 550
    control by, 548
  community power, 547, 557
  congressional influence,
    546, 551
  delegation of, 556, 615
  executive-legislative re-
    lations, 551
  governor, 558
  invisible, 541
  leadership, community and
    political, 545
  male-female power orienta-
    tion, 563
  management inefficiency, 542
  organizational power, 555
  political power, 552
  presidency, 436, 560, 611
  regulatory sprawl, 540
  two-dimensional approach to,
    539
Productivity, 284, 304, 312,
  313, 318, 334, 341, 342
  analysis, 293
  and information technology,
    325
  and intergovernmental fi-
    nance, 326
  and national economy, 314
  and private sector, 301
  and productivity bargain-
    ing, 327, 347
  challenge, 313
  environment for, 332
  ethic, 283
  flexitime, 351
  for NY city transit, 392
  improvement, 281, 282, 297,
    302, 308, 328, 329, 339
  issues in, 334
  lessons, 292
  measurements, 285, 306, 310

311, 331, 346
  problems, 312, 342, 347
  status, 342
  system 4, 328
  technological innova-
    tions, 349
  unbalanced incentives, 345
Professionalization, 610
  and protectionism, 240
  and external relations, 89
  for forest personnel, 207
  in state government, 12
  military professionals, 82
  of police, 79
  professional ethics, 223,
    224
  professionally-oriented,
    244
  professional standards,
    229
Promotions
  executive mobility, 66
  promotional exams, 69
  social workers, 299
  technical expertise, 56
Public executives
  and budgetary behavior, 147
  and innovation adoption,
    360
  and program implementa-
    tion, 31
  city managers, 63, 110,
    124, 444, 545, 550
  development of, 31
  evolution of ef execu-
    tives, 446, 470
  existentialist, 247
  federal executives, 66,
    435
  female executives, 315
  local chief executives,
    377
  municipal administrators,
    290
  professional administra-
    tors, 44
  Senior Executive Service,
    146

Public management
  and black perspective, 569
  and productivity improve-
    ment, 339
  and public revenue system,
    120
  and technology transfer, 365
  business involvement, 122,
    365
  implementation, 279
  muscle administration, 254
  space age management, 274
  versus corporate management,
    4, 94, 103, 193, 301, 337,
    432, 445, 613
Public relations
  city manager and council,
    549
  city manager and public,
    110, 124, 550
  city public relations prog-
    ram, 118, 132
  cultural activities, 104
  public image, 113

Recruitment
  administrative brainpower,
    23
  assistant positions, 20
  city managers, 42, 45, 49
  demographic factors, 21
  employment tests, 18
  employment validation pro-
    cedures, 30
  executive search, 46
  ex-offenders, 43
  federal positions, 47
  graduate students, 28
  guidelines for candi-
    dates, 17
  high school students, 26
  minorities, 22, 29, 32, 47
  MPA degrees, 25, 50
  part-time positions, 27
  personnel selection pro-
    cess, 33
  professional administra-
    tors, 44

public administration
  graduates, 45, 48
  trainees, 39
  undergraduate, 35
  unemployed, 37
  urban managers, 48
  volunteer military, 24, 38
  women, 29, 32
  young people, youth, 32, 40

Red tape, 193, 266
Reorganization, 256, 267,
  269, 273, 275
  and Administrative Proce-
    dures Act, 257
  reorganizers, 533
Responsibility
  and professionalism in
    state government, 12
  moral, 228
Retention
  alternatives to lay-offs,
    78
  constructive program, 65
  military, 309
  public workers, 55
  young employee, 54

SES, 74, 222, 425, 614
Social technology, 182
Survey-based change, 507
Staffing
  municipal employment, 57
Statistics
  managerial use, 604
Stress, 568, 573
Supreme Court, 102, 356, 409

Technology
  and government management,
    171
  and local government, 178
  and urban problems, 184
  computer usage, training,
    183, 185
  executive preparation,
    180
  impact, computers, 175

information system, 172,
  174, 177
in mass transit, 361
local budgetary system, 173
psychological weapons, 170
robotics, 176
social technology, 182
soldier-machine connection,
  186
technological innovations,
  349
technology assessment, 179
technology transfer, 365
Third sector organizations,
  272
Training
  administrative trainee
    program, 39
  aviation training, 64
  CETA program, 37
  executive training, 61, 62,
    67, 73, 76
  external management train-
    ing, 88
  for computer usage, 183, 185
  for decentralized organiza-
    tion, 80
  for interracial relations,
    87
  human relations, supervi-
    sors, 71, 593, 671
  in-service program, 68, 73,
    85, 86,
  management development, 68
  middle level managers, 81
  military, 51, 60, 72
  municipal, 53, 75, 84
  on labor relations, 401, 419
  professional women, 601
  replacements for key posi-
    tions, 84
  state employee union, 401

supervisors, 71
training institutes, 58
training workshops, 85
urban management educa-
  tion, 83

Unionism
  attitudes toward unions,
    404
  bargaining impasses, 418
  collective action, 396
  collective bargaining
    400, 402, 407, 411, 412
    419. 420, 570
  compulsory arbitration,
    397. 421
  EEO program, 408
  employee-management coope-
    ration, 417
  final offer arbitration,
    403
  fringe benefits, 422
  Hatch Act reform, 416
  joint union-management
    committees, 410
  labor relations, 398
    programs, 413
    training, 419
  mediation, 418
  motives for membership, 406
  municipal, 409
  recognition of unions, 414
  representation elections,
    399
  strikes, 405
  union agreements, 415

Waste
  fraud and abuse, 199
  in human services, 189
Whistle blowing, 220
Women, 29, 32, 59, 591